Social Attitudes
in
Northern Ireland

Social Attitudes
in
Northern Ireland

edited by

Peter Stringer & Gillian Robinson

1990-91
edition

THE
BLACKSTAFF PRESS
BELFAST

First published in 1991 by
The Blackstaff Press Limited
3 Galway Park, Dundonald, Belfast BT16 0AN, Northern Ireland
with the assistance of
the Policy Planning and Research Unit
under the Community Relations Programme

Typeset by Textflow Services Limited

Printed in Northern Ireland by
The Universities Press Limited

British Library Cataloguing in Publication Data
Social attitudes in Northern Ireland
1990–1991
1. Northern Ireland. Social life
941. 60824
ISBN 0-85640-477-2

Contents

The contributors

Mary Black
Co-ordinator of Health Promotion and Education, North and West Belfast, Eastern Health and Social Services Board.

Ed Cairns
Senior Lecturer in Psychology and member of the Centre for the Study of Conflict, University of Ulster.

Celia Davies
Professor of Women's Opportunities and Director of the Centre for Research on Women, University of Ulster.

S. Dunn
Director of the Centre for the Study of Conflict, University of Ulster.

Eileen Evason
Senior Lecturer in Social Administration and Policy, University of Ulster.

A.M. Gallagher
Research Officer at the Centre for the Study of Conflict, University of Ulster.

Mark Hart
Senior Lecturer in Applied Economics, University of Ulster.

John Kremer
Lecturer in Psychology, The Queen's University of Belfast.

Pamela Montgomery
Until January 1990, Research Officer at the Centre for Research on Women, University of Ulster; now Chief Investigation Officer, Equal Opportunities Commission, Belfast.

Edward Moxon-Browne
Senior Lecturer in Politics, The Queen's University of Belfast.

Liam O'Dowd
Senior Lecturer in Sociology, The Queen's University of Belfast.

R.D. Osborne
Director of the Centre for Policy Research, University of Ulster.

Gillian Robinson
Research Associate at the Northern Ireland Regional Research Laboratory, The Queen's University of Belfast and the University of Ulster.

Ian Sneddon
Lecturer in Psychology, The Queen's University of Belfast.

Peter Stringer
Professor in the School of Social Science and Director of the Centre for Social Research, The Queen's University of Belfast.

Kevin Sweeney
Head of the Central Survey Unit, Policy Planning and Research Unit.

Introduction

Peter Stringer

This book is the first of what we hope will be a long-running series. Each year we shall report the results of a survey of the attitudes of people in Northern Ireland towards issues of local, national and international significance. This report and its successors will be an important source of information to all those who have an interest in Northern Ireland, and not least to those who make decisions affecting our society.

The issues covered in this first volume are apparent from the table of contents: for example, community relations, fair employment, the position of women, poverty, and healthy eating. In future annual surveys, these issues will be reinvestigated from time to time and others will be introduced. In this way, a picture will be built up of trends or changes in social attitudes towards topical concerns.

The survey on which this book is based is an extension of the British Social Attitudes series. That series was started in 1983 by Social and Community Planning Research (SCPR), the London-based social survey organisation. Thanks to the interest of government's Central Community Relations Unit (CCRU) and Policy Planning and Research Unit (PPRU), and to the generosity of the Nuffield Foundation, it was possible in 1989 to include Northern Ireland in the survey for the first time.

Because a sample of nearly 900 adults was interviewed in Northern Ireland, it is possible to compare their attitudes with those of their British counterparts. Such a comparison has never before been feasible. In addition, in future years we shall be able to make international comparisons in relation to certain topics, with findings from countries such as the Republic of Ireland, Israel, the Netherlands, the USA and Germany.

The importance of the Social Attitudes series

When the British Social Attitudes series was first presented to the public in 1984, its directors pointed out the deficiencies which existed then in social reporting. Despite the importance of public attitudes, much less attention had been given to them than to behaviour patterns, social conditions or demographic characteristics. The government was, and still is, responsible for the great majority of national survey series. However, if it was to initiate a comprehensive attitudinal survey, it would run the risk of covering areas (such as, say, sexual lifestyles) which might be seen as too intrusive, sensitive or controversial. The public might consider such matters as being not the proper concern of government.

Much of what we do know about public attitudes is derived from opinion surveys. Because these surveys are frequently sponsored by newspapers, radio and television, they deal with newsworthy topics in such a way as to yield very quick results. Very little time or effort is available for covering and reporting topics in depth, or for the technical niceties of state-of-the-art survey work. There may even be a suggestion of survey questions being tailored to suit a client's interests.

The British Social Attitudes survey series was made possible initially by academic research funding, from a research council (the Economic and Social Research Council) and charitable foundations (the Nuffield Foundation and the Monument Trust). Its continuation relies heavily on such sources, though there is also a significant measure of support from government departments and the private sector. This pattern of funding has enabled the survey to remain independent: funders are invited to support the project, not to determine the questions it asks or the manner in which findings are reported.

The British surveys are now in their eighth year. This, and the fact that they are increasingly and manifestly gaining the attention of decision-makers in the public and private sectors, attests to their importance as a part of the information-base of contemporary and changing British society. The longevity of the series already means that Britain has a unique means of monitoring trends and changes in social attitudes.

Social attitudes in Northern Ireland

Against this background, it is interesting to note that much of the initiative to have the survey series extended to Northern Ireland originated with government. The suggestion that the extension might prove worthwhile was made by the former Policy Research Institute (PRI) of The Queen's University of Belfast and the University of Ulster to CCRU and PPRU. It was only their positive response to this suggestion, as well as their material support and professional resources, that made the survey and the present book possible. Equally, without the willingness of SCPR to undertake the considerable commitment entailed by the extension, it would never have been possible.

Independence has been maintained. This is a necessary condition of receipt of further financial assistance from the Nuffield Foundation. SCPR retain responsibility for the content, structure and wording of the questionnaire. As in Britain, there is no sense in which funders determine which questions are asked or which findings are reported.

PRI had a particular interest in this project as being one way of trying to extend the very slim coverage of Northern Ireland in nominally 'national' surveys. This deficiency in the past had been due to several factors. Many large-scale surveys are undertaken for government; but most Whitehall departments do not have a responsibility in Northern Ireland. In other cases, including Northern Ireland in a survey sample on a proportional basis would produce a very small sub-sample, too small to enable separate analysis to be carried out. The survey itself might entail unusual logistical problems. (For a

2

similar reason, surveys in Scotland are frequently restricted to that part which lies south of the Caledonian Canal.)

The fact that this survey of social attitudes has now been extended to Northern Ireland on a full-scale basis – at least for the three years 1989–91 – means that comparisons will be possible for the first time with attitudes in Britain. One set of such comparisons has already appeared in the book which reports on the 1989 British survey (Curtice and Gallagher, 1990). There are many reasons why such comparisons might or might not be interesting. Not all contributors to this book have chosen to place an emphasis on them, and readers will make their own interpretation of any comparative findings that are represented. But the survey is about *social* attitudes, and Northern Ireland is a distinctive society – culturally, demographically, economically, geographically, politically and in other ways. From a purely social perspective, it warrants comparison with other societies.

The possibilities for comparison go further than Britain. At about the same time as the British Social Attitudes survey series was launched, the International Social Survey Programme was founded (for further information, see Jowell et al, 1989). It is a voluntary grouping of teams in some fourteen countries, each of which has agreed to carry out each year the same short survey of attitudes to a particular topic. To date, the topics have been: the role of government (in 1985 and 1990), family networks and support systems, social inequality, women and the family, work orientations, and religion and religious belief. On the first and the last two topics, it will now be possible to place Northern Irish views in the perspective of views from a balanced collection of other societies.

The aim of this book

PRI was closed in July 1990. Its share of the responsibility for the social attitudes project was taken over by the newly formed Centre for Social Research at The Queen's University of Belfast and by the Economic and Social Research Council's Northern Ireland Regional Research Laboratory (NIRRL). Together with SCPR, they had to determine what should happen to all the information which was being collected.

It was decided to follow in broad outline the pattern which had already been set by SCPR. The principal objective of the project is to produce an annual data-set which is publicly available for all interested parties to use. To that end, the fully documented data-set is deposited by SCPR with the Economic and Social Research Council's Data Archive in Essex. In the case of Northern Ireland, local users may find it convenient to access the survey by way of NIRRL, which has taken on the responsibility for its data-processing. It is hoped that the NIRRL will be in a position to encourage and facilitate use of the data by interested academics, civil servants, journalists and others who wish to use it to answer their own questions.

Detailed analysis and application of the survey, then, is yet to come. What this book attempts to do is no more than to give a first taste of the kind of information the survey contains. One of the appendices reproduces the questionnaire and gives the marginal totals of answers to all the questions asked.

3

In each of the chapters which form the bulk of the book, contributors who have a particular interest in one of the survey topics give their own interpretation of the survey's findings. Because there are a limited number of chapters, the account of the survey is not comprehensive. Because authors selected their own topics and have dealt with them in their own way, there is a personal element in the treatment of material. At the same time, it is important to emphasise that the contributors were using material that was supplied to them: most of them had no hand in drawing up the questionnaire itself.

The task of the editors has been to recruit the contributions, and to transform them into as readable and uniform a style as possible, while respecting the academic interests of the authors.

The series

Funding has been guaranteed for two more editions of this book. They will report findings of the surveys carried out in early 1990 and 1991.

Preparation of the 1991/92 edition is already well underway. It will include chapters on mainstream economic, political and environmental issues, as well as more focussed reports of findings on attitudes to civil liberties, policing and various forms of crime.

By the time this book appears, the 1991 survey data will be being processed. Questions have been asked on attitudes to, in particular, community relations (repeating some of those asked in 1989), health, right and wrong, and religious belief.

In the course of time, we can expect that a range of other topics will be introduced for particular attention: for example, education, welfare, housing, employment and international comparisons.

It is important that the Social Attitudes project does produce a *series* of reports. It is in this way that we can begin to monitor and understand trends and changes in society. The great majority of social studies are investigations at one point in time and unrelated to one another. A sustained look is also necessary. The full value of these reports can only be tested in future years when there has been an opportunity to cover a wide range of public issues and to repeat questions on two or more occasions.

Acknowledgements

Unfortunately, protocol inhibits us from naming those individuals in the Civil Service whose interest was decisive in enabling this project to be launched. We have already referred to the main groupings to which we are indebted. A particular round of thanks is due to all members of the Central Survey Unit of PPRU, and to the interviewers in its field-force. The professional skills of all those people have been, and continue to be, invaluable.

The financial support of the Nuffield Foundation has been of considerable assistance to the Northern Ireland extension as well as to the British surveys.

Tony Gallagher and Eddie Moxon-Browne gave valuable advice on aspects of the questionnaire. They and all the other contributors made this book possible.

The staff of SCPR, and in particular its director Roger Jowell and his colleague Sharon Witherspoon, played a crucial role in seeing the survey through from beginning to end. They had no hesitation in allowing their 'child' to migrate across the Irish Sea. They were unstinting in giving their own time to make the same journey. Their guidance was expert and sympathetic. The efforts of SCPR's coding and data-processing staff ensured that the Northern Ireland survey is comparable with its British counterpart.

Caroline McCracken has borne the brunt of all manner of secretarial work which the project has thrown up at various times, sometimes under unexpectedly difficult circumstances.

We have no hesitation in following the convention of SCPR and reserving our last expression of thanks for the 4000 forever anonymous residents of Northern Ireland and Britain who were willing to reveal their attitudes and so provide the raw material for this book and for future reports.

References

CURTICE, J. and GALLAGHER, T., 'The Northern Irish dimension', in Jowell, R., Witherspoon, S. and Brook, L. (eds), *British Social Attitudes: the 7th report*, Gower, Aldershot (1990).

JOWELL, R., WITHERSPOON, S. and BROOK, L. (eds), *British Social Attitudes: special international report*, Gower, Aldershot (1989).

1

Community relations in Northern Ireland: attitudes to contact and integration

A.M. Gallagher and S. Dunn

If there is one single initiative that one can identify which, if taken 20 years ago, would have changed fundamentally what is happening today it is integrated education. Is it remotely conceivable that had integrated education been introduced at the outbreak of the troubles in 1969 that the divide between the communities would now be so great? Is it conceivable that the boys and girls that would have known each other at school could foster such deep sectarian animosity towards the opposite community as had occurred? Is it conceivable that the parents of such children, drawn together through the school system, could do likewise? [Vincent Browne, *Sunday Tribune*, 24 December 1989]

In a year which saw fundamental and sweeping change in the political face of Europe, Vincent Browne, editor of Ireland's *Sunday Tribune*, pointed to continued opposition to integrated education in Northern Ireland by the Catholic Church as evidence that Ireland remained 'largely unchanged and, apparently, unchangeable'. This call for a change in the system of Catholic and (by implication) Protestant schools in Northern Ireland is only the latest in a long line of such appeals (for example, Fraser, 1974; Heskin, 1980; Spencer, 1987). Survey evidence has suggested a fairly consistent level of support for integrated schools from two-thirds of respondents (Rose, 1971; Dunn, 1986; Darby and Dunn, 1987). At the same time, more recent research suggests that a much lower proportion than this of parents with school-age children intend to send them to an integrated school, where this is an available option (Cairns et al, 1989).

Proponents of integrated education are motivated by a range of considerations (Dunn, 1989). Among these are the right of parents to choose the type of education which their children receive; the high level of support for integrated education in opinion polls; the fact that integrated schools provide equal status for their pupils and teachers, through a balance in the numbers of Protestants and Catholics; and the fact that integrated schools encourage involvement in the school on the part of parents. In addition, integrated schools espouse a child-centred approach to education, helping children to cope with living in a plural society. Some hope that this will provide institutional support for a middle-ground in Northern Irish politics (Spencer, 1987).

However, the central argument for integrated schools is based on some variant of the 'contact hypothesis' (Spencer, 1987; Trew, 1986; Hewstone and Brown, 1986). This suggests that, under appropriate conditions, contact between members of opposing groups will help to ameliorate their conflict. Many advocates of the efficacy of contact look to integrated education, mainly, perhaps, because it promotes contact between young people, the future generation of Northern Ireland.

This pressure for change has not been without effect. In 1984, the first planned integrated secondary school in Northern Ireland, Lagan College, opened its doors. By the end of the decade, it had been joined by another integrated secondary school, Hazelwood College, and 10 integrated primary schools (Darby and Dunn, 1987; Dunn, 1989). Education reforms in 1989 committed government to support initiatives to establish integrated schools and introduced community relations cross-curricular themes into the proposed common curriculum (DENI, 1988a; 1988b; see also Education Reform (Northern Ireland) Order 1989 No. 2406 (NI 20)).

The concentration on education should not obscure the fact that other opportunities for cross-community contact are available in Northern Ireland. Detailed local studies have shown that there is contact between Protestants and Catholics in everyday life despite the social and cultural barriers (Harris, 1972; Burton, 1978; Donnan and MacFarlane, 1983; Hamilton et al, forthcoming). There is evidence of residential mixing in urban centres (Boal and Orr, 1978; Poole, 1982; Boal, 1982), even though widespread rioting in the early years of the present conflict aggravated residential segregation, particularly in working-class areas of Belfast (Boal, 1969; Darby, 1986). Mixed marriages are uncommon; but research points to an increase in recent years (Compton and Coward, 1989). Finally, despite evidence of Catholic disadvantage in employment opportunities (Cormack and Osborne, 1983; Osborne and Cormack, 1986), survey evidence has suggested that many people are employed in fairly mixed workplaces (Rose, 1971; Moxon-Browne, 1983).

The Northern Ireland Social Attitudes survey included questions on the extent of contact between Catholics and Protestants in a number of spheres of life in Northern Ireland, and on respondents' perceptions of the desirability (or undesirability) of such contact. It is possible to compare the results with those of two previous attitude surveys in Northern Ireland, which were carried out in 1968 (Rose, 1971) and 1978 (Moxon-Browne, 1983). Of the 866 respondents to the survey, this chapter will deal with the responses of the 422 (49%) who described themselves as Protestant and the 310 (36%) who described themselves as Roman Catholic. The section which follows will examine perceptions of prejudice and of community relations, which provide the attitudinal context for a consideration of perceptions of contact. Thereafter, perceptions of contact in the family, among friends and neighbours, in the workplace, and in the education system will be successively examined. The concluding section will draw the evidence together.

Prejudice and community relations

Previous Social Attitudes reports in Britain found that nine out of ten people believed there to be prejudice against Asians and Blacks, and about one-third admitted to being racially prejudiced themselves (Airey, 1984; Airey and Brook 1986). In these British surveys, respondents were asked about the extent and pattern of racial prejudice, before being asked whether they themselves were prejudiced. This order of questions was also used in the Northern Ireland survey, with the difference that respondents were asked about prejudice against Catholics and Protestants.

	Catholics	Protestants
	%	%
Perceived prejudice against Catholics		
A lot	38 ⎫ 84	26 ⎫ 63
A little	46 ⎭	37 ⎭
Hardly any	11	31
Perceived prejudice against Protestants		
A lot	15 ⎫ 62	26 ⎫ 69
A little	47 ⎭	43 ⎭
Hardly any	31	24

The majority agreed that there was some prejudice against both Protestants and Catholics. However, more prejudice was perceived to be directed at their own group. This effect was larger for Catholics than for Protestants. Protestant respondents felt that there was more prejudice against Protestants than did the Catholic respondents (69% versus 62%); Catholics, in turn, felt that there was more prejudice against Catholics than did the Protestant respondents (84% versus 63%).

There was little difference in respondents' perception of the pattern over time of prejudice against Catholics. Just over one-half of all respondents felt that religious prejudice against Catholics was about the same as five years ago, and a similar proportion thought that it would be the same in five years' time. Just under one in four Catholics and one in five Protestants felt that there was more prejudice against Catholics now than five years ago; while just under one in six Catholics and one in eight Protestants felt that prejudice against Catholics would be greater in five years' time.

A somewhat different pattern was found for perceptions of prejudice against Protestants. The majority of both groups felt that religious prejudice against Protestants was the same now as five years ago (66% Catholic, 55% Protestant), and would be about the same in five years' time (62% Catholic, 58% Protestant). However, proportionately twice as many Protestant as Catholic respondents felt that there was more religious prejudice now against their own group than five years ago (31% versus 16%), and they expected more in five years' time (20% versus 12%).

A majority of both groups agreed that there was some prejudice against Protestants and Catholics. While most felt that this was, at best, a static situation, sizeable minorities felt that prejudice had increased over the past five years and would increase over the next five. Particularly noteworthy were Protestant perceptions of prejudice against Protestants. Despite all this, only just over one in five Protestants and one in seven Catholics were prepared to admit to any personal prejudice, a somewhat lower figure than that found in British surveys of racial prejudice.

A further set of questions asked respondents about relations between Protestants and Catholics, and about the importance of religion in Northern Ireland. Some comparison is possible between these results and those of the 1968 survey (Rose, 1971). In addition, respondents were asked for their general view of the effect of mixing and separating the two communities.

Relations between Protestants and Catholics

	Catholics		Protestants	
	1968*	1989	1968*	1989
	%	%	%	%
Compared to five years ago				
better	65	23	56	20
worse	4	31	7	26
about the same	27	44	35	50
In five years' time				
better	–	30	–	22
worse	–	16	–	16
about the same	–	51	–	56

*Rose, 1971

The figures may reveal some of the impact of 20 years of violence. In 1968, only 4% of Catholics and 7% of Protestants felt that relations between the communities were worse than five years before, but in 1989 this was so for 31% of Catholics and 26% of Protestants. Similarly, while in 1968 a majority of both groups felt that relations between the communities were improving, by 1989 more felt that relations between the communities were getting worse rather than better. The 1989 respondents' expectations for community relations in five years' time show a similar lack of optimism: a majority of both groups expect no change.

The relative pessimism of respondents in 1989, in comparison with those in 1968, does not, however, show the entire picture. A survey in 1986 (Smith, 1987) found that 47% of Protestants and 46% of Catholics felt that relations between Protestants and Catholics were worse than five years previously. This particularly negative perception is likely to have been influenced by the protests which followed the signing of the Anglo-Irish Agreement in 1985. The present survey would suggest that, in comparison to 1986, perceptions of the relations between Protestants and Catholics in Northern Ireland have moved in a slightly more optimistic direction.

Respondents to the survey were asked whether they thought that religion would always make a difference to the way people felt about each other in Northern Ireland. Eighty-three per cent of Catholics and 89% of Protestants agreed with this statement. Overall, the findings do not suggest an encouraging climate for an improvement in community relations. A majority agreed that there was prejudice against Catholics and Protestants, that the level of prejudice had not decreased in the recent past and that it was not likely to decrease in the foreseeable future. Most respondents felt that relations between the communities had not improved and were unlikely to improve. A very large majority felt that religion would always have an impact on the way people in Northern Ireland felt about each other.

Despite this pessimistic climate, there was evidence that respondents did believe that relations between the communities could be improved. They were asked which of the two following statements came closer to their own view: *'Some people think that better relations between Protestants and Catholics in Northern Ireland will only come about through more mixing of the two communities. Others think that better relations will only come about through more separation.'* The response was unequivocal: 93% of Catholics and 87% of Protestants agreed with the former position; and only 3% of Catholics and 10% of Protestants agreed that more separation was needed to improve community relations. Although the greater Catholic support for more mixing of the communities is statistically significant, it is clear that a large majority of both groups agreed with the potential efficacy of integration.

The next four sections examine the extent to which integration was perceived to exist in 1989 in different aspects of everyday life.

Contact in families between Catholics and Protestants

Harris (1972) argued that the relative lack of intermarriage between rural Protestants and Catholics in Northern Ireland in the 1950s has provided the lynch-pin for maintaining community division. Even where it did occur:

> Intermarriage bridged no gaps. It was rare, but in so far as it is possible to generalise about such an occurrence, the couple were usually married in the wife's church and the husband dropped most of his former contacts even when he did not actually change to his wife's denomination. He ceased any attendance at his church and membership of the associated organisations and political groups. Most important was the fact that tensions were set up between him and his kinsfolk, and especially between them and his wife, that put all normal kin-based contacts between them out of the question. [Harris, 1972, chapter 7]

Of course, what was true of rural Ulster in the 1950s may not be so evident today (Donnan and MacFarlane, 1983; Hickey, 1984). There is evidence that the proportion of mixed marriages, while still small, has increased in recent years (Compton and Coward, 1989).

The Social Attitudes survey sought to establish the extent to which respondents had direct experience of mixed marriages, and also asked for their attitudes to the possibility of mixed marriages. Respondents were asked whether or not their parents were of the same religion as one another; and, if they themselves were married or living as married, whether or not their partner was of the same religion. For both questions the extent of mixing was very low: only 7% of Catholics and 2% of Protestants were the offspring of mixed marriages. Of those married or living as married, only 5% of Catholics and 3% of Protestants were themselves in mixed relationships. These results confirm the continuing infrequency of mixed marriages in Northern Ireland.

Respondents were also asked what proportion of their relatives, including relatives by marriage, was of the same religion. Again, the findings highlight the lack of cross-sectarian mixing within kinship networks. Eighty-two per cent of Catholics and 89% of Protestants said that all or most of their relatives were of the same religion. Although these figures are high, they

11

represent a slight movement towards mixing when compared with the situation in 1968. At that time, 87% of Catholics and 93% of Protestants said that all or most of their relatives were of the same religion (Rose, 1971).

Respondents were asked about what changes they favoured regarding mixed marriages.

*Are you in favour of more **mixing** or more **separation** in people's marriages?*

	Catholics	Protestants
	%	%
A bit, or much more mixing	54	34
Keep things as they are	38	49
A bit, or much more separation	5	15

There is a clear difference between the two communities. A majority of Catholics favour more mixing in marriage, while most Protestants want to keep things as they are. More Catholic support for mixed marriages has been found in earlier surveys (for example, Moxon-Browne, 1983; Hickey, 1984). However, it is noteworthy that the overall level of support for more mixing in marriages is considerably higher than the actual extent of mixed marriages.

Respondents were also asked how they felt most people in Northern Ireland would react if one of their close relatives were to marry someone of the other religion and how they themselves would react.

Attitudes to a close relative entering a mixed marriage

	Catholics	Protestants
	%	%
Most people in Northern Ireland		
would mind a lot	25	40
would mind a little	29	35
would not mind	43	18
You personally		
would mind a lot	6	25
would mind a little	10	21
would not mind	82	51

The results confirm the greater willingness of Catholics to countenance mixed marriages, both in terms of the respondents' perception of general opinion and of their personal opinion. The willingness of Catholics to accept mixed marriages may be associated with their expectation that, in religious matters, it is the Catholic partner who will be the dominant one (see Hickey, 1984, p.139). As with the issue of prejudice, personal opinions about mixed marriages seem to be more positive than perceptions of other people's opinions. This discrepancy may be due, of course, either to an unrealistically negative view of general opinion, or to an unrealistically positive report of personal opinion.

Contact among friends and neighbours

Just as people can choose to whom they wish to be married, so they can, within limits, choose where they wish to live. There is a degree of religious segregation in housing in Northern Ireland. The historical pattern of working-class, residential segregation in Belfast (Gray, 1985; Hepburn and Collins, 1981; Hepburn, 1983) increased in some areas during the 1970s and 1980s following periods of rioting (Boal, 1982; Darby, 1986). In 1989, the Berlin Wall was demolished; but the walls dividing Protestant and Catholic working-class districts of Belfast, rather incongruously known as the 'Peace Line', remained solidly intact. Nevertheless, residential segregation in Northern Ireland is not as general or as marked as the media may suggest (Poole, 1982).

The Social Attitudes survey asked a number of questions about the extent of mixing in the neighbourhood where respondents lived and about their attitudes to residential integration. One question asked whether respondents were in favour of more residential mixing or more separation where people live. A large majority favoured more mixing, with Catholics favouring significantly more.

Another question asked respondents if their personal preference was for a mixed or a non-mixed neighbourhood. Three-quarters of Catholics and two-thirds of Protestants said that, given the choice, they would prefer to live in a mixed neighbourhood. These preferences are not entirely satisfied by the perceived residential mix.

Support for more mixing/separation in residential areas

	Catholics	Protestants
	%	%
A bit, or much more mixing	79	66
Keep things as they are	17	29
A bit, or much more separation	–	2

People perceive a high degree of residential segregation. Most believe that they live in neighbourhoods that are dominated by their co-religionists (see also Smith, 1987). A comparison of the three sets of survey results suggests that between 1968 and 1978 there was an increase in perceived residential segregation, even though this was somewhat smaller for Catholics than Protestants. However, between 1978 and 1989 the extent of perceived residential segregation decreased for Protestants, but remained the same for Catholics.

How many of your neighbours would you say are the same religion as you?

	Catholics	Protestants
All or most	%	%
1968*	57	68
1978#	61	75
1989	62	67

* Rose, 1971; # Moxon-Browne, 1983

The Social Attitudes survey also asked about the proportion of respondents' friends who were of the same religion as themselves.

Religion of respondents' friends

	Catholics	Protestants
All or most the same	%	%
1968*	57	78
1978#	56	75
1989	63	72

* Rose, 1971; # Moxon-Browne, 1983

These results suggest that a sectarian bias in friendships is more marked for Protestants than for Catholics. However, it should be noted that changes over time move in the opposite direction for the two groups: while friendship patterns of Catholics appear to have become more homogeneous, those of Protestants have become less so.

Contact in the workplace

Allegations of discrimination against Catholics in employment played a central role in the Civil Rights campaign of the late 1960s. It has been claimed that several large engineering concerns in Belfast had, at least until recently, an almost exclusively Protestant workforce. Analyses of the 1971 and 1981 Census of Population have suggested that (particularly male) Protestant and Catholic workers were concentrated in different sectors of industry (Aunger, 1983; Osborne and Cormack, 1987). However, responses to the present survey suggest that workplaces provide greater opportunities for cross-sectarian contact than do family, friends or neighbours.

Thinking about people at your workplace – as far as you know, about how many are the same religion as you?

	Catholics	Protestants
	%	%
All or most	44	42
Half	29	23
Less than half	18	16
Don't know	10	19

Just over two-fifths of respondents believed that people at their workplace were mostly of the same religion as themselves. A slightly higher proportion of Catholics than Protestants thought that a half or less of their workmates were co-religionists.

The relatively high proportion of 'don't know' responses to this question is noteworthy. Why this proportion is so high is not immediately obvious. It may be related to a well-established finding in social anthropological studies in Northern Ireland: in certain contexts, people avoid talking about the issues of religion and politics (Harris, 1972; Burton, 1978; Donnan and MacFarlane,

1983). It may be that in workplaces, which appear to be one of the most integrated areas of social activity, minority group members, of whatever religion, maintain a low visibility. As a result, it may be unclear just how many of them there are. By contrast, in other areas of social life, there may be cues which enhance the visibility of minority group members. In residential neighbourhoods, for example, the school uniform worn by children provides a cue to religious affiliation. Similarly, in schools special arrangements for religious education may make minority group members more visible.

As in the case of the other areas of social life referred to above, respondents expressed generally favourable attitudes to the possibility of increased cross-sectarian contact in the workplace. Eighty-five per cent of Catholics and 72% of Protestants said that they were in favour of a bit or much more mixing where people worked. Similarly, when respondents were asked whether, if they had to change their job, they would prefer a workplace with people of their own religion or a mixed-religion workplace, 86% of Catholics and 81% of Protestants said that they would prefer the latter. In line with the results already discussed, Catholic respondents had a generally more favourable attitude to mixing.

Contact in schools and educational settings

It was pointed out at the beginning of this chapter that most concern about the need for Protestant/Catholic integration in Northern Ireland has focussed on educational settings. The great majority of pupils are educated in either predominantly Catholic or predominantly Protestant schools (Gallagher, 1989a). The recently founded, integrated secondary and primary schools in Northern Ireland have an enrolment which is about 1% of the total pupil population. These schools are sometimes described as 'planned integrated' schools, to indicate that they were founded specifically as integrated schools. The label highlights their commitment to reflect both cultural traditions in their organisation and curriculum (Dunn, 1989). It differentiates them from the small number of schools, mainly grammar schools, which have at least some pupils on their rolls from both communities. It seems likely that the number of planned integrated schools will rise in the near future. The government is committed in the 1989 Education Reform Order to support initiatives to establish integrated schools.

The Social Attitudes survey asked respondents about their experience of and attitudes towards integration in schools. Excluding those respondents who had no children, a surprisingly high proportion (21%) claimed to have sent their children to 'a mixed or integrated school'. The same proportion claimed to have attended a mixed or integrated school themselves. By comparison, Rose (1971) found that 13% of Protestants and Catholics claimed to have attended a mixed school at some point, although even this figure seems high for 1968 (see Darby et al, 1977). The most likely explanation for these unexpectedly high figures lies with respondents' interpretation of the question. An affirmative answer may have been given when respondents believed there to have been at least some pupils from both communities at their school. This reflects two differing perceptions of what is meant by an 'integrated' school (see Dunn et al, 1989).

A majority of the respondents said they were in favour of more mixing in schools: 68% of Catholics and 65% of Protestants favoured more mixing in primary schools, and 73% of Catholics and 68% of Protestants favoured more mixing in secondary schools. These figures are consistent with the results of other surveys and of numerous public opinion polls. When respondents were asked whether they would send their own children to a mixed-religion or own-religion school, the proportion favouring mixed schooling dropped a little; but it still remained at slightly over half of both Protestants and Catholics.

Respondents were also asked whether the government should encourage mixed schooling, discourage mixed schooling or leave things as they were. Once again, a clear majority indicated support for integrated schooling. Only a small minority said that the government should discourage mixed schooling. This result suggests that there is a positive climate for the government's educational reform of support for integrated schools. However, it remains to be seen how this opinion will be affected when the support is actually provided. If the relevant questions in the Social Attitudes survey are repeated in a few years' time, we shall be able to judge.

What the government should do on mixed schooling

	Catholics	Protestants
	%	%
Encourage it	67	57
Discourage it	5	9
Leave things as they are	28	33

The impact of government reforms on attitudes to educational pluralism can be assessed through several other questions. Perhaps the principal educational reform is the proposal for a common curriculum for all pupils. This differs in some important respects from the national curriculum in England and Wales. In particular, the common curriculum proposes to include two cross-curricular themes, Education for Mutual Understanding (EMU) and Cultural Heritage, which incorporate elements of community relations. Part of the rationale for this is that, despite the relative rise in the 1980s in the small number of integrated schools, for the foreseeable future most pupils will continue to be educated in predominantly Protestant or predominantly Catholic schools. The government felt that this should not preclude schools from playing some role in encouraging better community relations: hence, the two cross-curricular themes.

The survey did not ask for opinions on these themes directly. However, it did ask respondents whether they agreed or disagreed that all secondary school pupils should be taught particular subject-matter: that is, the history of Northern Ireland, British history, and the history of the Republic of Ireland. This focus reflects a concern which has been expressed over the curriculum in Northern Irish schools, at least in the time of the present 'troubles'. Magee (1970), for example, argued that much history teaching was partisan and encouraged community division.

Do you agree or disagree that all secondary school pupils should have to study the history of:

	Northern Ireland		Britain		Republic of Ireland	
	Cath.	Prot.	Cath.	Prot.	Cath.	Prot.
	%	%	%	%	%	%
Strongly agree/agree	69	73	63	80	71	50
Neither agree nor disagree	10	10	13	11	9	13
Strongly disagree/disagree	20	14	23	7	18	33

These figures appear to support a plural history curriculum. A majority of Protestants and Catholics agreed that all three aspects of history should be studied by all pupils. Within that overall agreement, however, there are differences in emphasis which reflect the different cultural traditions of the communities. While there was agreement about the teaching of Northern Ireland history, significantly more Protestants felt that British history and significantly more Catholics felt that the history of the Irish Republic should be taught to all pupils. Attitudes on the teaching of the history of the Irish Republic were most polarised. It attracted the highest extent of Catholic agreement and Protestant disagreement.

Respondents were also asked whether they agreed or disagreed that all secondary pupils should study Protestant, Catholic, and non-denominational religious beliefs. Compared with attitudes to the teaching of history, responses showed a greater level of disagreement between Protestants and Catholics. A majority of Catholics agreed that all pupils should study all three sets of religious belief. The greatest agreement was in their attitudes to the teaching of Catholic religious beliefs. By contrast, more Protestants disagreed than agreed with the proposition that all pupils should study Catholic or Protestant religious beliefs; only slightly more agreed than disagreed that they should study non-denominational religious beliefs.

Attitudes to the teaching of religious beliefs

	Protestant religious beliefs		Catholic religious beliefs		Non-denominational religious beliefs	
	Cath.	Prot.	Cath.	Prot.	Cath.	Prot.
	%	%	%	%	%	%
Strongly agree/agree	52	37	60	29	53	39
Neither agree nor disagree	17	15	15	15	20	20
Strongly disagree/disagree	27	43	22	52	22	37

The most interesting feature of these results was the pattern of Protestant responses. That the majority did not wish Catholic religious beliefs to be taught in schools can be attributed, in part, to the frequency of fundamentalist Protestantism (or anti-Roman Catholicism) in Northern Ireland (Bruce, 1986; Morrow, forthcoming). On the other hand, this does not explain more Protestants opposing than supporting the teaching of Protestant religious beliefs. That may be due to the denominational heterogeneity of Protestantism, which is obscured by the use of the umbrella term 'Protestant'. 'Protestant'

encompasses a variety of denominational categories (Church of Ireland, Presbyterian, Methodist, Free Presbyterian, etc.). While they all have major theological differences from Catholicism, they also have denominational differences from one another (Morrow, forthcoming). There is no single set of
'Protestant religious beliefs', but rather a plethora of theological nuances.
Respondents might have felt that these would not be fully incorporated within
a curriculum subject. Gallagher (1989a) found that there was a major curriculum difference between Protestant and Catholic schools in Northern Ireland
in the amount of the timetable devoted to religious education: Catholic schools
allocated up to four times more to this subject.

An alternative explanation is that, in the context of the conflict in Northern
Ireland, the teaching of Protestant religious beliefs is viewed by Protestants
as threatening: it might highlight in-group differences and implicitly, at least,
challenge the notion of a shared identity. Although this suggestion is specula-
tive, there is some evidence for it. Bruce (1986), for example, has pointed to
the frequency and importance of disputes between different Protestant denominations and sects over doctrinal issues and membership. In a situation
of crisis, when a premium is placed on in-group unity, there may be a motiva-
tion to avoid anything that could challenge the basis of that unity.

Respondents were asked whether they agreed or disagreed that all secondary
pupils should study the Irish language and culture. Again, there was considerable difference between Protestants and Catholics. Over two-thirds of Protestants disagreed, while almost three-fifths of Catholics agreed with the
proposition. Of all parts of the curriculum areas examined in the survey, this
one provoked the greatest difference in attitudes.

*Do you **agree** or **disagree** that **all** secondary school pupils should **have** to study Irish
language and culture?*

	Catholics	Protestants
	%	%
Strongly agree/agree	59	23
Neither agree nor disagree	16	14
Strongly disagree/disagree	22	69

Answers to the questions on mixed or integrated education suggest that a
somewhat higher proportion of respondents saw opportunities for mixing in
schools than other evidence suggests. However, the majority agreed that most
people did not meet those of the opposite religion in schools. Despite this, a
majority of Protestants and Catholics supported more mixing in schools and
agreed that the government should encourage more mixing.

Attitudes towards a plural curriculum were somewhat more ambivalent.
Catholics were more supportive of curricular pluralism, although this may
have been a feature of the particular subjects about which opinions were
asked. With this caveat in mind, it is clear that the Protestants' attitude to
curricular pluralism is one of 'so far, but no further'. Half the Protestants
agreed that all pupils should study the history of the Irish Republic, but just
over half did not agree that all pupils should study Catholic religious beliefs,

and over two-thirds did not agree that all pupils should study the Irish language and culture.

As educational reforms, and in particular the common curriculum and its cross-curricular themes, come into place in the schools of Northern Ireland over the next few years, it seems likely that most pupils will spend at least some time studying elements from all the curricular areas identified in the Social Attitudes survey. It will be interesting to see in future surveys whether this has any impact on attitudes.

Conclusion

A number of broad conclusions about attitudes to contact and integration between Catholics and Protestants can be drawn from the results of the first Northern Ireland Social Attitudes survey. The general perception of community relations in Northern Ireland was not very positive. A majority agreed that there was prejudice against both Catholics and Protestants, although somewhat fewer admitted to personal prejudice. Most respondents believed that the level of prejudice had not changed over the past five years; and most also believed that it would not change over the coming five years. In addition, most believed that relations between the communities had not improved and were unlikely to improve, and that religion would always have an impact on the way people felt about each other.

In this unfavourable climate, most respondents agreed that improved relations between the communities would only come about through more mixing. This view was reinforced by answers to questions about mixing in particular spheres of daily life. Most respondents favoured more mixing where people lived and worked; and most agreed that the government should encourage more mixing in schools. In other words, if one were looking for a general attitude towards contact and integration in Northern Ireland, it would be that there should be more of it and that it should improve community relations. Despite the perception of a high level of prejudice and poor community relations, only a very small minority advocated increased separation of the two communities in Northern Ireland.

A number of caveats need to be entered. The results suggest that, despite generally favourable attitudes to contact, relatively few people have had experience of direct contact with members of the opposite religion. Few were the offspring of a mixed marriage or were themselves in a mixed marriage; few suggested that there was much mixing within their family networks; most believed that they lived in areas dominated by their co-religionists and that most of their friends were co-religionists; few respondents had attended a mixed school, or had sent their children to one; and a large proportion, although not a majority, believed that most of the people in their workplace were co-religionists. If these perceptions are accurate, it is possible that people's belief in the efficacy of increased contact is based more on hope than on experience. It is possible, of course, that the continuing conflict had led respondents to believe that they had fewer contacts in certain spheres of life than was actually the case. Such a belief might be enhanced by a general avoidance of politics and religion as topics of everyday conversation (Harris, 1972; Burton, 1978; Donnan and MacFarlane, 1983).

The deliberate avoidance of these topics, particularly in conversations with strangers or in public places, may reduce the visibility of minority group members. A relatively high proportion of respondents did not know the extent to which people in their workplaces were co-religionists. Workplaces, in comparison with other areas of social activity, may provide relatively few cues to religious affiliation.

Secondly, there was a pattern of difference in the attitudes of Protestants and Catholics. Simply stated, Catholics tended to favour increased contact to a greater extent than Protestants. This was particularly true in response to questions about marriage and education: a majority of Catholics favoured more mixed marriages. The largest proportion of Protestants wanted things left as they were. Catholics showed more support for a plural curriculum, although this may have been a function of the particular curricular areas which respondents were asked to consider.

The greater support for contact among Catholics is perhaps a little surprising. Within Northern Ireland, Catholics are in the minority, and as such might be expected to view contact with suspicion. It could lead to assimilation into the majority group. However, the trend would be more understandable if Protestant attitudes were based on their position as a minority on the island of Ireland (Cairns, 1987; Gallagher, 1989b). An alternative explanation for the finding refers to the overtly anti-Catholic belief system of Protestant fundamentalists (Bruce, 1986). Although they are in a minority in the survey sample, there are enough of them to produce a picture of Protestants being less in favour of contact. A third explanation relies on the consequences of majority–minority contact in any plural society (Smith, 1987). Minority group members (that is, Catholics in Northern Ireland) will necessarily have more contact with majority group members (that is, Protestants) than vice-versa, the effect being more pronounced the smaller the minority is. The greater experience of contact by minority group members may predispose them towards more favourable attitudes to contact generally. The efficacy of each of these three explanations could be explored in further analysis of the survey results.

The analyses above are based on the responses of those who classified themselves as either Protestant or Catholic. About 16% of the respondents did not classify themselves into either category, although most of them did describe themselves as having been brought up in one of the two communities. It would be interesting to see whether the attitudes and experience of these respondents, who appear to have rejected the traditional identities of Northern Ireland, are any different from those who still adhere to them.

To date, most research on cross-sectarian contact has concentrated on children and young people (Trew, 1986, 1989). Most advocates of contact look to the schools to provide the main institutional context for contact. However, the results of the present survey suggest that the area of social activity which provides the most opportunities for contact is the workplace. The Fair Employment (Northern Ireland) Act (1989) has introduced religious monitoring of employment and has probably heightened the awareness of religious identity among employees. It is a particularly appropriate time to begin an examination of the dynamics of Protestant–Catholic relations in mixed workplaces.

References

AIREY, C., 'Social and moral values', in Jowell, R. and Airey, C. (eds), *British Social Attitudes: the 1984 report*, Gower, Aldershot (1984).

AIREY, C. and BROOK, L., 'Interim report: social and moral issues', in Jowell, R., Witherspoon, S. and Brook, L. (eds), *British Social Attitudes: the 1986 report*, Gower, Aldershot (1986).

AUNGER, E.A., 'Religion and class: an analysis of 1971 census data', in Cormack, R.J. and Osborne, R.D. (eds), *Religion, Education and Employment: aspects of equal opportunity in Northern Ireland*, Appletree Press, Belfast (1983).

BOAL, F.W., 'Territoriality on the Shankill–Falls divide, Belfast', *Irish Geography*, 6, 30–50 (1969).

BOAL, F.W., 'Segregating and mixing: space and residence in Belfast', in Boal, F.W. and Douglas, J.N.H. (eds), *Integration and Division: geographical perspectives on the Northern Ireland problem*, Academic Press, London (1982).

BOAL, F.W. and ORR, J.A.E., 'Ethnic and temporal dimensions of regional residential preferences: a Northern Ireland example', *Irish Geography*, 11, 35–53 (1978).

BRUCE, S., *God Save Ulster! The Religion and Politics of Paisleyism*, Clarendon Press, Oxford (1986).

BURTON, F., *The Politics of Legitimacy: struggles in a Belfast community*, Routledge and Kegan Paul, London (1978).

CAIRNS, E., *Caught in Crossfire: children and the Northern Ireland conflict*, Appletree Press, Belfast (1987).

CAIRNS, E., DUNN, S., MORGAN, V. and GILES, M., 'Integrated education in Northern Ireland: the impact of real choice', *Education North*, 1(2), 20–23 (1989).

COMPTON, P. and COWARD, J., *Fertility in Northern Ireland*, Gower, Aldershot (1989).

CORMACK, R.J. and OSBORNE, R.D. (eds), *Religion, Education and Employment: aspects of equal opportunity in Northern Ireland*, Appletree Press, Belfast (1983).

DARBY, J., *Intimidation and the Control of Conflict in Northern Ireland*, Gill and Macmillan, Dublin (1986).

DARBY, J. and DUNN, S., 'Segregated schools: the research evidence', in Osborne, R.D., Cormack, R.J. and Miller, R.L. (eds), *Education and Policy in Northern Ireland*, Policy Research Institute, Belfast (1987).

DARBY, J., MURRAY, D., BATTS, D., DUNN, S., FARREN, S. and HARRIS, J., *Education and Community in Northern Ireland: schools apart?*, New University of Ulster, Coleraine (1977).

DENI (DEPARTMENT OF EDUCATION NORTHERN IRELAND), *Education in Northern Ireland: proposals for reform*, DENI, Bangor (1988a).

DENI (DEPARTMENT OF EDUCATION NORTHERN IRELAND), *Education Reform in Northern Ireland: the way forward*, DENI, Bangor (1988b).

DONNAN, H. and MacFARLANE, G., 'Informal social organisation in Northern Ireland', in Darby, J. (ed), *Northern Ireland: the background to the conflict*, Appletree Press, Belfast (1983).

DUNN, S., 'Public opinion and integrated schools', unpublished paper, University of Ulster (1986).

DUNN, S., 'Integrated schools in Northern Ireland', *Oxford Review of Education*, 15(2), 121–8 (1989).

DUNN, S., MORGAN, V. and WILSON, D., 'Perceptions of integrated education', *Collected Original Resources in Education* (1989).

FRASER, R.M., *Children in Conflict*, Penguin, Harmondsworth (1974).

GALLAGHER, A.M., *Majority Minority Review 1: education and religion in Northern Ireland*, Centre for the Study of Conflict, University of Ulster (1989a).

GALLAGHER, A.M., 'Social identity and the Northern Ireland conflict', *Human Relations*, 42(10), 917–35 (1989b).

GRAY, J., *City in Revolt: James Larkin and the Belfast Dock Strike of 1907*, Blackstaff Press, Belfast (1985).

HAMILTON, A., McCARTNEY, C., FINN, A. and ANDERSON, A., *Violence and Communities*, Centre for the Study of Conflict, Coleraine (forthcoming).

HARRIS, R., *Prejudice and Tolerance in Ulster*, Manchester University Press, Manchester (1972).

HEPBURN, A.C., 'Employment and religion in Belfast, 1901–1951', in Cormack, R.J. and Osborne, R.D. (eds), *Religion, Education and Employment: aspects of equal opportunity in Northern Ireland*, Appletree Press, Belfast (1983).

HEPBURN, A.C. and COLLINS, B., 'Industrial society: the structure of Belfast, 1901', in Roebuck, P. (ed), *Plantation to Partition*, Blackstaff Press, Belfast (1981).

HESKIN, K., *Northern Ireland: a psychological analysis*, Gill and Macmillan, Dublin (1980).

HEWSTONE, M. and BROWN, R., *Contact and Conflict in Intergroup Encounters*, Basil Blackwell, Oxford (1986).

HICKEY, J., *Religion and the Northern Ireland Problem*, Gill and Macmillan, Dublin (1984).

MAGEE, J., 'The teaching of Irish history in Irish schools', *Northern Teacher*, 10(1), 15–21 (1970).

MORROW, D., *The Churches and Inter-community Relationships*, Centre for the Study of Conflict, Coleraine (forthcoming).

MOXON-BROWNE, E., *Nation, Class and Creed in Northern Ireland*, Gower, Aldershot (1983).

OSBORNE, R.D. and CORMACK, R.J., 'Religion and unemployment in Northern Ireland', *Economic and Social Review*, 17(3), 215–25 (1986).

OSBORNE, R.D. and CORMACK, R.J., *Religion, Occupations and Employment 1971–1981*, Fair Employment Agency, Belfast (1987).

POOLE, M., 'Religious segregation in urban Northern Ireland', in Boal, F.W. and Douglas, J.N.H. (eds), *Integration and Division: geographical perspectives on the Northern Ireland problem*, Academic Press, London (1982).

ROSE, R., *Governing Without Consensus: an Irish perspective*, Faber and Faber, London (1971).

SMITH, D.J., *Equality and Inequality in Northern Ireland. Part 3: perceptions and views*, Policy Studies Institute, London (1987).

SPENCER, A.E.C.W., 'Arguments for an integrated school system', in Osborne, R.D., Cormack, R.J. and Miller, R.L. (eds), *Education and Policy in Northern Ireland*, Policy Research Institute, Belfast (1987).

TREW, K., 'Catholic–Protestant contact in Northern Ireland', in Hewstone, M. and Brown, R. (eds), *Contact and Conflict in Intergroup Encounters*, Basil Blackwell, Oxford (1986).

TREW, K., 'Evaluating the impact of contact schemes for Catholic and Protestant children', in Harbison, J. (ed), *Growing Up in Northern Ireland*, Stranmillis College, Belfast (1989).

2

National identity
in Northern Ireland

Edward Moxon-Browne

National identity assumes an importance in Northern Ireland not evident elsewhere in the United Kingdom. In Britain, for the most part, lines of ethnicity, class and religion run across the preponderant 'British' identity. That identity itself encapsulates wide variations of racial and national origin: Jewish, Jamaican, Scots, Bangladeshi and Hong Kong Chinese. For all these groups, and indeed the hundreds of other ethnic minorities living in Britain, 'British' national identity can be regarded as a primordial umbrella under which subordinate ethnic identities can co-exist with reasonable ease.

In Northern Ireland, by contrast, primordial national identity is an exclusive and divisive concept. Moreover, national identity in Northern Ireland is not simply a reflection of diverse ethnicities based on successive waves of immigration. It is rooted in the colonisation of Ulster by Protestants; and, consequently, by opposing views of the legitimacy of the state and its boundaries.

In Britain, political conflict is largely mediated by rules and institutions that command widespread consent; in Northern Ireland, the conflict is rooted in rules and institutions. For example, in the present survey, when respondents were asked if they thought that *The law should always be obeyed, even if a particular law is wrong*', there was a stark contrast between Catholic and Protestant responses, with almost half (49%) of Protestants agreeing, while only 28% of Catholics did so. Likewise, when asked about the death penalty for terrorism, while 71% of Catholics oppose it, only 19% of Protestants do so – the same as in Britain as a whole. Not only does divided national identity lie at the heart of the political conflict in Northern Ireland, but also it informs and underlies other social divisions, not to mention strong divergences of attitude towards many basic issues.

The differences between the two communities in Northern Ireland are palpable. The lines of division tend to reinforce each other. There are few, if any, overarching institutions or foci of loyalty that can transcend the cleavages. Although the lines of division are often considered to be religious in character, religion is best seen as a badge of difference – the visible symbol of deeper and less tangible attachments to national 'roots'. These roots derive from historical events whose interpretation is itself a subject of conflict. Today, these conflicting interpretations manifest themselves in two sets of apparently irreconcilable political aspirations: unionists determined to maintain Northern Ireland's position within the United Kingdom, and nationalists aiming at some kind of all-Ireland structure.

At least two major surveys have previously examined the salience of national identity in Northern Ireland. Rose (1971) and Moxon-Browne (1983) report the results of attitude surveys carried out, respectively, in 1968 and 1978. Both surveys interviewed around 1300 respondents.

Rose's interviews were fortuitous in their timing: they took place a few months before the 'troubles' began in 1968. As one commentator has observed, they 'embalm for us a permanent record of attitudes in Northern Ireland at the last moment when the region was still at peace' (Whyte, 1990, p.6). The main value of the Moxon-Browne survey, carried out in the midst of the 'troubles' exactly 10 years later, was in the replication of certain key questions.

The present survey asks virtually the same questions as both Moxon-Browne and Rose, but uses a slightly different set of response-categories. For example, while all three surveys ask *Which of these (terms) best describes the way you usually think of yourself?*, the Social Attitudes survey substitutes 'Northern Irish' for 'Anglo-Irish' and does not include 'sometimes British – sometimes Irish'. Although such differences mean that findings across the three surveys can never be precisely comparable, it is nonetheless possible to draw useful conclusions from them as a series.

This chapter examines three aspects of national identity in Northern Ireland: the overlap between religion and national identity; the impact of social class on national identity; and the relationship between party political allegiance and national identity. It concludes with some comments on the evolution of national identity.

National identity and religion

The dichotomy between 'British' and 'Irish' national identity in Northern Ireland might have become less sharp had it not been for high rates of intra-group marriage (that is, endogamy). Most ethnic groups show a strong preference for endogamy. American Jews and American Blacks marry preponderantly within their own group. There is an underlying fear that the ethnic group will not survive in the next generation if only one parent is of that group. In colonial situations, or where there is a stark contrast in the respective sizes of two or more ethnic groups or, more particularly, in the gender composition of the groups, interbreeding often developed and was condoned.

In Northern Ireland, however, despite a Protestant majority, endogamy has been preserved. This has been due partly to an adequate gender balance within each community and partly to religious and political objections to intermarriage. By contrast, in the Republic of Ireland, where the Protestant minority is very small and the political implications of intermarriage are perceived as unimportant, much more intermarriage takes place. In any society in which the boundaries between communities are clearly defined, endogamy is frequently the single most important factor in maintaining the boundaries.

In Northern Ireland, endogamy is both a reflection and a cause of strong communal identity.

Rose (1971) found that only 5% of marriages crossed the communal divide; 10 years later, Moxon-Browne (1983) found the proportion to be the same, and the figure in the current survey is only slightly less (4%). The consistency of these figures reflects not only the crystallisation of the sectarian division in Northern Ireland, but a strong belief in maintaining such a division.

This lends support to the conclusions of a recent discussion (Whyte, 1986) of the factors which may be responsible for delineating boundaries between the two communities in Northern Ireland. Educational segregation and high rates of endogamy were considered to be more pertinent than party political affiliations, residential segregation, economic status or membership of the Orange Order. Much earlier, Harris (1972) had found endogamy to be the single most powerful factor in maintaining the divide between the two communities in the rural area she studied. The supremely important ties of kinship never crossed the sectarian divide. The fundamental relevance of sectarian identity patterns is underlined by Whyte's observation that when intermarriage did occur, 'it bridged no gaps, for usually the husband cut off all ties with his own kin' (Whyte, 1986, p.230). This fear of 'diluting' the prime reference-point for identity points to its significance. Marriages across social class boundaries do not arouse the same negative reactions.

Given the clearly delineated boundaries between the two communities in Northern Ireland, it might be assumed that national identity and religion are virtually synonymous. Indeed, 'Catholic' and 'nationalist', and 'Protestant' and 'unionist', respectively, are often used interchangeably. However, the evidence from four attitude surveys, including the present one, shows that there are important exceptions to this. It can be seen that, although most Protestants feel 'British' and most Catholics feel 'Irish', it is far from being a universal rule. In 1968, just before the onset of civil unrest in Northern Ireland, 20% of Protestants claimed to feel 'Irish'. Ten years later, after having borne the brunt of the IRA campaign, Protestants have swung more definitely towards adopting the label 'British'. This swing is confirmed by the David Smith survey of 1986 reported in Whyte (1990) and by the present survey.

Religion and national identity

	1968[1]		1978[2]		1986[3]		1989	
	Prot.	Cath.	Prot.	Cath.	Prot.	Cath.	Prot.	Cath.
	%	%	%	%	%	%	%	%
British	39	20	67	20	65	9	68	8
Irish	20	76	8	69	3	61	3	60
Ulster	32	5	20	6	14	1	10	2
Northern Irish	–	–	–	–	11	20	16	25

[1]Rose, 1971; [2]Moxon-Browne, 1983; [3]Whyte, 1990

National identity and social class

If social class is a part of the Northern Irish identity, its importance is obscured, in the political domain at least, by religion. Rose (1971) found that Northern Irish people are well aware of a class structure which approximates to that found in the rest of the United Kingdom. This was true of both Protestants and Catholics. However, in response to questions about their self-identification in class terms, Protestants placed themselves disproportionately in the middle and upper classes. Even when class was assigned more objectively, there was still 'a limited tendency for Protestants to have a higher occupational class than Catholics' (Rose, 1971, p.280). This socio-economic imbalance in favour of the Protestant community, as well as its relatively lower unemployment rates, was confirmed both by Aunger (1975) and Moxon-Browne (1983). Rose's famous dictum that there are 'more poor Protestants than poor Catholics in Northern Ireland' (Rose, 1971, p.289) was not supported. In the 1989 Social Attitudes survey, 47% of Catholic respondents ascribed themselves to the working class, compared with 33% of Protestants; and one in six Catholics and one in ten Protestants were unemployed. These figures suggest a narrowing of the gap between the socio-economic positions of the two communities.

National identity and social class

	Protestants				
	I	II	IIINM	IIIM	IV
	%	%	%	%	%
British	82	60	72	65	69
Irish	18	8	3	1	4
Ulster	–	8	6	17	12
Northern Irish	–	21	13	18	11
British/Irish	–	5	4	1	3

	Catholics				
	I	II	IIINM	IIIM	IV
	%	%	%	%	%
British	–	14	14	10	6
Irish	56	44	55	65	63
Ulster	–	–	7	–	3
Northern Irish	44	34	16	22	26
British/Irish	–	8	8	4	2

Is social class a barrier to social relationships? Rose asked his respondents whether they thought that they had more in common with people of the same class but a different religion, or with people of the same religion but a different class. Thirty-nine per cent of both Protestants and Catholics felt that they had more in common with those of the same class as themselves, irrespective of religion. Only 15% thought that they had more in common with co-religionists of a different class. Thirty-six per cent said that neither religion nor class makes any difference to social relations. In all three cases, there were no great differences between Protestant and Catholic views. Rose concluded from this that there was a sense of community among people in Northern Ireland and that religion played a relatively small role in their day-to-day lives. Religious differences only became important in the domain of politics. But, as Harris tells us, politics is normally a taboo subject in contacts between people of different religions in Northern Ireland, and great efforts are made to avoid controversial topics in 'mixed company' (Harris, 1972, pp.146–8).

The Social Attitudes survey suggests that both religion and class are important in social relationships. In answer to the question *How close would you say you feel towards people who have the same religious background as yours?*', and *'to people who have the same social class background as you?*', 65% said 'close' or 'very close' to both. Both religion and class were more important in this respect than area of residence, area of birth, or political beliefs.

Who do you feel closest to?

	Northern Ireland		Britain
	Prot.	Cath.	
'Very close'/'Fairly close'	%	%	%
People born in the same area	57	63	49
People of the same social class	68	65	59
People of the same religion	67	70	36
People of the same race	65	67	56
People of the same political beliefs	54	52	34
People who live in the same area	55	66	46

Rose found that political attitudes were much less affected by class than by religion (1971, pp.280–1). Within the two religious communities he found virtually no differences in socio-economic status that explained extreme or moderate political positions. In the late 1970s, however, class clearly did have an impact on national identity, political party affiliation, and attitudes towards constitutional solutions. Among Catholics, self-perceptions of being 'British' were more common among middle-class Catholics than among their working-class co-religionists (Moxon-Browne, 1983). Among Protestants the 'Ulster' label was adopted by more working-class than middle-class respondents. These contrasts are further emphasised by the social structure of support for the main political parties. The proportion of voters who were working class was greater in the Democratic Unionist Party (DUP) and Sinn Féin than in either the Official Unionist Party (OUP) or the Social Democratic and Labour Party (SDLP). Among the predominantly middle-class supporters of the Alliance Party, Catholics were noticeably more likely to see themselves as 'British' than in either the SDLP or Sinn Féin (Moxon-Browne, 1983; Moxon-Browne and Munday, 1984).

The present survey found that an Ulster identity is still relatively attractive to lower-class Protestants, though as many referred to themselves as Northern Irish, an alternative that was not available to respondents in the two earlier surveys. The 'British' label is still as strong among Protestants as it was in 1978 and 1968. Among Catholics, if the 'British' label is applied, it is more likely to be by middle-class than working-class respondents. The 'Northern Irish' label is attractive to many middle-class Catholics.

The reasons for class attachments to different national labels is a matter for speculation. It seems reasonable to suppose that middle-class Protestants benefit from the union with Britain more directly than those who are less well-off. The latter, and especially unemployed Protestants, would feel no great affinity with the status quo and still less with any attempts to extend political or economic opportunities to the Catholic community. An Irish identity is rejected by almost all Protestants. The more disadvantaged groups reject a British identity as well, perhaps because Britain is perceived to be acting in a way that is not conducive to the best interests of the Protestant working class. The claim to an 'Ulster' identity may be in protest against what are seen as alien 'English' policies. For the Protestant, national identity is a pragmatic issue. Waddell and Cairns (see Whyte, 1990, p.71) argue that national identity is more 'situationally determined' for Protestants than for Catholics. They cite the familiar observation that Protestants feel most Irish when 'watching Ireland play rugby'. Since the imposition of direct rule in 1972, a shift towards 'Ulster nationalism' has coincided with the growth of Loyalism. Both can be seen as a reaction to the more 'neutral' – and, therefore, less anti-Catholic policies – pursued by government in Northern Ireland since 1972.

What emerges unmistakeably from the present survey is the attractiveness of the 'Northern Irish' label. As a badge of identity, it is clearly less divisive than many others. Its attractiveness rests on an inherent ambiguity. Catholics can see the label as referring geographically to the northern part of Ireland. As such it can be taken to include, say, the counties of Donegal, Sligo, Cavan, Monaghan and Leitrim, all of which are politically in the Republic. This interpretation of 'Northern Ireland' avoids any legitimisation of the border; Catholics' Irishness is thus not compromised. Protestants, on the other hand, see the term as adjectivally derived from 'Northern Ireland', the official nomenclature for a part of the United Kingdom; thereby, they do not compromise their British identity.

It might be expected that the sentiment of feeling Northern Irish would be related to supporting an independent Northern Irish state. But the general weakness of support for this constitutional option and its relatively greater unpopularity among Catholics confound such a hypothesis. Support for an independent Northern Ireland has remained consistently in single figures, among both Catholics and Protestants. Asked which of seven constitutional options they would least like to see, 48% of Catholics chose an independent Northern Ireland, but only 31% of Protestants did so (Moxon-Browne, 1983, p.105).

National identity and political partisanship

In the 1978 survey (Moxon-Browne, 1983), a polarisation of national identity deflected party political support. Seventy-six per cent of SDLP supporters chose an Irish identity, while 71% of OUP respondents chose a British one. More interesting was the relatively stronger preference for an Ulster identity among DUP (34%) than among OUP supporters (21%). This asymmetry reflected the much stronger tendency for the DUP than the more moderate OUP to take 'direct action' against British government policies. The Alliance

28

Party, befitting its trans-sectarian base, incorporated both British (43%) and Irish (29%) identities and, more significantly, a higher proportion than other parties of respondents unwilling to commit themselves to either the 'British', 'Ulster' or 'Irish' labels – 17%, as against 4%, 3% and 8%, respectively, for the OUP, DUP and SDLP.

A survey of local council representatives in 1984 produced the same predictable cleavages: SDLP and Irish Independence Party (IIP) councillors were almost entirely 'Irish'. The OUP (80%) and DUP (65%) opted heavily for a 'British' identity, though one-third of the DUP described themselves as having an 'Ulster' identity. Alliance supporters were divided more or less equally between an Irish and British identity, though the largest proportion of them (36%) felt that they were 'sometimes British/sometimes Irish' (Moxon-Browne and Munday, 1984).

By 1989 the disparity between the DUP and OUP over Ulster identity has disappeared. Arguably, both parties have become alienated by the Anglo-Irish Agreement, and are equally anxious to resist any weakening of the link between Northern Ireland and the rest of the United Kingdom. The SDLP remains substantially 'Irish'. But about a quarter of supporters of the SDLP, as well as of the Alliance Party and Sinn Féin, are attracted by the notion of 'Northern Irish' identity. The complete absence of a 'British' identity among Sinn Féin supporters, and the 8% of 'British' respondents in the ranks of SDLP supporters, may reflect their differing faiths in the possibility of reform within existing political institutions (Moxon-Browne, 1986).

Political parties and national identity

	Alliance	DUP	OUP	SDLP	Sinn Féin
	%	%	%	%	%
British	54	70	71	8	–
Irish	10	6	3	65	73
Ulster	2	14	13	2	–
Northern Irish	26	10	14	24	27

Conclusion: the evolution of identity

In his pioneering study in 1968, Rose found that there were three national labels of importance in Northern Ireland: 'British', 'Irish' and 'Ulster'. Ten years later these had virtually collapsed into 'British' and 'Irish'. Protestants had become more inclined to see themselves as British, and less as identified with Ulster, while Catholics overwhelmingly saw themselves as Irish. The violence of the intervening period had undoubtedly made Protestants less inclined to see themselves as Irish, and more likely to cling to a British identity. This may, however, have derived from a perception that the Ulster identity was linked to a 'weak' political unit and that Britain, although constituting an untrustworthy custodian of Ulster's political future, was the stronger of the two contenders for control over Northern Ireland.

The present survey shows that the polarisation between Catholic Irishness and Protestant Britishness is as strong as before. The Protestant identity may be negatively based – that is, Protestants are more sure of what they are not than of what they are; their perceptions of self-identity rest on constitutional arrangements, and not on 'being born and bred', as Rose (1971) pointed out. But it shows no signs of having weakened. The fact that more Protestants now vote for the Conservative Party in Northern Ireland than vote for the Alliance Party could be interpreted as one sign of the persistence of the British attachment in the Protestant community.

References

AUNGER, E., 'Religion and occupational class in Northern Ireland', *Economic and Social Review*, 7, 1–18 (1975).

HARRIS, R., *Prejudice and Tolerance in Ulster*, Manchester University Press, Manchester (1972).

MOXON-BROWNE, E., *Nation, Class and Creed in Northern Ireland*, Gower, Aldershot (1983).

MOXON-BROWNE, E., 'Alienation: the case of the Catholics in Northern Ireland', *Journal of Political Science*, 14, 74–88 (1986).

MOXON-BROWNE, E. and MUNDAY, J., 'Bridges and chasms: cross-cutting attitudes among district councillors in Northern Ireland', *Administration*, 32, 55–75 (1984).

ROSE, R., *Governing Without Consensus: an Irish perspective*, Faber and Faber, London (1971).

WHYTE, J., 'How is the boundary maintained between the two communities in Northern Ireland?', *Ethnic and Racial Studies*, 9, 219–34 (1986).

WHYTE, J., *Interpreting Northern Ireland*, Clarendon Press, Oxford (1990).

3

Discrimination and fair employment

R.D. Osborne

This chapter examines the perception of religious discrimination in employment and attitudes to fair employment policy. In Northern Ireland, fair employment policy has been designed to improve the equality of opportunity of Protestants and Catholics. Religious discrimination in employment has long been a controversial topic of public debate. The debate was especially vigorous during the period which led up to the passing of the Fair Employment (Northern Ireland) Act: that is, around the time of the 1989 Social Attitudes survey. Thus, the views and attitudes of survey respondents were measured at a time when the principles and details of the new policy were highly salient. The chapter outlines some key elements of the policy debate and of the new legislation, before considering the relevant findings of the survey.

Fair employment: the debate and emerging policy

Allegations of unfairness in employment on the basis of religious discrimination, and the rebuttal of those allegations, formed a constant refrain during the 50 years of Unionist-dominated, devolved government. The Cameron Commission (1969), set up by the Unionist government to investigate the outbreak of disturbances at the end of the 1960s, provided evidence of malpractice in the allocation of jobs and public-sector housing by local authorities (including some which were not Unionist-controlled).

Whyte (1983) has provided the most comprehensive examination of the range of areas in which discrimination was alleged to have occurred. After systematically reviewing the available evidence for the period of devolved government in Northern Ireland, he concludes with a list of 'demerit' where evidence of discrimination is most marked: electoral practices, public employment, policing, private employment, public housing and regional policy. Whyte suggests that many of the complaints of discrimination arose as a result of the practices of Unionist-controlled local authorities, especially in the west of the Province.

> The Unionist Government must bear its share of responsibility. It put through the original gerrymander which underpinned so many of the subsequent malpractices, and then, despite repeated protests did nothing to stop those malpractices continuing. [Whyte, 1983, p. 31]

At the end of the 1960s, the Unionist government began to institute a range of reforms, stimulated partly by its own hesitant agenda, but more especially by pressure from the British government. The latter completed the reforms after the institution of direct rule in 1972. Major responsibilities of local authorities were transferred to other bodies. For example, new statutory boards were set up, for education, health and personal social services and housing. The Fair Employment (Northern Ireland) Act of 1976 made illegal religious discrimination in public and private sector employment. The Act brought into being the Fair Employment Agency (FEA), which had the duties of eliminating religious discrimination and of promoting equality of opportunity in employment. It was responsible for the investigation of individual complaints of discrimination and was also empowered to conduct investigations into individual employers. A central point in the directions issued by the FEA was that employers should institute religious monitoring of their employees.

Essentially, the 1976 legislation sought voluntary compliance in the institution of equality of opportunity. However, even the Civil Service was slow to respond to the legislation; like other employers it only responded after an FEA investigation (FEA, 1982). No significant organisation or employer 'took the lead' in implementing an equal opportunity policy with monitoring as its central component. By the mid-1980s, there was a widespread feeling that the 1976 initiative had failed. There was new evidence from the government's Continuous Household Survey (CHS) of continuing and significant Catholic labour-market disadvantage, especially in terms of unemployment. (For a full assessment of the factors leading to the decision to reform see Osborne and Cormack, 1989.) Catholics experience substantially higher rates of unemployment, are more likely to be dependent on social benefits and have lower household incomes than Protestants (Osborne and Cormack, 1986; Harbison, 1989).

New legislation, the Fair Employment (Northern Ireland) Act, was passed in 1989. By having monitoring at the centre of its informing policy, the Act is in advance of equal opportunity policy in the rest of the United Kingdom. Specifically, the Act requires all employers with 25 or more employees to monitor their religious affiliation and to submit an annual return to the Fair Employment Commission (FEC). Larger private-sector companies and all public-sector organisations are also required to monitor applications and appointments. By far the most significant innovation of this new legislation is the institution of employment monitoring.

Attitudes to fair employment

Some of the questions in the Social Attitudes survey relating to the issue of fair employment replicated questions in an earlier survey conducted by the Policy Studies Institute (PSI) (Smith, 1987). The PSI survey of 1672 adults, conducted in 1986, covered a wide range of social and economic issues. Perceptions of discrimination formed a major focus of the survey. Whereas the PSI survey measured attitudes at the end of the first decade of fair employment intervention and prior to the period leading to the revised legislation, the Social Attitudes survey was carried out while the Fair Employment (Northern Ireland) Bill was before Parliament. Responses to the two surveys will be compared where appropriate.

Perceptions of discrimination

Perhaps the most basic issue to be assessed is the extent to which respondents believe there to be religious discrimination in employment in Northern Ireland. Respondents were asked their opinion of the relative chances in the job market of Protestants and Catholics.

*On the whole, do you think the Protestants and Catholics in Northern Ireland who apply for the same jobs have the **same** chance of getting a job or are their chances of getting a job different?*

	Social Attitudes Survey		PSI Survey	
	Cath.	Prot.	Cath.	Prot.
	%	%	%	%
Same chance	30	60	26	68
Different chance	60	30	67	27
Don't know	10	10	7	5
If different:				
Protestants favoured	89	34	84	28
Catholics favoured	1	43	–	25
Depends	4	12	16	28
Don't know	6	10	–	18

The responses correspond quite closely to those in the PSI survey. A high proportion of Catholics believe that labour-market chances vary according to religion, as do a significant minority of Protestants. A large majority of Catholics believe Protestants to be favoured, as do one-third of Protestants. Overall, Protestants tend to see advantages in the labour-market for both Protestants and Catholics. Catholics are more likely to perceive job opportunities as being weighted against them, whereas a significant proportion of Protestants see this as being the lot of both Protestants and Catholics. These differences suggest that Protestants have a view of a segregated society in which each community 'looks after its own'; Catholics perceive a society which inflicts substantial disadvantage on their own community.

Respondents were also asked about employers' employment practices with regard to Protestants and Catholics.

*Some people think that many employers are **more** likely to give jobs to Protestants than to Catholics. Do you think this happens?*

	Catholics	Protestants
	%	%
A lot	26	6
A little	54	43
Hardly at all	13	42
Don't know	8	8

A substantial majority of Catholics believe that employers favour Protestants. Moreover, virtually half the Protestant respondents also believe that employers favour Protestants, although this is seen as happening 'a little' rather than 'a lot'.

Respondents were asked why employers might favour Protestants. Of those respondents who believed that Protestants were favoured, a clear majority of both Protestants and Catholics believed this to be due to discrimination on the part of employers, though a much higher proportion of Catholics held this view.

Reasons employers favour Protestants

	Catholics %	Protestants %
Employers discriminate	87	67
Catholics not qualified	2	12
Both reasons	4	8
Don't know	6	13

When respondents were asked whether employers favoured Catholics, the pattern of replies showed a greater similarity between the two groups. Slightly less than half of Catholic respondents believed that employers favour Catholics, compared with more than half of Protestants. On this question, in which they were asked specifically about the actions of employers, more Catholics indicated that some employers favour Catholics than when they were asked the more general question about the respective chances of the two communities in the labour-market.

*Some people think that many employers are **more** likely to give jobs to Catholics. Do you think this happens?*

	Catholics %	Protestants %
A lot	6	13
A little	43	44
Hardly at all	42	33
Don't know	10	10

Of those who believe that employers are more likely to give jobs to Catholics, a clear majority of both Protestants and Catholics believe that this happens because employers discriminate, rather than because Protestants are not qualified.

Reasons employers favour Catholics

	Catholics %	Protestants %
Employers discriminate	83	76
Protestants not qualified	4	6
Both reasons	6	6
Don't know	7	12

Perhaps the most important finding from the answers to these questions is the high proportion of both Protestants and Catholics who believe that discrimination operates in the labour-market. There are relatively more Catholics who believe that there is discrimination against Catholics than Protestants who believe that Protestants are unfairly treated. However, a significant proportion, approaching half, of Protestants believe that Protestants are advantaged in the competition for jobs and that employers favour Protestants. (They also believe, in similar proportions, that employers favour Catholics.)

Employment status

The question arises as to whether the differential economic position of Catholics and Protestants influences people's attitudes towards relative opportunities in the labour-market. In their answers to a question on whether Protestants and Catholics have the same chance of getting a job, the two groups of respondents showed a marked difference. Employed Catholics are significantly more likely than unemployed Catholics to believe that Protestants and Catholics have the same chance, though even a majority of Catholics who are employed believe that the chances of the two communities are different. Unemployed Catholics are far less likely to believe that the two groups have the same chance of a job than unemployed Protestants.

Perceptions of relative labour-market opportunity, by employment status

	Catholics		Protestants	
	Employed	Unemployed	Employed	Unemployed
	%	%	%	%
Same chance	34	22	55	66
Different chance	57	70	34	28
Don't know	9	8	10	8

When respondents were asked specifically whether Protestants are favoured by employers, the effect of employment status is not so clear-cut. Some 85% of unemployed Catholics believe that Protestants are favoured by employers, compared with three-quarters of Catholics in employment. On the other hand, fewer Protestants, and almost the same proportions of employed and unemployed Protestants, believe that Protestants are favoured by employers.

Perceptions of whether employers favour Protestants, by employment status

	Catholics		Protestants	
	Employed	Unemployed	Employed	Unemployed
	%	%	%	%
A lot	18	36	6	7
A little	58	49	52	52
Hardly at all	16	13	38	34
Don't know	8	3	5	7

Fair employment

A substantial proportion of both Protestant and Catholic respondents believes that there is unfairness and discrimination in the labour-market and that it variously gives advantages and disadvantages to both groups. How do respondents view the fair employment legislation? Half of all respondents show some support for the legislation, but there are major differences in attitude between Protestants and Catholics. Almost two-thirds of Catholics support the legislation, with nearly half showing strong support. On the other hand, only two-fifths of Protestants support fair employment, and only one in five shows strong support. Strong opposition, on the other hand, is expressed by one-third of Protestants, but by only one-sixth of Catholics. Unemployed Catholics show the strongest support for the fair employment law, whilst unemployed Protestants divide equally between those in support of and those against the legislation.

Monitoring

A central feature of the new fair employment legislation was the introduction of monitoring. All employers with 25 or more employees (from 1992 this lower limit will be reduced to 10) are required to file an annual return to the Fair Employment Commission on the religious composition of their workforce. Larger employers and public-sector organisations are also required to monitor the religion of job applicants.

Attitudes towards monitoring were elicited by two questions. One question related monitoring to the requirements of the fair employment law.

Do you generally support or oppose a fair employment law in Northern Ireland, that is a law which requires employers to keep records on the religion of their employees and make sure there is no discrimination?

	Catholics %		Protestants %	
Support strongly	47		20	
Support just a bit	16	64	21	42
Support	1		1	
Oppose	1		2	
Oppose just a bit	10	27	14	49
Oppose strongly	16		33	
Don't know	10		9	

Support for a fair employment law that incorporates monitoring receives significantly stronger support from Catholics than Protestants. Only one-fifth of Protestant respondents strongly support monitoring, compared with nearly one-half of Catholics. One-third of Protestants strongly oppose monitoring, compared with approximately one-sixth of Catholics. Perhaps surprisingly, however, over one-quarter of Catholics do not support monitoring.

The other question sought to measure attitudes towards monitoring more directly.

*Some people say that all employers should keep records on the religion of their employees to make sure there is not discrimination. Other people say this is not necessary. What about you – do you think employers **should** or **should not** keep records about their employees' religion?*

	Catholics		**Protestants**	
	%		%	
Strongly should	17 ⎫		8 ⎫	
Just a bit should	14 ⎬ 31		13 ⎬ 22	
Should	* ⎭		* ⎭	
Should not	1 ⎫		1 ⎫	
Just a bit should not	19 ⎬ 64		22 ⎬ 73	
Strongly should not	44 ⎭		50 ⎭	
Don't know	6		6	

For a number of reasons, the responses to this question are the most interesting to be reported in this chapter. Their pattern suggests that monitoring, when not specifically related to the fair employment legislation, is unpopular. A majority of both Protestants and Catholics do not support monitoring in this context – a clear contrast with attitudes to monitoring when it is linked explicitly to fair employment. For many respondents, especially Catholics, the idea of employers undertaking a religious head-count outside the provisions of fair employment legislation may recall the days when it was believed that many employers kept such records to assist in discriminatory behaviour.

However, this interpretation sits rather awkwardly with the findings of Smith's (1987) survey. His respondents were asked whether records of employees' religion should be kept by employers.

Would you be prepared for your employers to keep a record of your religion?

	Catholics	**Protestants**
	%	%
Yes	70	67
No	27	31
Don't know	3	2

(Based on respondents economically active in employment.)

Responses in this earlier survey give clear support to monitoring on the part of both Protestants and Catholics. Has there, perhaps, been a fall in support for monitoring? The answer is not clear. A high level of support may have been expressed in response to Smith's question because it linked monitoring to the respondent's own employer ('my employer is OK – but employers in general are less trustworthy'). It may be that monitoring for positive reasons

37

represents such a new concept that attitudes and opinions are both volatile and also very sensitive to the particular structure of questions. It will be interesting to see how people's attitudes responded to the reality of monitoring when employers undertook it for the first time in the early part of 1990.

Conclusions

Attitudes and opinions are shaped both by individuals' characteristics (attitudes are related to values and experiences, etc.) and by the public discussion of issues – with family, friends, neighbours and in the media. In Northern Ireland, the communal division produces a basic dichotomy in the perception and discussion of many issues. Traditionally, there has been little common ground between most Catholics, who believe that there has been and continues to be extensive discrimination in employment against Catholics, and most Protestants, who believe the Catholic claims to be greatly exaggerated. To a degree, the traditional parameters of this debate have been reflected in the attitudes recorded in this survey. However, there may also be some evidence that more Protestants are beginning to recognise the existence of discrimination and the disadvantages faced by Catholics. As the new fair employment legislation is implemented, it will be important to assess whether there is an increasing sense of fairness and equality in the labour-market. It may be that, for Catholics, this will only occur if the new policy can actually be seen to deliver greater opportunity for them. In the case of Protestants, perceptions of unfairness in the labour-market may increase if greater fairness for Catholics is perceived as being achieved only at Protestants' expense.

Note

This chapter analyses the responses only of those who indicated a religious affiliation. Of the 866 respondents 85% indicated a Protestant or Catholic affiliation (61% of these being Protestant and 39% Catholic).

References

CAMERON COMMISSION, *Disturbances in Northern Ireland*, Cmd 532, HMSO, Belfast (1969).

FEA (FAIR EMPLOYMENT AGENCY), *Report of an Investigation by the Fair Employment Agency into the Non-industrial Northern Ireland Civil Service*, FEA, Belfast (1982).

HARBISON, J., 'The social and economic context of growing up in Northern Ireland', in Harbison, J.(ed), *Growing Up in Northern Ireland*, Stranmillis College, Belfast (1989).

OSBORNE, R.D. and CORMACK, R.J., 'Religion and unemployment in Northern Ireland', *Economic and Social Review*, 17(3), 215–25 (1986).

OSBORNE, R. D. and CORMACK, R. J., 'Fair Employment: towards reform in Northern Ireland', *Policy and Politics*, 17(4), 287–94 (1989).

SMITH, D., *Equality and Inequality in Northern Ireland: perceptions and views*, Policy Studies Institute, London (1987).

WHYTE, J., 'How much discrimination was there under the Unionist regime, 1921–1968?', in Gallagher, T. and O'Connell, J. (eds), *Contemporary Irish Studies*, Manchester University Press, Manchester (1983).

4

Social class

Liam O'Dowd

Sociological dimensions of class

Debates on the nature, measurement and significance of class continue to be a central preoccupation of the international sociological literature (Marshall et al, 1988; Wright et al, 1989; Breen et al, 1990; Marshall and Rose, 1990; Emmison and Western, 1990; Pawson, 1990). A recent survey carried out by researchers at the University of Essex challenges assertions that class has become irrelevant or anachronistic in Britain in the 1980s. The survey could find no evidence that 'class has lost its salience as the foremost source of social identity' (Marshall et al, 1988, pp. 225–6). It concluded that 'differences in attitudes and values are structured more obviously by class than by other possible sources of social cleavage'. While these conclusions have been challenged (see, for example, Emmison and Western, 1990), a strong case has nevertheless been made that class still exerts a strong influence on voting behaviour in Britain (see Marshall et al, 1988; Marshall and Rose, 1990).

In Northern Ireland, by contrast, the debate over the role of class has been much more muted. Apart from a large-scale survey of class and mobility undertaken in 1973 (see Miller, 1986), there have been no major studies of class structure. The absence of such studies is a reflection of the conventional wisdom, which sees class as considerably less significant than forms of identity based on ethnicity, religion or nationality. Moreover, to argue that Northern Ireland is a class-based society seems to invoke an undesirable similarity to other societies, including Britain. Class is neglected in order to emphasise what apparently makes Northern Ireland different – the intense ethnic–national conflict.

Among the more explicit reasons for the neglect of class is the absence of any support for socialist parties of the British and European variety. This absence may also be used as evidence for a lack of political activism based on class. This is despite the fact that simply voting for a political party that has a class rhetoric is a very inadequate indicator of class activism or class politics.

While the Essex survey (Marshall et al, 1988) found that class influenced voting behaviour, it also found little evidence of a link between class identity and class activism in a broader sense. Britain, it suggested, is not a nation of class warriors. Nevertheless, the Essex researchers do see the prevalence and persistence of class identity as significant in a society in which the organised pursuit of pecuniary self-interest is a central feature. Taking up this theme, Pahl (1989) has recently argued that class has ceased to be useful as a means of explaining how consciousness is transformed into action, although he is prepared to accept that it is a useful concept for understanding macro-historical change. Heath and Topf (1987, p. 61), in their discussion of British Social Attitudes data, suggest that radical views of social order are influenced by class and are associated with cynicism towards government, but that they are not 'at all strongly associated with activism'.

The purpose of this chapter is to explore several dimensions of class identity and class awareness in Northern Ireland. It will for the most part leave aside the question of the links between these concepts and class activism. It tests the view that other more powerful identities diminish the significance of class identity. Using comparable data from Britain, it seeks to examine whether class identity is more muted in Northern Ireland. The chapter concludes with a brief discussion of how the links between class identity, class politics and class activism might best be understood in the context of Northern Ireland.

Locating class identity

It is now possible to make an initial comparison of Northern Ireland with Britain as regards the self-assignment of class. Airey and Brook (1986, p.151), in presenting data for 1983–5 from the British Social Attitudes surveys, have noted the relatively unchanging patterns of self-assignment of class over time. The 1989 data demonstrate that Northern Ireland deviates little from the British pattern. It is not surprising that more people in Northern Ireland see themselves as working class, given the substantial gap in average household income between Britain and Northern Ireland, the consistently higher unemployment and greater reliance on state benefits (Curtice and Gallagher, 1990). Figures derived from the survey of Marshall et al (1988) in Britain show a higher middle-class identification. However, the form of the question posed in that study was somewhat different: 'Suppose you were asked to say which class you belonged to which would you say?' (p.295). All the surveys reveal an almost universal willingness among respondents to assign themselves a class identity.

Self-assigned class in Northern Ireland and Britain

	Northern Ireland (1989)		Britain (1989)		Britain (1984)	
	%		%		%	
Upper middle class	1	} 25	2	} 29	3	} 38
Middle class	24		26		35	
Upper working class	17	} 69	19	} 66	11	} 49
Working class	52		47		38	
Poor	4		3		4	
Don't know	2		2		8	

What is striking in Northern Ireland is that more people seem to embrace a class identity than either a religious or political identity. Thus, 98% of respondents saw themselves as having a class identity, 85% defined themselves as having a particular religion (36% Catholic, 49% Protestant and 15% other), and only 54% claimed to be either unionist or nationalist.

Interpretation of these differences needs to be cautious. The question on self-assigned class identity was more directive than those about religious or political identity: *'Most people see themselves as belonging to a particular social class. Please look at this card and tell me which social class you would say you belong to?'* The religious and political questions were: *'Do you regard yourself as belonging to any particular religion? If yes, which?';* and *'Generally speaking, do you think of yourself as a unionist, a nationalist or neither?'.*

Substantial majorities of both non-manual (67%) and manual worker Protestants (75%) identified themselves as unionists. Yet, remarkably, only 32% of non-manual and 45% of manual worker Catholics identified themselves as nationalists, with 67% and 55% respectively identifying themselves as neither unionist nor nationalist. Both Protestant and Catholic manual workers were more likely than their non-manual counterparts to identify themselves as unionists or nationalists.

The low proportion claiming a political affiliation must be seen in a political context in which the great majority have voted for either unionist or nationalist parties and have consistently rejected alternatives. While failure to assert a political affiliation might demonstrate political flexibility, especially among Catholics, the data do show clear evidence of sharp underlying polarisation. No Protestant (non-manual or manual) worker claimed to be nationalist and only one Catholic (non-manual) worker claimed to be a unionist.

There are some differences across political affiliations with respect to the self-assignment of class. Only 14% of those who claim nationalist affiliation see themselves as middle class, compared with 24% of unionists and 28% of those who claim no political affiliation. Of the middle class, 47% claimed a political affiliation, compared to 58% of those who saw themselves as working class.

Self-assigned class by political affiliation

	Unionists	Nationalists	Neither
	%	%	%
Middle class	24	14	28
Working class	73	80	63
Poor	1	4	7
Don't know/Other	2	2	2

When we look more closely at the 85% of respondents who claimed to be either Protestant or Catholic, we see substantial differences between the two groups in terms of the self-assignment of class. A half of Protestants see themselves as either middle class or upper working class, compared to 31% of Catholics. Similarly, 67% of Catholics see themselves as working class or poor, compared to 48% of Protestants.

41

Self-assigned class by religion

	Protestants	Catholics
	%	%
Middle class	28	19
Upper working class	22	12
Working class	46	61
Poor	2	6
Don't know/Other	2	2

The next table suggests that the much-criticised manual/non-manual distinction (for example, Saunders, 1990, p. 27ff) has some roots in class identity. Over twice as many manual (76%) as non-manual workers (37%) saw themselves as working class or poor. Conversely, 72% and 69%, respectively, of those who assigned themselves to the middle and upper working classes were non-manual workers. Only 32% of those claiming a working-class identity were non-manual workers.

Self-assigned class by manual/non-manual status

	Non-manual	Manual
	%	%
Middle class	35	12
Upper working class	26	10
Working class	36	70
Poor	1	6
Don't know/Other	2	2

Although respondents embrace class identities, it is clear that they are shaped in different ways by political affiliation, religious allegiance and non-manual/manual status.

Perceived importance of class

The existence of class identity guarantees nothing about its significance. Is class identity perceived as any more or less important than, for example, being a certain height or having a particular colour of hair? Nearly two-thirds (64%) of respondents in Northern Ireland felt that a *person's social class affects his or her opportunities a great deal or quite a lot*. The comparable British figure is 59%.

There is a considerable degree of cross-class consensus on this point in Northern Ireland (see Tables 4.1, 4.2 and 4.3 at the end of this chapter). About two-thirds of middle-class, working-class, non-manual and manual worker respondents believed that class affects opportunities a great deal or quite a lot. Approximately one-third felt that class matters not very much or not at all.

The perceived importance of class remains remarkably consistent when other variables are controlled for. In terms of the manual/non-manual distinction, the greatest difference is between male and female non-manual respondents, with the latter being more likely to stress the effect of class. This is not surprising in view of the nature and poor pay of much of women's non-manual work. In terms of political affiliation, the biggest gap is between male unionists and nationalists: the latter are more likely to stress the influence of class. For those respondents who report no political affiliation, controlling for gender makes little difference to the importance attributed to class.

What of the perceived importance of class by occupational categories? The largest difference is between professionals/employers and manual workers. Only 19% of the former believe that class affects opportunities a great deal, compared to about one-third of the latter. From their position at the top of the class structure, professionals and employers see class as less significant than do groups lower down the hierarchy. Yet when opinions are dichotomised (a great deal/quite a lot versus not very much/not at all), it is the intermediate non-manual group that attributes the most significance to class – 69%, compared with 62% of the two categories of manual workers and 59% of professionals/employers.

Perceived impact of class by occupational categories

	Professionals/ employers etc.	Intermediate non-manual	Skilled manual	Semi/ unskilled manual	Other
	%	%	%	%	%
A great deal	19	24	35	33	33
Quite a lot	40	45	27	29	29
Not very much	35	26	28	27	23
Not at all	6	5	5	8	7
Don't know/Other	–	–	5	3	8

Despite some variation in this table there is an underlying consistency with the data in Tables 4.1 and 4.2. Across all categories, approximately two-thirds believe that class matters a great deal or quite a lot, and one-third that it matters not very much or not at all. Significantly, only a small proportion in all categories (less than 10%) believes that class has no effect upon opportunities.

The strong sense that class affects opportunities co-exists with a profound conviction of the significance of religion in Northern Ireland. When respondents were asked whether *'religion will always make a difference in Northern Ireland'*, 87% answered in the affirmative, with only 8% saying 'no'. There was little variation between manual and non-manual workers, and little variation was evident when the significance attributed to class was controlled for. For example, 90% of manual workers and 87% of non-manual workers who thought that class affected opportunities a great deal also thought that religion would always make a difference. Of the much smaller numbers of manual and non-manual workers who thought that class did not affect opportunities, 80% thought that *'religion will always make a difference'*. This evidence lends support to the thesis that consciousness of class is not an alternative to consciousness of religion; rather, they co-exist.

Egalitarianism

The fact that respondents in Northern Ireland embraced class identities and generally perceived class to be important in affecting opportunities is not necessarily evidence for a class-conflict model of society. Heath and Topf (1987, p.59) note that there has been much debate about the nature of class consciousness in British society: that is, about whether the working class has a conflict model of society and holds radical values, or whether it accepts the 'dominant ideology' which endorses the existing and unequal economic order. It might be argued that the existence of strong cross-class, communal identities in Northern Ireland diminishes awareness of an unequal economic order.

The next table allows us to make a direct comparison of Northern Irish and British attitudes to economic inequality. The data demonstrate that people in Northern Ireland show a greater tendency to be egalitarian or radical than their British counterparts, on three of the five statements to which they responded. This suggests that cross-class communalism has not dulled perceptions of economic inequality.

Attitudes to economic inequality, Northern Ireland and Britain

	Agree		Neither		Disagree	
	NI	GB	NI	GB	NI	GB
	%	%	%	%	%	%
One law for rich, one for poor.	65	67	16	14	17	16
Big business benefits owners at expense of workers	56	53	20	24	22	21
Ordinary people do not get their fair share of the nation's wealth	69	65	16	18	14	16
Management will always try to get the better of workers if it gets the chance	56	58	22	21	21	19
Management and workers are always on opposite sides	45	38	20	19	29	39

Another issue is whether there are differences across classes in terms of radical or egalitarian opinion. Are any such class differences more or less important in Northern Ireland than in Britain? We can roughly follow Heath and Topf's (1987, p.60) breakdown of classes into salariat (professions, managers, employers), intermediate classes (intermediate/junior non-manual) and working class. There are interesting, if relatively small, differences between Britain and Northern Ireland, as shown in the next table. The Northern Ireland salariat is rather less egalitarian or radical than its British counterpart, while the intermediate classes in Northern Ireland are more radical/egalitarian. In the working class, there is little difference.

However, this table does demonstrate that class divisions on these questions are at least as deep in Northern Ireland as in Britain. In both Northern Ireland and Britain, there are substantial differences between the working class and the other classes, with the former being far more likely to have egalitarian or radical attitudes. Interestingly, the salariat in Northern

Ireland differs more from the other two classes than it does in Britain – holding relatively more conservative views on all three of the statements. The intermediate classes in Northern Ireland hold views which are closer to those of the working class than is the case in Britain: in Britain there is a relatively greater difference in attitude between these two groups.

Agreeing with radical alternative

	Salariat		Intermediate classes		Working class	
	NI	GB	NI	GB	NI	GB
	%	%	%	%	%	%
Nation's wealth unfairly distributed	42	48	67	60	77	75
One law for rich, one for poor	42	54	63	63	75	79
Management/workers are always on opposite sides	29	30	37	27	54	53

Curtice and Gallagher's (1990) analysis of the 1989 Social Attitudes surveys in Britain and Northern Ireland underlines the above findings. They conclude that attitudes to economic equality are as strongly related to class in Northern Ireland as in Britain.

What did respondents feel should be done about economic inequality? Northern Ireland is more heavily dependent on public expenditure, state transfers and subsidies than any other part of the UK (Rowthorn and Wayne, 1988; O'Dowd, 1989; Curtice and Gallagher, 1990). Some interesting comparisons on people's attitudes to redistribution of income by government are summarised in the next table.

The government should redistribute income

	Agree		Neither		Disagree	
	NI	GB	NI	GB	NI	GB
	%	%	%	%	%	%
Salariat	37	39	20	16	43	43
Intermediate classes	52	45	21	22	27	32
Skilled manual	55	53	18	22	27	24
Semi/unskilled manual	74	60	15	20	11	18

There is a considerable difference between the ends of the class spectrum, in both Northern Ireland and Britain. The gulf is even more marked in Northern Ireland, where proportionately twice as many semi/unskilled workers favour the redistribution of income by government as do members of the salariat. Conversely, in Northern Ireland members of the salariat are four times more likely than semi/unskilled workers to oppose the proposition compared to two-and-a-half times more likely in Britain.

Northern Ireland is a major beneficiary of redistributive public expenditure. The high level of dependency on state transfer payments is consistent with semi/unskilled manual workers favouring the redistribution of income by government. However, the relatively high measure of opposition to government intervention among the Northern Ireland salariat is more surprising, given the extent to which professionals and the self-employed (including relatively large numbers of farmers) also rely on public expenditure and subsidies. It is tempting to suggest that the salariat are opposed only to those forms of redistribution which impact elsewhere in the class hierarchy. However, even though the salariat in Northern Ireland is more conservative than its British counterpart, the difference in attitudes to economic inequality and state intervention in Northern Ireland and Britain is relatively narrow (see also Curtice and Gallagher, 1990).

In both sets of data there are sharp class differences. In view of the cross-class communalist nature of politics in Northern Ireland, it might be expected that these differences would be more muted when responses are broken down by political affiliation. On the contrary, the findings suggest that there are substantially different responses across political affiliations. Nationalists are more radical, and unionists less radical, than the Northern Ireland average in their responses to the five propositions. Those who claim no political affiliation are close to the average in each case. Political affiliation moderates, but does not obliterate, the differential responses noted in the previous tables. Nationalists show a radical profile, whilst unionists are relatively more conservative. Significantly, the gulf between nationalists and others is widest on the question of whether the government should redistribute income. This is also the issue that sharply discriminates between the classes. Unionists share with the salariat an antipathy to the redistribution of income by government. The profile of nationalist responses is remarkably close to that of semi/unskilled manual workers.

These findings provide a reminder of the extent of social disaffection shared by nationalists and semi/unskilled manual workers, and of the distance between these two groups and unionists and the salariat. The impact of unemployment and social deprivation on semi/unskilled manual workers and on the nationalist community make these responses understandable.

Agreeing with radical alternative

	Unionist	Nationalist	No stated affiliation	Total
	%	%	%	%
Government should redistribute income	48	70	57	55
Big business benefits owners at expense of workers	50	69	57	56
Ordinary people do not get their fair share of the nation's wealth	63	78	70	69
Management will always try to get the better of workers if it gets the chance	52	70	54	56
One law for rich, one for poor	55	77	70	65

Summary and conclusion

Much more analysis of the available data is needed if we are fully to probe the various dimensions of class differentiation in Northern Ireland. The evidence here suggests that, far from class identification being more muted in Northern Ireland, it is in some respects more sharply articulated than in Britain. Class identity persists, even though, as in Britain, the organised pursuit of pecuniary self-interest is one of the central features of the society.

More important, it may be asked why the existence of powerful cross-class, communal identifications has not undermined class awareness and consciousness. The evidence suggests that communal identifications are not alternatives to class identity; rather, they co-exist with it. Class differentiation and division may sustain rather than undermine these identities, and vice-versa. Class profile varies across political and religious affiliations and across the manual/non-manual distinction. Nevertheless, the overwhelming majority of respondents acknowledged a class identity. Roughly two-thirds of respondents in all the categories analysed thought that class affected opportunities. This view represents a broad cross-class and cross-community consensus.

Comparisons between British and Northern Ireland survey data suggest that, in broad terms, respondents in Northern Ireland adopt more radical (or cynical?) and egalitarian attitudes to the economic system. Perceptions of economic inequality are more marked in Northern Ireland and the gulf between the classes is wider on their response to a number of key propositions.

There are major differences between the salariat and semi/unskilled manual workers on responses to inequality: that is, on whether the government should redistribute income. Differences also exist between nationalists and unionists on this issue. Semi/unskilled manual workers and nationalists are notably more radical and egalitarian on the propositions examined than their middle-class and unionist counterparts. The data suggest, therefore, that the Northern Ireland class structure contains a relatively conservative middle class (salariat) and a working class that is relatively radical and egalitarian on social questions. It seems clear that the middle classes have not been able to establish hegemony: they have failed to generate widespread ideological acceptance of a status quo that is perceived to be unequal. This is an interesting finding in an area where cross-class communal organisation seems to be so strong. There is little evidence, however, that this has led to a reduction in the salience of the communal divide.

The data demonstrate the strength of class identity and class awareness at several levels in Northern Ireland, and raise important questions about how links there between class identity (awareness), class activism and class politics might be understood. Superficially, there appears to be a much more tenuous link between class identity and class politics in Northern Ireland than in Britain. Nonetheless, Northern Ireland's political parties do provide environments for the articulation of class identity. It is interesting, for example, that those who explicitly claim a unionist or nationalist affiliation are more likely to be manual workers and to see themselves as working class.

Class politics may mean something quite different in Northern Ireland than in Britain. It may be misleading to define class politics in such narrow terms as, for example, support or involvement in parties that claim to be left-wing. Curtice and Gallagher's (1990) analysis provides an interesting confirmation of this point. They examine the responses of people who identify with the major Northern Ireland parties to two propositions: one, that the government should redistribute income; and, two, that ordinary people do not get their share of the nation's wealth. Seventy per cent of those identifying with the SDLP or DUP agreed with the first proposition and 80% of both groups agreed with the second. This marked them out as having more 'left-wing' views on these issues than people identifying with the OUP or Alliance Party. The DUP, however, would scarcely claim to be a left-wing party, even though it is supported by a disproportionately large sector of the Protestant working class. Although many socialists within and without Northern Ireland regularly question the left-wing credentials of the SDLP, it does seem to represent the relatively egalitarian and radical perceptions of most nationalists across the class spectrum. Had the survey sample been on sufficiently large a scale to include enough Sinn Féin supporters, we might have found that their perception of these issues scarcely differed from that of their most bitter opponents – the DUP.

Will the substantial degree of class awareness revealed in the above data provide a platform for class activism or class politics? An answer to this question depends crucially on how such activism or politics is defined. Class awareness may be present in political parties which are militantly anti-socialist or which give priority to constitutional or national questions. It is beyond the scope of this chapter to examine the extent to which class activism is also evident in these parties, and thereby to assess the extent to which class awareness is linked to class activism. However, in Britain links between class identity and class activism have proved notoriously difficult to establish.

For these reasons, it may be misleading to suggest (as do Curtice and Gallagher, 1990) that it is only the strength of the religious divide in Northern Ireland that prevents a version of British 'class politics' emerging there. Using British 'class politics' as an abstract measuring stick to assess a degree of cultural and political lag in Northern Ireland is a questionable procedure. Electoral behaviour is an inadequate measure of class politics, or of class activism in a wider sense. Moreover, it seems likely that voting behaviour and party affiliation have a rather different meaning in Northern Ireland than in Britain. Voting in Northern Ireland is a way of affirming ethnic–national and religious solidarity, as well as a plebiscite on the territorial boundaries of the state.

The recent willingness to introduce the Conservative Party into Northern Ireland might appear to indicate a modernisation of local politics, bringing them more into line with those in Britain. It seems more plausible, however, to suggest that this is simply a traditional articulation of ethnic–national, religious and class identities under a new guise. Indeed, the Social Attitudes survey lends support to this interpretation.

The major contrast drawn by Curtice and Gallagher (1990) is between a Northern Ireland sharply polarised on religious grounds and a Britain polarised, although less sharply, by class. Yet, in terms of class awareness at least, Northern Ireland is as polarised as Britain. One might assume that the direction of change will be away from ethnic–national or religious division towards a more class-based politics – the laggard 'province' will 'catch up' with the 'mainland'. An alternative and perhaps more convincing interpretation recognises that class identity has always articulated with other identities in Northern Ireland, and will continue to do so. Perhaps it is necessary to look beyond the British interpretations of 'class politics' and 'class activism' and to treat the British 'measuring stick' more sceptically. Class politics in Northern Ireland operate through parties whose primary rhetoric is not that of class. Similarly, forms of violent conflict should be understood not merely as ethnic–national politics but also as forms of class activism. Stated alternatively, if everyone in Northern Ireland was miraculously translated into the middle class, it is likely that the ethnic–national division would persist, but that many of its violent forms which are associated with contemporary working class communities would disappear.

The conclusion to be drawn from the Northern Ireland data is that class does not exist in abstraction from other forms of identity that are based on nationality, religion and ethnicity. It articulates with them in complex ways. These need to be studied further in a comparative context which transcends intra-UK comparisons.

References

AIREY, C. and BROOK, L., 'Interim report: social and moral issues', in Jowell, R., Witherspoon, S. and Brook, L. (eds), *British Social Attitudes: the 1986 report*, Gower, Aldershot (1986).

BREEN, R., HANNAN, D., ROTTMAN, D. and WHELAN, C., *Understanding Contemporary Ireland: state, class and development in the Republic of Ireland*, Gill and Macmillan, Dublin (1990).

CURTICE, J. and GALLAGHER, T., 'The Northern Irish dimension', in Jowell, R., Witherspoon, S. and Brook, L. (eds), *British Social Attitudes: the 7th report*, Gower, Aldershot (1990).

EMMISON, M. and WESTERN, M., 'Social class and social identity: a comment on Marshall et al', *Sociology*, 24, 241–53 (1990).

HEATH, A. and TOPF, R., 'Political culture', in Jowell, R., Witherspoon, S. and Brook, L.(eds), *British Social Attitudes: the 1987 report*, Gower, Aldershot (1987).

MARSHALL, G., NEWBY, H., ROSE, D. and VOGLER, C., *Social Class in Modern Britain*, Hutchinson, London (1988).

MARSHALL, G. and ROSE, D., 'Out-classed by our critics', *Sociology*, 24, 255–67 (1990).

MILLER, R., 'Social stratification and social mobility', in Clancy, P., Drudy, S., Lynch, K. and O'Dowd, L. (eds), *Ireland: a sociological profile*, Institute of Public Administration, Dublin (1986).

O'DOWD, L., 'Employment and unemployment since 1968', *Revue Française de Civilisation Britannique*, 5, 73–89 (1989).

PAHL, R., 'Is the emperor naked? Some questions on the adequacy of sociological theory in urban and regional research', *International Journal of Urban and Regional Research*, 13(4), 709–20 (1989).

PAWSON, R., 'Bias in sociological methods: half-truths about bias', *Sociology*, 24, 229–40 (1990).

ROWTHORN, B. and WAYNE, N., *Northern Ireland: the political economy of conflict*, Polity Press, Cambridge (1988).

SAUNDERS, P., *Social Class and Stratification*, Routledge, London (1990).

WRIGHT, E. O., BECKER, U., BRENNER, J., BURAWOY, M., BURRIS, V., CARCHEDI, G., MARSHALL, G., MEIKSINS, P., ROSE, D., STINCHCOMBE, A. and VAN PARIJS, P., *The Debate on Classes*, Verso, London (1989).

Table 4.1 Perceived impact of class, by self-assigned class. Does social class affect opportunities?

	Middle %	Working %	Poor %	Other/Don't know %
A great deal	23 } 64	31 } 65	53 } 67	13 } 38
Quite a lot	41	34	14	25
Not very much	32 } 35	26 } 32	19 } 33	25 } 31
Not at all	3	6	14	6
Other/Don't know	1	3	–	31

Table 4.2 Perceived impact of class, by non-manual/manual workers. Does social class affect opportunities?

	Non-manual %	Manual %	Other/Don't know %
A great deal	22 } 64	35 } 64	34 } 64
Quite a lot	42	29	30
Not very much	29 } 34	26 } 32	24 } 31
Not at all	5	6	7
Other/Don't know	2	3	5

Table 4.3 Perceived impact of class, by gender, manual/non-manual and political affiliation. Does social class affect opportunities?

	A great deal/ Quite a lot %	Not very much/ Not at all %
Male manual	65	33
Female manual	63	33
Male non-manual	58	39
Female non-manual	68	33
Male unionists	57	39
Male nationalists	69	28
Female unionists	64	34
Female nationalists	64	33
Male/no political affiliation	67	31
Female/no political affiliation	63	32

5

A decade of enterprise in Northern Ireland?

Mark Hart

Without doubt the 1980s were a highly favourable decade for small enterprise and self-employment, as the dramatic increase in the numbers involved in small-scale economic activities demonstrated (Johnson, 1989; Curran and Blackburn, 1990). In addition, since 1979, the concept of the 'enterprise culture' was one of the dominant principles of the project of Thatcherism. The policies of the Conservative government over three terms have sought to promote the enterprise culture, by heralding it as the guiding principle for all sectors of the economy.

Furthermore, against the background of major economic, social and political change in Britain in the 1980s, the proponents of the enterprise culture have sought to present it as an antidote to these deep-rooted restructuring processes. The justification and validity of this connection has yet to be adequately debated; yet it remains at the forefront of government policy for the 1990s (Burrows, 1989). The spirit of enterprise has thus become closely associated in the United Kingdom's economy with industriousness, regeneration and national recovery. Such a strategy is seen as being of particular significance for the lagging peripheral regions, which include Northern Ireland.

The Enterprise Initiative, which was set out in the Department of Trade and Industry's White Paper in January 1988, demonstrated the commitment of the present government to new and small firms, as part of their strategy to promote enterprise and reduce unemployment (DTI, 1988). Within Northern Ireland, the Department of Economic Development (DED) produced a document in 1987 known as 'Pathfinder', which reported the progress of its new economic development strategy (DED, 1987). In essence, this document concentrated on the means by which indigenous potential could be harnessed in the regeneration of the regional economy. Pathfinder established a number of taskforces to find new and better ways of achieving economic growth in the Province. Its proposals included the stimulation of a more positive attitude to enterprise; a change in attitudes to competitiveness; the encouragement of export activity; exploitation of the strengths of the public sector; and a better targeting of public funds.

Arising out of Pathfinder, the Enterprise Taskforce produced a major initiative to foster a more positive attitude to enterprise in Northern Ireland. The Enterprising Northern Ireland Campaign was launched in July 1988, with the task of promoting and developing enterprise. It was intended to add to the current level of entrepreneurial activity (that is, self-employment), and to target underdeveloped sources of enterprise ability: young people, women, people in employment and unemployed people. Continued support for the encouragement of enterprise has been acknowledged in the most recent strategy document to emerge from the Department of Economic Development (DED, 1990).

In the light of these policy developments it is pertinent to examine how far enterprise, and self-employment in particular, is finding acceptance among the public in Northern Ireland. This chapter will report people's attitudes to their current position in the labour-market and will assess the degree to which that might change in the future. We need to establish whether the rapid increase in the numbers of small-business start-ups and of the self-employed, both nationally and regionally, will continue. The rapid increase in the numbers of self-employed in the United Kingdom in the 1980s may have been a function only of the dramatic restructuring processes at work within the economy as a whole, rather than evidence for the rise of an enterprise culture as such (Burrows, 1989).

This chapter also seeks to present an overview of attitudes to other important aspects of economic policy being pursued by the Conservative administration. Despite the fact that the people of Northern Ireland in practice play no part in the political process associated with the selection of the governing party and its range of macro-economic policies, their attitudes to the broad approach adopted for the management of the United Kingdom economy are important in at least one major respect. A 'North–South Divide' has been emerging in the economic prosperity of the United Kingdom since the early 1980s. Northern Ireland provides an extreme example of this growing division in a period of national economic boom (Gudgin and Roper, 1990). Attitudes to national economic policy in a lagging peripheral region will illustrate the degree to which this divide is being reflected in an emergent dissatisfaction with current economic policies.

The self-employed workforce

Labour-market analysis has only very recently begun to focus on the self-employed workforce, as a direct result of the phenomenal growth in its relative and absolute size in Britain during the 1980s. There are many problems associated with the use of available information, due to deficiencies in measurement and identification (Hakim, 1988). Nevertheless, it is still possible, through large-scale public attitude surveys, to question whether the government is succeeding in creating a new enterprise culture that encourages entrepreneurial activity and produces a more positive image for the self-employed.

In the Northern Ireland Social Attitudes survey 11% of respondents classify themselves as self-employed. This is a marginally lower figure than that quoted in government statistics (PPRU, 1989) for the whole labour-market in Northern Ireland (12%). Survey respondents include all those currently in paid work, those about to take up paid work, and those who are either unemployed, retired or looking after the home. For the latter three groups data refer to their last job.

The majority of people who describe themselves as self-employed have no employees at all – not even a part-time assistant. Just over two-thirds of self-employed respondents work alone, while just under one-third have less than 25 employees: typically, this means one, two or three employees. This pattern is similar to that observed in Britain (Hakim, 1988) and in other industrialised industries (OECD, 1986). It is repeated when one examines only those respondents who describe themselves as currently self-employed. Of these, 66% report that they have no partners and 61% that they have no employees. It should be stressed that the vast majority of those who are currently self-employed (91%) view self-employment as their main job and work more than 30 hours per week.

Self-employed: number of employees

	%
None	67
1–24	29
25 or more	3

In the particular context of Northern Ireland, it should be noted that 32% of respondents classified as self-employed were in the agricultural sector, the majority of them having no employees. This proportion of the self-employed has remained static throughout the 1980s. It represents the traditional form of economic activity in many parts of a predominantly rural region (Humphreys et al, forthcoming). Overall, then, a significant proportion of the growth in self-employment in the 1980s in Northern Ireland, as in the rest of the United Kingdom, has consisted of single-person businesses. As Hakim (1988, p. 430) argues:

> ... it cannot be assumed that the self-employed are invariably entrepreneurs who are building businesses that will eventually employ more people than themselves. The evidence to date suggests that most of the self-employed are only providing themselves with an alternative to the employee job.

The move into self-employment

Of central concern to the stimulation of greater levels of entrepreneurial activity is the process whereby individuals move from paid employment (or unemployment) into self-employment (Harrison and Hart, 1983). The desirability of a move away from a present employer, and the ease with which an individual can make that move, is seen as a function of a complex series of interacting factors. They may *push* an individual away from one organisation towards the attractions (*pull*) of another organisation or some other form of employment (including self-employment and the establishment of a new business).

Those currently in self-employment were asked to indicate whether they had either worked as an employee in their main job or been unemployed and seeking work, for any period in the previous five years (that is, since March 1984). The responses indicate that there has been some movement from the position of paid employment (or unemployment) to self-employment within the Northern Ireland labour-market in the latter half of the 1980s. Although categories are not mutually exclusive, the figures suggest that approximately one-fifth of those currently self-employed had made the decision to be so relatively recently. The majority, therefore, of the self-employed have been occupying that position in the labour-market for some considerable time (more than five years). They represent evidence which refutes the view of a resurgence of the enterprise culture.

Self-employed: previous economic position within previous five years

	%
Employee	23
Unemployed	18

A question can also be raised about the motivations and skills of the new recruits to self-employment. Movement into self-employment from a position of inactivity in the labour-market may not necessarily make a positive contribution to the regeneration of the local economy. Indeed, it could well be that some proportion of this group transfers back to employee jobs when the economy improves. Other research has shown that businesses set up by the unemployed tend to suffer more difficulties from lack of resources and experience than businesses set up by people who transfer to self-employment from an employee job (Hakim, 1988). However, the data in this survey are not sufficiently detailed to allow the exact route into self-employment to be established. For example, individuals who are currently self-employed could have experienced a period of unemployment followed by some time as an employee, before occupying their current economic position.

The decision to move into self-employment may have more to do with changes taking place in the wider economy than with the creation of a new climate of opinion which encourages the entrepreneurial spirit. The sudden rise in self-employment in the 1980s could equally be explained by employers sub-contracting more tasks and functions, either to self-employed individuals or to independent companies. The causes of growth in the number of the self-employed will only be understood if further research is carried out.

Turning to those who are currently in paid employment (that is, employees) or are unemployed, what are their expectations about their future role in the labour-market? Employees were asked to state how likely or unlikely it was that they would leave their current employer over the next year and to indicate their reasons for that change. One in four employees indicated that they expected to be leaving their current position in paid employment within the next 12 months. The reasons for this movement reflect a mixture of voluntary and compulsory factors. Over two-thirds of those who expected to leave their current employment would do so voluntarily, with the majority expecting to maintain their position in the labour-market as a paid employee. The remaining one-third would be forced to leave as a result of business closure, redundancy or an expiring contract. In the context of the present discussion, the most significant finding is the extremely low number who, having indicated they are likely to leave their current employer, consider self-employment to be a viable option. This signals the reluctance of the more mobile employees in the labour-market to embrace the concept of the enterprise culture and actively pursue self-employment.

Employees: propensity to leave current employer

	%
Very likely	12
Quite likely	13
Not very likely	30
Not at all likely	45

Employees: reasons for leaving current paid employment

	%
Firm will close down	2
Made redundant	20
Contract expires	12
To seek another employer	61
To become self-employed	4
Domestic responsibilities	7

(NB: more than one reason may be indicated.)

This point was investigated further by asking all employees how seriously they had considered, in the last five years, working as a self-employed person. The answers are unequivocal and support the view expressed above. Despite a decade of policy designed to promote entrepreneurial activity and self-employment in the national and local economy, the majority (approximately four out of five) of those occupying a position as an employee in the labour-market in Northern Ireland have not seriously considered moving into self-employment. However, this response could represent a realistic and rational assessment by employees of the risks associated with self-employment; it does not necessarily point to a lack of enterprise or initiative. If that is the case, more careful targeting of enterprise initiatives is called for, rather than the current tendency towards a blanket coverage of the whole working population. Nevertheless, in the future, sudden changes in the workplace or wider economy, culminating in redundancy or business closure, may well force more employees to consider the benefits of self-employment over paid employment.

Employees: considered move to self-employment?

	%
Very seriously	8
Quite seriously	11
Not very seriously	12
Not at all seriously	70

The extent to which the entrepreneurial culture of the self-employed workforce has been weakened by the influx of new recruits, some of whom are involuntary recruits to self-employment, has begun to be raised as an issue by researchers (Hakim, 1988). It has long been the view that self-employment entails a distinctive set of attitudes, values, motivations and ambitions which together make up the ideology of self-employment. The self-employed are seen as possessing more 'individualistic' attitudes and values. Data on trade-union membership from the Northern Ireland Social Attitudes survey tends to support that view. Only 1% of the self-employed are currently members of a trade union compared to 48% of employees. Even more revealing is the fact that 60% of the self-employed state that they have never been members of a trade union, compared to 31% of employees.

One way of crudely assessing the validity of that issue is to examine differences between employees and the self-employed in their basic work ethic, as expressed in their perception of paid work. When they were asked what they would do if 'without having to work, you had what you would regard as a reasonable living income', some interesting differences emerged between the self-employed, employees and the unemployed.

Still prefer a paid job

	%
Self-employed	91
Employees	83
Unemployed	85

Although the great majority of all three groups would prefer to have a paid job (or do paid work, in the case of the self-employed) rather than stop working, the self-employed have a slightly higher regard for paid work. When they were asked whether their current (or most recent) job was 'just a means of earning a living' a clear difference emerged between the self-employed and employees. The self-employed were less likely to agree with this statement (22%) than their employee counterparts (31%). More important, nearly two-thirds of the self-employed agreed with the statement that 'work is a person's most important activity', compared to only 40% of employees. Furthermore, three-quarters of the self-employed said that 'I make a point of doing the best work I can, even if it does interfere with the rest of my life', compared with just over half of employees.

Finally, when asked to assess the importance to their current job of a range of characteristics, the self-employed and employees produced broadly similar responses. The most significant divergence in opinion arose, not surprisingly, with respect to the statement, 'I can work independently'. Thirty-nine per cent of the self-employed strongly agreed with this statement, compared with only 18% of employees. The self-employed were also more likely to agree strongly that their job was more interesting: 30% compared with 20% of employees. On all other variables, such as job security, income level, career opportunities, leisure time, flexible working hours, usefulness to society and helping other people, the difference in views expressed by the two groups was negligible.

Thus, despite the tendency for some degree of transfer of individuals between employment categories in recent years, the self-employed do seem to exhibit slightly different attitudes and values. These may be different from the work orientations of the employee, and may support the contention that an ideology of self-employment or enterprise culture exists. However, the existence of such differences does not necessarily support the contention that such a culture has only emerged in the last decade. It could simply reflect the values, attitudes, motivations and ambitions traditionally held by the self-employed. Only through consistent serial surveys can one begin to provide an adequate discussion of these issues. Evidence from the British Social Attitudes surveys (Hakim, 1988) tends to undermine the existence of an ideology of self-employment: the attitudes and perspectives of employees and the self-employed are very similar.

Economic attitudes

Recent analyses of the Northern Ireland economy have demonstrated the extent to which it has become detached in the 1980s from the economic performance of the rest of the United Kingdom (Gudgin and Roper, 1990; Hart and Harrison, forthcoming). The unique features of the regional economy have meant that there has been little evidence of Northern Ireland participating in the period of rapid growth of the rest of the national economy between 1983 and 1989. This situation has arisen despite very high levels of public-sector support in Northern Ireland to the economy as a whole, and to industry in particular. The recession of the early 1980s has become transformed into a period of slow growth in Northern Ireland, relative to the rest of the United Kingdom.

In stark terms, the socio-economic position of the Province at the start of the 1990s can best be summarised as follows: unemployment remains high, at over 14%; out-migration runs at persistently high levels; participation rates are low; and incomes are falling even further behind the national average.

Given this situation, Northern Ireland residents might be less optimistic about the economic future, and more concerned, for example, about unemployment than their counterparts in Britain. The discussion which follows presents evidence on perceptions, attitudes and values towards basic economic trends and macro-economic policy options. In the absence of a comparative regional dimension to this analysis it is not possible to integrate the findings into a broader commentary on the 'North–South Divide'. The reader is referred to the British Social Attitudes survey for an analysis of regional variations in attitudes in Britain.

People in Northern Ireland did not express much confidence in the ability of the United Kingdom's industrial performance to improve in the year to come. From the perspective of people in an economically lagging peripheral region this viewpoint is not surprising. Whatever growth has taken place in the national economy in the latter half of the 1980s, in a period now commonly referred to as the Lawson Boom, has not been transmitted to Northern Ireland. Perceptions of the future are characteristically not optimistic.

UK's industrial performance in next 12 months?

	%
Improve a lot	3
Improve a little	21
Stay much the same	48
Decline a little	17
Decline a lot	3

In addition to giving a general prediction for the national economy, people were asked specific questions about future trends in inflation, unemployment and household income. The most interesting trend to emerge from the responses is that the pessimistic assessment of the future of the United Kingdom economy is supported by views on the key economic indicators of inflation. Furthermore, inflation is of greater concern to those living in Northern Ireland than unemployment. This is perhaps surprising given the persistently high levels of unemployment in Northern Ireland, though it could simply reflect the widespread acceptance that unemployment has always been, and will continue to be, a major weakness in the local economy. Of greater concern is the capacity of household income, from whatever source (including benefits), to meet expenditure. In the context of rising inflation in the national economy, this concern is certainly realistic.

Economic evaluations: next 12 months

	%
Expect prices to go up a lot next year	43
Expect unemployment to go up a lot next year	20
Inflation of greater concern to me and my family than unemployment	55
Household income fell behind prices last year	52
Expect household income to fall behind prices next year	52
Living on household income difficult or very difficult	28

However, less than one-third of respondents indicate that they have experienced any degree of difficulty in having to live on their current household income. Although 52% stated that their household income had fallen behind prices in the previous 12 months, only some of them experienced financial difficulties. The extent to which the availability of credit, the chance to economise, and/or the use of savings has served to defer these difficulties is open to question.

It is useful to investigate the extent to which the characteristics of class and income affect the evaluations of inflation, unemployment and household income. The findings confirm the view that the working class tends to possess a much more pessimistic attitude than members of the salariat, who tend to have a more secure basis to employment and a higher income.

Economic evaluations: next 12 months

	Salariat	Working class
	%	%
Expect prices to go up a lot next year	13	46
Expect unemployment to go up a lot next year	8	56
Inflation of greater concern to me and my family than unemployment	21	32
Household income fell behind prices last year	14	45
Expect household income to fall behind prices next year	14	45
Living on household income difficult or very difficult	7	48

Attitudes towards more fundamental issues concerning the role of the state in the management of the national economy were also addressed. A clear theme dominates the findings. Although the Conservative administration has spent a decade implementing policies designed to roll back the level of state involvement in the management of the economy, this strategy has not gained widespread acceptance in Northern Ireland. There is a marked ideological gulf between this part of the Thatcherite experiment and the views of those people living in the most deprived region of the United Kingdom.

This finding is further supported by responses to questions on the state ownership of industry, income distribution and current levels of taxation. Two-thirds of Northern Ireland respondents are not prepared to support the 'rolling programme' of privatisation embarked upon by Conservative administrations of the 1980s. The need for greater economic equality in society, as reflected in income distribution, is endorsed by the great majority of respondents (86%). Furthermore, progressive changes in the tax system have produced a regime that is particularly undesirable to low-income households.

Overall, the attitudes and perceptions of those living in Northern Ireland support action by the government to reduce inequality in society as a whole. They see greater state involvement in the management of the economy as a critical factor in this process, in preference to allowing the operation of the free market to produce a more egalitarian society (see Tables 5.1–5.4). These views have probably been shaped by the unique economic circumstances of Northern Ireland and might contrast significantly with the views expressed by the residents of other regions of the United Kingdom, particularly in the Southeast.

Conclusion

The implications of these findings for current government policy in Northern Ireland are of major interest in the light of recent policy statements. The size of the public sector and an overdependence on public funds have been pinpointed as two of the major weaknesses of the local economy (DED, 1987; 1990). As the government seeks to move away from this overdependence and identify a more strategic role for the private sector and individual enterprise, the views and perceptions of those living in Northern Ireland appear to run counter to the government's strategy. The lack of full participation in the decision-making processes of the state, and of access to national political parties, gives added significance to these findings.

In the case of Northern Ireland, the experiment of 10 years of Thatcherism seems to have had little impact on attitudes towards individual enterprise and the role of the market in economic development. This situation obtains despite an active campaign by government, both nationally and regionally, to promote the individualistic philosophy of the private sector and the market place (DTI, 1988; DED, 1987; 1990). The extent to which the scale of the economic problem in Northern Ireland demands a large and significant role for the public sector remains a matter of some debate. Nonetheless the attitudes expressed by people in Northern Ireland on a range of economic topics clearly reflect the deep-rooted nature of the economic problem.

With the data drawn on here as a benchmark it will be possible to monitor in the years ahead the extent to which attitudes change to any significant degree. This longitudinal analysis will be of major importance to government, given their identification of attitude-change towards economic development as a key policy objective for the 1990s (DED, 1987). In addition, the findings in Northern Ireland will need to be placed within a national context, in order to separate out spatial effects from those of, for example, income and class.

References

BURROWS, R., 'The restructuring of Britain and the discourse of the Enterprise Culture: a polemical contribution', paper presented to a workshop on The Small Enterprise in the Year 2000, held at Kingston Polytechnic, 21–2 September 1989.

CURRAN, J. and BLACKBURN, R., *Small Business 2000: socio-economic and environmental factors facing small firms in the 1990s*, Small Business Research Trust, London (1990).

DED (DEPARTMENT OF ECONOMIC DEVELOPMENT), *Building a Stronger Economy: the Pathfinder initiative*, HMSO, Belfast (1987).

DED (DEPARTMENT OF ECONOMIC DEVELOPMENT), *Northern Ireland: competing in the 1990s: the key to growth*, HMSO, Belfast (1990).

DTI (DEPARTMENT OF TRADE AND INDUSTRY), *DTI – the Department for Enterprise*, HMSO, London (1988).

GUDGIN, G. and ROPER, S., *The Northern Ireland Economy: review and forecasts to 1995*, Northern Ireland Economic Research Council, Belfast (1990).

HAKIM, C., 'Self-employment in Britain: recent trends and current issues', *Work, Employment and Society,* 2(4), 421–50 (1988).

HARRISON, R. T. and HART, M., 'Factors influencing new business formation: a case study of Northern Ireland', *Environment and Planning A*, 15, 1395–412 (1983).

HART, M. and HARRISON, R. T., 'Northern Ireland: recession to stagnation – the economic reality of the 1980s?', in Townroe, P. and Martin, R. (eds), *Regional Development in the British Isles in the 1990s*, Jessica Kingsley Publishers, London (forthcoming).

HUMPHREYS, P., BAILEY, E. and HAASE, T., *Agricultural Change and Rural Employment within Northern Ireland, 1971–87*, Northern Ireland Economic Research Centre, Belfast (forthcoming).

JOHNSON, S., 'Small firms and the UK labour market in the 1990s', paper presented to a workshop on The Small Enterprise in the Year 2000, held at Kingston Polytechnic, 21–2 September 1989.

OECD (ORGANISATION FOR ECONOMIC CO-OPERATION AND
   DEVELOPMENT), *Employment Outlook*, OECD, Paris (1986).
PPRU (POLICY PLANNING AND RESEARCH UNIT), *Monthly Economic Report:
   September 1989*, PPRU, Department of Finance and Personnel, Belfast (1989).

Table 5.1 Support for economic policy options

	%
Control of wages by law	36
Control of prices by law	67
Reducing the level of government spending on health and education	7
Government controls to cut down goods from abroad	70
Increasing government subsidies for private industry	66
Reducing government spending on defence	56
Government schemes to encourage job-sharing	76
Government to set up construction projects to create more jobs	90
Government action to cut interest rates	87
Government controls on hire-purchase and credit	82

Table 5.2 Preferred state ownership of industry

	%
More	15
Less	22
Same amount as now	51

Table 5.3 Income distribution

Gap between high and low incomes:	%
Too large	86
About right	10
Too small	2

Table 5.4 Levels of taxation

	Income group		
	High	Middle	Low
	%	%	%
Much too low	16	*	*
Too low	36	4	2
About right	32	55	13
Too high	9	32	38
Much too high	4	5	46

6

Perceptions of poverty

Eileen Evason

Since the early 1960s there has been a continuing academic debate about the definition of poverty and about its extent. More recently, the New Right has issued its own challenge by attempting to redefine poverty as synonymous with destitution and as a phenomenon affecting only a tiny minority of people – a definition which has a hint of victim-blaming. The Social Attitudes survey data allow us to assess the degree of support that the protagonists in this debate command among the population of Northern Ireland. Interviewees were questioned on what they thought constituted poverty; the extent of real poverty in the United Kingdom today; past and future trends in the prevalence of poverty; the causes of poverty; and how often they themselves felt poor. As a preliminary to a discussion of the survey findings, this chapter begins with an outline of the academic and political background of the debate.

Theoretical and political context

It is now nearly 30 years since Townsend reopened the debate on poverty in Britain. He was challenging earlier perspectives, which had sought to define poverty by reference to the minimum levels of income required for the maintenance of physical efficiency. This approach had been pioneered by Rowntree. In his later work, he had extended the definition of necessities and made some concessions to custom and culture. Townsend (1979) argued for a complete shift in the definition of poverty, on the grounds that necessities were relative. People were poor if they lacked access to those items which were considered normal and customary in any society at any given point in time. Townsend's definition overlaps, but does not completely coincide with, a concept of inequality. A society may have a degree of income inequality even though it does not contain persons or households which conform to Townsend's definition.

The difference between the positions of Rowntree and Townsend has perhaps been exaggerated. Townsend followed Rowntree's search for an objective, scientific method of measuring the extent of poverty, culminating in the massive work he published in 1979. Townsend concluded not only that deprivation increased as income diminished, but also that there was a clear cut-off point

– a poverty threshold – which corresponded to 150% of the supplementary benefit standard.

Townsend's work was subsequently criticised by Piachaud (1981), who questioned the existence of the threshold and Townsend's failure to allow for people's tastes and choices. The root of the definitional problem is that poverty is a political issue and a moral concept. The label 'poverty' implies that a state of affairs is wrong and that action should be taken. As Piachaud (1981) puts it:

> The term poverty carries with it an implication and a moral imperative that something should be done about it. The definition by an individual, or by society collectively, of what level constitutes 'poverty' will always be a value judgement. Social scientists have no business trying to pre-empt such judgements with 'scientific prescriptions'.

Townsend's valuable work needed to be complemented by information about the perception and values of the general population with regard to the nature and extent of poverty in society. The development of a social consensus approach by Mack and Lansley (1984) was of great significance in this respect. Crucially, their research allowed survey respondents to select from a range of items those which *they* thought constituted necessities. A deprivation index was constructed from the items that were chosen by a majority of the respondents. Mack and Lansley's research, in fact, reinforced Townsend's conclusions. They demonstrated that people's perceptions of necessities are grounded in a relative perspective. Their study also suggested that a poverty threshold existed at around 133% of supplementary benefit rates – a point not far from Townsend's figure.

Piachaud (1987, p.150) has warned that there is a danger of the debate on the definition of poverty becoming a narrow 'semantic and statistical squabble . . . part of the problem rather than part of the solution'. The significance of this observation has been particularly apparent in the decade since it appeared. Have the poor paid the price of academic disagreements about the definition of poverty? The 1988 cuts and restructuring of benefits were preceded by the Green Paper *Reform of Social Security* (1985), which noted that 'there is no universally agreed standard of poverty', and was thus able to conduct its debate in terms of targeting, priorities and efficiency rather than need or adequacy. Ministers now eschew the very word 'poverty'. The statistical series on low-income families, which used to indicate the number of people living on or below the 140% supplementary benefit standard, has been scrapped and replaced by a series 'likely to lead to an underestimate of the numbers living on low incomes' (Social Services Committee, 1988).

Moreover, the objective has been to change not just how things are done, but how people think: to suggest that 'real' poverty is synonymous with actual destitution (Moore, 1989), that greater inequality is desirable and benefits those on low incomes through the 'trickle-down' effect, and that 'those who are living in need are fully and properly provided for' (Mack and Lansley, 1984, p.11).

Within the context of these academic debates and political developments, data on pertinent social attitudes have a considerable role to play. First and foremost, they allow us to chart the progress made by contemporary ideologies and policies. In addition, they are of importance in suggesting fruitful directions for the development of theory and research. For, as Desai (1986) has pointed out, 'only those definitions which appeal to the widest possible audience will stick'.

The perceived extent of poverty

Sixty-three per cent of the Northern Ireland sample thought that there is quite a lot of real poverty in the United Kingdom today. While we do not know precisely how respondents interpreted the term 'real poverty', it seems unlikely that they had in mind only those people who are actually destitute. In Northern Ireland, then, people would appear to view relative poverty as a fairly widespread phenomenon in the United Kingdom today. With two exceptions, this perception varies little with the income and class of respondents. Relatively more poverty is perceived by those in the middle-income bracket, which includes many retired people, and less by upper-working-class respondents.

Perceptions of extent of real poverty in the UK, by household income (£)

	Very little %	Quite a lot %	Don't know %
Less than 5000	36	62	2
5000–7999	38	61	1
8000–11999	21	77	2
12000–17999	41	58	1
18000 or more	40	59	1
Don't know/Not answered	34	62	3

Perceptions of extent of UK poverty, by self-rated social class

	Very little %	Quite a lot %	Don't know %
Upper middle/middle	35	64	1
Upper working	41	55	4
Working	34	64	2
Poor/Don't know	30	70	–

Details of the relationship between respondents' current economic status and their perception of poverty show that, not surprisingly, it is the unemployed who are most likely to view poverty as extensive. Retired persons, whose perceptions may well be influenced by comparisons with the past, are much more likely than employees to think that there is very little poverty. Most striking, however, are the attitudes of the small sub-sample of self-employed, more than half of whom reject the view that there is quite a lot of poverty.

Perceptions of extent of UK poverty, by current economic position

	Very little	Quite a lot	Don't know
	%	%	%
Employee full/part-time	31	67	2
Self-employed full/part-time	59	41	–
Unemployed	28	71	1
Full-time home care	31	68	1
Retired	47	48	4
Other	31	69	–

Comparable data in terms of political affiliation show that supporters of all parties who believe that there is very little poverty are in a minority. The difference in perception is narrowest among Northern Ireland supporters of the Conservative Party, but even in this case 51% of those expressing a view consider poverty to be an extensive phenomenon, as do roughly the same proportion of Official Unionists.

Perceptions of extent of UK poverty, by party support

	Very little	Quite a lot	Don't know
	%	%	%
Conservative	48	50	3
Labour	17	83	–
Alliance (NI)	37	63	–
DUP	30	70	–
OUP	44	54	2
Sinn Féin	21	79	–
SDLP	30	70	–
None	29	66	4
Others/Don't know/ Not answered	36	61	2

In relation to other variables, there were only a few significant variations from the above pattern. Not surprisingly, for example, a majority (53%) of those who opposed the redistribution of income by government (24% of the total sample) took the view that very little poverty existed. On the other hand, on two questions which one would expect to reflect some support for Thatcherism, the results were the reverse of what might have been predicted. A clear majority (61%) of those who thought that taxation of high incomes was 'too high' or 'much too high' (14% of the total sample) also thought that there was quite a lot of poverty in the UK. This view was shared by 60% of those who thought that social class had 'not very much' or 'no impact' on opportunities (33% of the total sample). Otherwise, perceptions of poverty varied little with such variables as union membership, educational level and receipt of social benefit.

To summarise, the majority of interviewees thought that there is quite a lot of poverty in the UK today. Assertions that poverty is confined to a very small number of persons, who are actually destitute, and that those in need are fully and properly provided for, appear to command limited support in Northern Ireland.

Past and future trends

Consistently, across all socio-economic categories, only a minority of respondents believed that poverty had been decreasing over the past 10 years. Overall, only one-fifth considered that there had been a decline in the level of poverty. Nearly one-half (49%) thought that poverty had increased, and 29% thought that there had been no change. These figures represent a remarkable verdict on the past 10 years. Nor is the majority of respondents more optimistic about the next 10 years. Only 17% believed that poverty would decrease, 30% thought it would stay at about the same level, and the largest single group (48%) thought that poverty would increase.

Table 6.1 gives details of the past and future perceptions of respondents with different household incomes. Those who have higher incomes are more positive about the past 10 years and more optimistic about the next decade. Nevertheless, those who believe that poverty has decreased or will decrease constitute small minorities of all income groups.

On other socio-economic variables, too, there are some interesting differences between groups. The retired and self-employed differ markedly from other groups: more of them thought that poverty has decreased over the past 10 years. The self-employed are more hopeful about the future. Only 14% of Catholics thought that poverty had decreased, compared to nearly twice as many non-Catholics. Little over one in ten Catholics expected poverty to decrease, while for non-Catholics the figure was one-fifth. Conservative Party supporters stood out, in as much as 29% thought that poverty had decreased; the highest figure otherwise in terms of political affiliation was 18% (Official Unionist). The latter group was also more likely to think that poverty would decrease over the next 10 years (see Table 6.2).

Despite these variations, the trends are in the same direction for all socio-economic groups. In the debate that has taken place over the past 10 years, government has argued that standards have been rising and benefits improving. Academics and campaigners, on the other hand, have challenged those views. It appears that the perspective of the majority of the population, as represented in the present sample, is closer to that of the academics and campaigners.

Defining poverty

The two questions that were asked in the survey about people's definition of poverty are of particular relevance to the academic debate on poverty. Respondents were asked first if they thought that people were poor if they could buy *'the things they really needed'* but not *'the things most people take for granted'* (definition A). This statement approaches Townsend's position: it is an overtly relative definition which appears to blur differences between the concepts of poverty and inequality. The second question asked respondents whether they thought that people were poor if they had *'enough to eat and live, but not enough to buy other things they needed'* (definition B).

People are poor if they can't buy things most people take for granted. Responses by household income (£)

	Yes	No	Don't know
	%	%	%
Less than 5000	27	68	5
5000–7999	32	67	1
8000–11999	34	66	–
12000–17999	27	73	–
18000 or more	23	76	1
Don't know/Not answered	25	67	8

People are poor if they can't buy things most people take for granted. Responses by self-rated social class

	Yes	No	Don't know
	%	%	%
Upper middle/middle	27	72	1
Upper working	22	77	1
Working	29	67	4
Poor	48	51	1
Don't know/Not answered	24	65	12

People are poor if they can't buy things most people take for granted. Responses by current economic position

	Yes	No	Don't know
	%	%	%
Employed	28	71	1
Self-employed	26	70	3
Unemployed	49	50	1
Full-time home care	27	71	3
Retired	18	75	8
Other	26	71	3

The first definition (A) was fairly firmly rejected, though there were some differences of opinion between those with incomes below and above £12000. The upper working class was the group most opposed to this definition. Only the unemployed gave it any significant support (49%). Otherwise, the proposition was rejected by 70% of the self-employed, 71% of employees, 75% of the retired and 71% of those engaged in full-time home care.

These findings do not mean that the population defines poverty in absolute terms of physical efficiency. The view of a majority of the sample, that there is a great deal of poverty, implies that people have a relative perspective. Responses to some other questions support this interpretation.

The second definition (B) received more general support. Across the board, a majority of respondents thought that the people it describes are indeed poor. The majority view would appear to be that necessities go beyond those items required for survival. As the figures indicate, this perspective commands less support among self-employed, upper working class and Official Unionist groups.

People are poor if they have enough to eat and live but not enough to buy other things they need. Responses by self-rated social class

	Yes %	No %	Don't know %
Upper middle/middle	62	37	1
Upper working	56	44	1
Working	63	34	3
Poor	85	13	1
Don't know/Not answered	47	35	18

People are poor if they have enough to eat and live but not enough to buy other things they need. Responses by current economic position

	Yes %	No %	Don't know %
Employed	62	37	1
Self-employed	53	38	8
Unemployed	75	25	1
Full-time home care	61	36	3
Retired	54	39	6
Other	74	26	–

People are poor if they have enough to eat and live but not enough to buy other things they need. Responses by political affiliation

	Yes %	No %	Don't know %
Conservative	59	39	2
Labour	66	30	5
DUP	58	39	3
OUP	51	48	2
SDLP	74	25	–
Other	67	31	2
None	65	31	4

Respondents were also asked whether they believed that people were in poverty if their incomes were insufficient to *'eat and live without getting into debt'*. With no significant variations, the great majority (93%) of those interviewed agreed that persons in such circumstances were in poverty.

The data clearly indicate that Townsend's definition is generally unacceptable: they strengthen the position of consensus theorists. In future, more research effort needs to be devoted to elucidating people's understanding of phrases such as 'other things they need'. In this way our definitions of poverty can be more explicitly based on popular perceptions. The majority of those who were interviewed conceive of basic necessities in relative terms. However, they reject definitions which overtly connote egalitarianism.

Why are people poor?

The causes of poverty have been the subject of rather less academic disagreement. By demonstrating the tendency of the poor to fall within such categories as the unemployed and the elderly, poverty surveys have undermined explanations which focus on the individual. Cultural explanations, which enjoyed some popularity in the 1960s and early 1970s, have similarly been undermined, both by research (Holman, 1978) and by experience – the American war on poverty, for example. Structural explanations, which view poverty as the inevitable and predictable outcome of economic and social structures and policies, have come to dominate theory. How do these explanations relate to popular perceptions?

In Northern Ireland, victim-blaming explanations enjoy little support. Most support for the individualistic, 'laziness' explanation is to be found among the upper middle and middle classes; though only one-fifth of respondents in these categories made this attribution and they were outnumbered by those who selected social injustice as the main cause of poverty. The most favoured explanation among all social groups, apart from those describing themselves as poor, was that poverty is an inevitable part of modern life.

Perceptions of the causes of poverty, by self-rated social class

	Been unlucky	Laziness	Social injustice	Inevitable	Other
	%	%	%	%	%
Upper middle/middle	12	20	24	37	8
Upper working	10	18	19	48	5
Working	12	17	25	40	5
Poor	13	3	57	25	1
Don't know/Not answered	6	47	18	12	18

Interestingly, when respondents' perceptions of the causes of poverty are related to their current economic position, we find that, while the self-employed might have been expected to opt for the individualistic explanation, the group which in fact stands out is the retired.

Perceptions of the causes of poverty, by current economic position

	Been unlucky	Laziness	Social injustice	Inevitable	Other
	%	%	%	%	%
Employed	12	16	25	41	6
Self-employed	18	16	19	44	3
Unemployed	12	10	24	50	4
Full-time home care	11	22	28	33	7
Retired	9	28	16	37	10
Other	10	7	43	36	3

An examination of perceptions in terms of political affiliation shows that a predictable gap exists between Conservatives and Unionists, on the one hand, and supporters of other parties. Even among Conservative Party supporters, the laziness explanation has few adherents.

Perceptions of the causes of poverty, by political affiliation

	Been unlucky	Laziness	Social injustice	Inevitable	Other
	%	%	%	%	%
Conservative	13	21	13	45	8
Labour	15	13	43	26	2
Alliance (NI)	12	7	28	43	10
DUP	8	38	20	33	2
OUP	11	23	15	46	6
SDLP	8	11	38	40	3
None	21	13	23	35	8
Other/Don't know/ Not answered	4	15	34	38	10

The findings offer limited support for loose attributions of the cause of poverty that point to the individual. Social injustice is a more popular view. But the most popular view of poverty is that it is an inevitable part of modern society. Further research to elucidate how 'inevitability' was interpreted would be valuable, since this is perhaps the alternative most open to varying interpretation. It may have been used as an escape-route from having to express fairly crude moral or political views. Strong support for a structural explanation devoid of overtly political overtones (that is, poverty is an inevitable part of modern life) does, of course, echo respondents' definitional preferences.

Subjective poverty

One reason given for taking the term 'poverty' out of the broader political debate has been that the use of the word is insensitive to, and rejected by, those actually living on low incomes. It is interesting, therefore, that 16% of the survey respondents reported that they felt poor 'often' or 'almost all the time', while a further 46% felt poor 'now and then'. There is, perhaps surprisingly, no overwhelming rejection of the label of 'poverty'. People's subjective assessments are consistent with research findings that associate poverty with unemployment, disability, etc. People in these categories are more likely to say that they feel poor. At the same time, however, self-assessed poverty does appear to cover a slightly broader front than academic judgements would suggest.

The Social Attitudes survey enables us to relate subjective assessment of poverty to self-rated social-class membership. Only 30% of those who consider themselves to be of the working class never feel poor. However, 42% of those who rate themselves as upper middle or middle class feel poor 'now and then', and a small minority feel poor 'often' or 'almost all the time'.

Subjective assessment by self-rated social class

	Feels poor			
	Never	Now and then	Often/Almost all the time	Don't know
	%	%	%	%
Upper middle/middle	51	42	4	3
Upper working	50	40	9	1
Working	30	52	17	1
Poor	4	23	73	–
Don't know/Not answered	47	24	29	–

The unemployed are the group least likely to 'never feel poor'. The difference between the unemployed and the sick and disabled may be the result of the more generous provision of benefits to the latter group.

Subjective assessment by main economic activity of respondent, previous seven days

	Feels poor			
	Never	Now and then	Often/Almost all the time	Don't know
	%	%	%	%
Paid employment	43	48	8	1
Unemployed	14	52	34	–
Permanently sick/disabled	36	44	19	1
Retired	47	34	19	–
Full-time home care	28	48	23	1
Other	61	39	–	–

Conclusion

This chapter has reviewed academic research and recent political developments with regard to several aspects of poverty, and has sought to relate them to the Social Attitudes data. The data suggest that a surprisingly large proportion of the population considers poverty to be an extensive problem in the United Kingdom. The majority also believes that the level of poverty has increased, or at least stayed the same, over the past decade. Only a minority of respondents are optimistic about the future. Most probably view those necessities without which people are poor in relative terms. Equally firmly, the population rejects efforts to integrate the concepts of poverty and inequality. There is little support for blaming the victims of poverty for its occurrence. While some would explain poverty as the result of social injustice, the most favoured interpretation is one that locates poverty within a structural perspective, shorn of overt political overtones.

Respondents showed a clear, but subtle, combination of attitudes. They must give more comfort to academics and campaigners on the left of the political spectrum than to those who have pursued the radical transformation of attitudes, as well as policies, over the past 10 years.

References

DESAI, M., 'Drawing the line: on defining the poverty threshold', in Golding, P. (ed), *Excluding the Poor*, Child Poverty Action Group, London (1986).

HMSO, *Reform of Social Security*, vol. 1, Cmnd 9517, HMSO, London (1985).

HOLMAN, R., *Poverty: explanations of social deprivation*, Martin Robertson, London (1978).

MACK, J. and LANSLEY, S., *Poor Britain*, Allen and Unwin, London (1984).

MOORE, J., Secretary of State for Social Security, Speech, 11 May 1988, discussed by Fran Bennett in 'Comment', *Poverty*, no. 73, p.1 (1989).

PIACHAUD, D., 'Peter Townsend and the Holy Grail', *New Society*, 10 September 1981.

PIACHAUD, D., 'Problems in the definition and measurement of poverty', *Journal of Social Policy*, 16(2) (1987).

SOCIAL SERVICES COMMITTEE, *Families on Low Income, Low Income Statistics*, HMSO, London (1988).

TOWNSEND, P., *Poverty in the United Kingdom: a survey of household resources and standards of living*, Penguin, Harmondsworth (1979).

Table 6.1 Perceptions of poverty (past and future), by household income (£)

	Over the past 10 years poverty has:			
	Increased	**Stayed the same**	**Decreased**	**Don't know/ Not answered**
	%	%	%	%
Less than 5000	48	29	19	5
5000–7999	56	23	17	4
8000–11999	59	24	15	1
12000–17999	43	34	23	–
18000 or more	38	39	23	–
Don't know/Not answered	50	24	21	5

	Over the next 10 years poverty will:			
	Increase	**Stay the same**	**Decrease**	**Don't know/ Not answered**
	%	%	%	%
Less than 5000	44	31	14	11
5000–7999	52	28	14	6
8000–11999	56	33	8	3
12000–17999	44	33	21	2
18000 or more	39	36	23	2
Don't know/Not answered	51	13	25	10

Table 6.2 Perceptions of poverty (past and future) by current economic position

	Over the past 10 years poverty has:			
	Increased	**Stayed the same**	**Decreased**	**Don't know/ Not answered**
	%	%	%	%
Employed	50	29	19	2
Self-employed	40	30	27	3
Unemployed	65	17	17	1
Full-time home care	51	28	17	5
Retired	36	20	40	4
Other	60	17	22	–

	Over the next 10 years poverty will:			
	Increase	**Stay the same**	**Decrease**	**Don't know/ Not answered**
	%	%	%	%
Employed	52	27	18	4
Self-employed	38	33	23	6
Unemployed	53	32	12	3
Full-time home care	47	31	12	10
Retired	37	34	20	10
Other	48	28	17	7

7

A woman's place in Northern Ireland

Pamela Montgomery and Celia Davies

Commentators have frequently drawn attention to the traditionalism and conservatism of Northern Ireland, particularly with regard to family issues, sexuality and women's role in society (see, for example, Ward and McGivern, 1980; Edgerton, 1986; Roulston, 1989; McWilliams, forthcoming). It has been argued that this conservatism is rooted in, and reinforced by, the influence of the Churches, which advocate a traditional role for women as wives and mothers within the family. Strong religious conservatism might be inferred from the widespread opposition to recent legislative changes in Northern Ireland on divorce, homosexuality and domestic violence.

However, little is actually known about the extent to which the attitudes of both women and men may be changing, and about how these changes may affect and be affected by behavioural changes, such as in women's participation in paid work. There have been few attempts systematically to examine attitudes to these and other issues, or to explore the frequently expressed view that attitudes to women are more traditional in Northern Ireland. One notable exception to this is the work of Kremer and Curry (1986). By drawing attention to considerable empirical diversity, their study of attitudes to women and work challenged the view that attitudes in Northern Ireland are always more traditional.

We begin this chapter by considering women's participation in paid and unpaid work in Northern Ireland, and how it compares with the situation in Britain. We then turn to findings on the nature and level of the commitment that women display towards paid work. The findings seem to contest traditionalism and confirm the growing insistence in the literature that it is the similarities rather than the differences between women and men in their attitudes to work that are striking. The lengthiest section of the chapter discusses issues of sexual relationships, divorce, abortion and pornography. These matters are central to the construction and reconstruction of gender norms in a society. We shall see that with these issues the traditionalism thesis apparently finds rather more support. However, once we go beyond global comparisons between Northern Ireland and Britain, to look at the findings in terms of age, gender and religious affiliation, a more complex pattern emerges.

Women's work: paid and unpaid

Whatever else women do in Northern Ireland, participation in paid work is the experience of the majority. Over half of the women aged 18–59 in the Northern Ireland sample were economically active – that is, in a paid job or available for employment, and as many as 46% were in a paid job at the time of interview. Much is made of the lower level of women's economic activity in Northern Ireland than in Britain. Comparisons with the British Social Attitudes survey data for 1989 confirm the picture found in other statistical sources (see, for example, Trewsdale, 1987). In Northern Ireland, some 10% fewer women than in Britain are economically active.

Economic activity of respondents

	Women, 18–59	Men, 18–64
	%	%
Full-time paid work	28	69
Part-time paid work	18	3
Unemployed	9	17
Total economically active	55	89
Economically inactive	43	8
Full-time students	2	3

The figures also show that part-time work is important for women. By contrast, male employment conforms overwhelmingly to a model of full-time employment. While, overall, part-time work may appear somewhat less important in Northern Ireland than in Britain (see Table 7.1), a consideration of those actually in employment reveals that in both samples around 40% of women who have a paid job work part-time.

It is well-known that part-time work is generally characterised by low pay and poor conditions and prospects. The situation is bleakest for those who work for less than 16 hours a week. They have fewer statutory rights: for example, entitlement to redundancy compensation, maternity leave or minimum periods of notice (see, for example, Beechey and Perkins, 1987). A detailed comparison of the hours worked by part-timers in the Northern Ireland and British samples suggests that a somewhat higher proportion of the female workforce in Northern Ireland falls into the category that is excluded from minimum employment rights.

Women working part-time, 18–59

Hours worked	Northern Ireland	Britain
	%	%
10–15	15	11
16–23	18	17
24–29	7	10
30 or more	61	62

Is there a discernible age-pattern that may account for the lower activity rate in Northern Ireland? Whilst economic activity rates are higher across all age groups in Britain, the age-patterns are indeed rather different. The particularly striking differences are amongst those aged 35–44 and 45–54, where the Northern Ireland participation levels are considerably lower. For British women in these two age groups, the proportions economically active are 71% and 67% respectively; in Northern Ireland they are 57% and 49% (Table 7.1).

A considerable number of research findings are now available for Britain that demonstrate the increasing participation of women in the labour-market at all stages of the life-cycle. Describing trends in Britain since the Second World War, Joshi has concluded:

> Motherhood replaced marriage as the occasion for leaving paid work and seldom marked the end of a woman's labour force membership . . . Mothers of younger and younger children have been taking on the dual burden of paid work and child-rearing. [Joshi, 1989, p.159]

The age of the youngest child, rather than the woman's own age, marital status or the number of her children, has been shown to be the factor most closely associated with reduced labour-market participation in Britain (Martin and Roberts, 1984). More recent data have shown that relatively few mothers of children under five (less than 30%) are in employment in either Britain or Northern Ireland (Cohen, 1988). However, they have also shown that in Northern Ireland the rates do not increase to the same extent as in Britain when children are of school age. It is this feature, in particular, which contributes to an overall percentage gap.

We can also ask questions about occupational segregation between women and men: that is, horizontal segregation by occupation, and vertical segregation by grade within occupation. These questions were explored in some detail in the British Social Attitudes survey of 1988. Marked differences in the distribution of men and women across eight occupational categories were found. In full-time work there was a concentration of women in fields such as clerical work, health, education and welfare. Women working part-time were also over-represented in these fields and in jobs with low pay and little security (Witherspoon, 1989).

Whilst we have not carried out the same detailed comparison in Northern Ireland, a crude examination of the occupational distribution of women shows a similar concentration in clerical and sales jobs and in a broadly defined 'working class' grouping that includes personal-service occupations (Table 7.2). Results from the Labour Force Survey in Northern Ireland point in the same direction. About one-quarter of women are in clerical work, a further quarter in catering, cleaning and other personal-service work, and 18% in health, education and welfare occupations (cited in EOCNI, 1988). However, all these findings must be viewed in the light of the continuing controversy (see, for example, Martin and Roberts, 1984; Abbott and Wallace, 1990) over the adequacy of classifying women's jobs in the same way as men's.

Is women's increased involvement in the world of work matched by an increased involvement of men in the domestic sphere? The survey contained two questions that are pertinent. Respondents were asked who in the household is mainly responsible for general domestic duties and who is mainly responsible for child-care. We looked at the answers of married couples and those living together as married, for men and women separately.

Who is mainly responsible for:	Men %	Women %	Total %
general domestic duties			
mainly women	84	89	87
shared equally	10	8	8
mainly men	4	3	4
general care of children			
mainly women	79	89	84
shared equally	18	11	15
mainly men	3	–	1

It is clear that women have the primary responsibility for both domestic duties and child-care. The tendency for more men than women to report that domestic duties and child-care are shared equally with their partner also emerged in the 1984 and 1988 Social Attitudes surveys in Britain. The largest difference between men's and women's reports involved child-care. Commenting on the more detailed information collected on this topic in the 1984 British survey, Witherspoon (1985) notes that men may well be exaggerating their participation in tasks in which they do have some involvement. There is no similar discrepancy in reporting in respect of traditionally more female tasks, such as making the evening meal or washing and ironing.

A similar, detailed breakdown by individual tasks was not possible with the 1989 survey data. However, analyses by age of the two questions that were asked did produce interesting results. First, there was no marked tendency for younger respondents to report more sharing of either set of tasks. Even among those aged 18–24, only 16% of men and women said that domestic tasks were shared equally with their partners and only 20% that child-care was shared equally. Second, there were discrepancies in the reports of men and women. For example, nearly one-quarter of women under 25 reported that these tasks were shared equally, whereas no men in this age group did so. In relation to shared child-care, there are similar gender differences in reports by the younger age group; yet among the other respondents it is the men who are more likely than the women to report that child-care is shared (see Table 7.3).

Men's contribution to domestic labour is clearly small. Regardless of age or the presence of children, women have by far the greater responsibility for the home. A recent review of research on these issues reaches four conclusions: even when employed, women continue to bear the main burden of domestic work; men have increased their participation in domestic work, but not to an extent sufficient to offset women's increased time in employment; women in part-time work with young children fare worst; though this does not preclude the possibility that men are more involved in domestic work at this stage of the life-cycle (Morris, 1990, p.90). Cell sizes are too small to attempt comparable analyses of the Northern Ireland data. Nonetheless, they seem to have a similar pattern: in particular, those in a part-time job are least likely to report that either domestic duties or child-care are shared equally (details in Table 7.4).

To summarise, the majority of women in Northern Ireland are now in the labour-market, though their participation rate is lower than in Britain. Women's work is concentrated in certain sectors of employment. As in Britain, there is little evidence that women's increasing involvement in paid work is accompanied by a more egalitarian distribution of domestic work.

Attitudes to paid work

It has long been the practice of industrial sociologists and psychologists to regard women workers as marginal. They either see women's commitment to work as less than that of men or ignore women's attitudes to work altogether. A warning was issued more than a decade ago, by Feldberg and Glenn (1979), that it was inconsistent to apply a 'job model' to men and a 'gender model' to women: that is, to explore men's attitudes to work as a function of circumstances, and women's attitudes to work as a function of their gender. The warning has now begun to be heeded. Dex, in a review of the recent research, has concluded that there is generally more support for considering both men and women as workers than as 'gendered beings': 'When women and men are compared in similar situations what seems notable is the similarity in their responses' (Dex, 1988, pp. 80–1).

The present data offer some scope for examining women's commitment to paid work. We have selected three items for consideration. Questions were asked about the importance to respondents of a range of factors relating to a paid job; about the importance of unemployment; and, for women not currently in paid employment, about reasons for their situation.

The percentage of women and men rating each of nine items as important or very important factors for them in a job is shown below.

Important factors in a job

	Very important or important	
	Men	Women
	%	%
Job security	98	96
Interesting job	94	93
Good opportunities for advancement	90	90
High income	85	83
A job that is useful to society	72	80
A job that allows someone to help others	69	77
A job that allows someone to work independently	66	63
A job with flexible working hours	40	53
A job that leaves a lot of leisure time	42	38

Job security, an interesting job, good opportunities for advancement and a high income were perceived by the majority both of men and women to be important aspects of work. However, there was a difference in the importance they attached to a job that involves helping others or that is useful to society, a job that offers flexible working hours, and a job that leaves a lot of leisure time. The latter difference is not large and there are studies that suggest that women with domestic responsibilities anyway enjoy very little 'leisure' as such (see, for example, Green, Hebron and Woodward, 1987; Wimbush, 1987).

It is not altogether surprising, given women's responsibilities in the home, that women were more likely than men to rate flexible working hours as important. Both flexible working hours and 'leisure-time' are likely to be used by women to enable them to combine domestic responsibilities and employment, rather than for recreation or social activities.

Women's responses showed virtually no variation with age. Women in all age groups agreed in rating a high income, good opportunities for advancement, job security and job interest as important to them. Nor were the part-time employed noticeably different in their assessments of what was important in a job. Factors such as security, interest and opportunity for advancement were, if anything, slightly more likely to be chosen as important by part-timers than full-timers. The one point on which they did differ was flexible working hours, something which probably reflected a preference for part-time work. Not surprisingly, those who were not in employment less frequently attached importance to a high income. Otherwise they showed similar priorities.

The importance of a job that helps others or is useful to society not only distinguished women from men, but also was rated more highly by older women, women working part-time, and those looking after the home. This finding is consistent with the rich ethnographic literature on caring and on married women's sense of obligation and dependency, and with debates about women's altruism (see, for example, Graham, 1983; Land and Rose, 1985; Ungerson, 1987; Lewis and Meredith, 1988). Choosing work which helps others can be seen as a mode of dissonance-reduction for women.

The salience of work for women can also be examined in terms of attitudes to unemployment and perceptions of the consequences of being unemployed. Respondents were presented with a series of factors associated with unemployment and asked to rank order the three worst things about being unemployed. This table shows the percentage of men and women who selected each item as among the three worst factors.

Worst thing about being unemployed

Respondents mentioning:	Men %	Women %
Not enough money	76	77
Loss of self-confidence	59	55
Family tensions	46	44
Not knowing how to fill one's time	28	17
Lack of contact with people at work	27	35
Loss of job experience	20	21
Loss of respect from friends and acquaintances	15	10

Once again, men and women were similar in many of their perceptions. Not enough money, loss of self-confidence and family tensions were the three most commonly perceived negative consequences of unemployment for both men and women. There were some differences in the relative importance of the remaining factors. For men, not knowing how to fill one's time was the fourth most serious consequence of unemployment; for women, it was loss of contact with people at work.

There were no very clear age-effects. But it was notable that, while lack of contact with co-workers was an important factor for almost all age groups of women, only the older men mentioned this with any frequency. Again, the patterns of response for women working full-time and part-time were very similar.

By focussing on women who were not currently in employment, we can explore whether they conform more to a 'gender' than a 'job' model of commitment to work. Women who had stated that they were looking after the home were asked why they were currently not in a paid job.

Main reasons of women who do not have a paid job

	%
Raising children	33
Prefer to look after home	36
No jobs available	4
Unsuitability for available jobs	2
Pregnancy/ill-health	4
Dependent relative	9
Poverty trap	6
Work less than 10 hours a week	3
Child-care costs	2
Unpaid work for family	1

Raising children, preferring to look after the home and looking after a dependent relative accounted for 78% of the responses. The unpaid, often unacknowledged, domestic work that women perform in the home is the most important reason for women not being in a paid job.

Witherspoon (1989), in her overview of data from the 1988 British survey, has distinguished between family responsibilities as a *constraint* on undertaking paid work and family responsibilities as a *preference*. Younger women and women with younger children are more likely to mention child-care as the main reason for not working, whilst older women and those whose youngest child is at least of secondary-school age are more likely to say that they prefer not to work. The smaller sample size of the Northern Ireland survey, combined with a low response-rate to this question, results in an effective sample here of only 69 women aged between 18 and 59. Comparisons should therefore be viewed with caution. Within this limitation, however, the evidence suggests that the constraint/preference pattern observed in Britain is also evident in Northern Ireland. Even for older women, constraining factors were still important: this was the case, for example, for nearly half of those aged over 35. Family responsibilities were a major constraining factor, with a quarter of the group absent from the labour force for this reason (Table 7.5).

The material analysed so far in this chapter confirms recent British studies, which find more similarities than differences in women's and men's attitudes to work. In addition, and notwithstanding the greater labour-market participation gap, there is little in the data so far to support the thesis of women's markedly greater traditionalism in Northern Ireland – in the sense of a lower commitment to paid work or a stronger preference for looking after the home. The traditionalism thesis does find some support, however, in the material presented in the next section.

Attitudes to social issues

This section examines responses to a number of social issues, such as sexual relationships, divorce, abortion and pornography. It concentrates both on comparisons within Northern Ireland and on comparisons with British data.

Attitudes to pre-marital, extra-marital and same-sex sexual relationships were measured by asking respondents to describe them in terms of one of five options, ranging from 'not wrong at all' to 'always' wrong. The table gives the results for all respondents.

Sexual relationships 'always' or 'mostly' wrong

	Northern Ireland	Britain
	%	%
Pre-marital	43	22
Extra-marital	90	84
Same-sex	82	68

Attitudes in this area are more conservative in Northern Ireland than in Britain, with attitudes to pre-marital sexual relationships showing the greatest difference. Attitudes to pre-marital sexual relationships were more conservative in Northern Ireland across all age groups: even among the youngest respondents (18–24 years), only 52% regarded such relationships as 'rarely wrong' or 'not at all wrong', compared with 75% of the same age group in Britain. Disapproval increases fairly uniformly with age in Northern Ireland, whereas in Britain the most notable age difference is between the more liberal under-45s and the more conservative older group (see Table 7.6 for details).

Women appear to be more traditional in their attitudes to pre-marital sexual relationships than men. However, further analysis of male and female attitudes by age reveals a more complex picture. Young men and women held similar attitudes towards pre-marital sexual relationships. It is only in the older age groups that women's greater traditionalism becomes apparent, and particularly in those aged over 55.

Whilst same-sex sexual relationships are generally thought to be wrong by both samples, in Northern Ireland attitudes are particularly conservative. Homosexuality was only legalised in Northern Ireland in 1982, after a case had been successfully taken to the European Court of Human Rights. While disapproval of homosexuality increased with age in Northern Ireland (as in Britain), even among the youngest age groups disapproval was widespread: 73% of those aged 18–24 stated that homosexual relationships are always or mostly wrong.

The survey also explored the issue of discriminatory attitudes towards homosexuals, through a series of questions which asked whether it is acceptable for homosexuals to occupy certain functions and roles.

It is acceptable for a homosexual person:

	Northern Ireland %	Britain %
To be a teacher in a school	35	45
To be a teacher in a university	44	55
To hold a responsible position in public life	48	58

A homosexual couple should be allowed to adopt a baby under the same conditions as other couples when:

	Northern Ireland %	Britain %
The couple are female	11	18
The couple are male	5	10

The findings suggest that discriminatory attitudes towards male and female homosexuals are more widespread in Northern Ireland than in Britain, though their pattern is similar. Functions or roles involving contact with children are least likely to be viewed as acceptable for homosexuals, particularly the parenting role. Although adoption was perceived as slightly more acceptable for female than male couples, attitudes to a homosexual couple adopting a child were strongly conservative both in Northern Ireland and Britain.

Attitudes on these questions, when differentiated by gender, age and religious affiliation, are broadly similar in the two samples. However, in comparison with others in Northern Ireland, young women tended to hold more liberal views on homosexuals holding positions of responsibility.

As with the reform of the law relating to homosexuality, attempts to reform divorce law, to bring it into line with that in England and Wales, has generated considerable controversy in Northern Ireland. Reform was opposed by both Protestants and Catholics and on both sides of the main political divide. Irreconcilability as grounds for divorce was finally recognised in Northern Ireland in 1978, 10 years after it had been in England and Wales.

Respondents stating that divorce should be:

	Northern Ireland %	Britain %
Easier to obtain than it is now	16	13
More difficult to obtain	32	30
Should remain the same	46	53

The evidence suggests that support for further liberalisation is relatively low in Northern Ireland and Britain. It is outweighed by those who want to see a tightening up of the legislation, as well as by those who are satisfied with the current situation.

Women were slightly more conservative than men on the matter of divorce, with more than one-third of them wanting to see it made more difficult. Again, it was among the younger women that the greatest support for liberalisation was found, with support dropping sharply with increasing age. By contrast, the greatest support among men for liberalisation occurred in the age group 35–54. Young women in both samples were more dissatisfied with the status quo than were men, and especially so in Northern Ireland. They were divided, however, in their attitudes to ease of divorce (Table 7.7). In addition, there were interesting religious differences. In Britain, Catholics were more likely than Protestants to say that divorce should be more difficult. In Northern Ireland, the converse held, with Protestant women being particularly opposed to easy divorce (Table 7.8).

In contrast to the public debates on homosexuality and divorce in recent years, a 'conspiracy of silence' has surrounded the issue of abortion (Northern Ireland Abortion Law Reform Association, 1989). The provisions of the 1967 Abortion Act have still not been extended to Northern Ireland. Public debate has been forced into the open only occasionally. Most recently, it was prompted by the successful campaign in 1984 in the Republic of Ireland for a constitutional amendment to make abortion illegal.

Attitudes to abortion were investigated in the Social Attitudes survey by focussing on the circumstances in which a woman should be permitted by law to obtain an abortion.

Respondents agreeing that abortion should be allowed by law when:

	Northern Ireland %	Britain %
The couple cannot afford any more children	24	57
The woman is not married and does not wish to marry	28	57
The woman decides on her own she does not wish to have a child	29	49
The couple agree they do not wish to have a child	30	59
There is a strong chance of a defect in the baby	60	87
The woman's health is seriously endangered by the pregnancy	76	92
The woman becomes pregnant as the result of rape	70	91

Attitudes to abortion were in all circumstances more traditional in Northern Ireland. Differences between the two samples were greatest when personal preference was involved: less than one-third of Northern Ireland respondents thought that the law should permit abortion in such circumstances. In the remaining cases, respondents in both samples were more likely to agree that the law should permit abortion. However, its acceptability in Britain was much more pronounced than in Northern Ireland.

A major gender difference was found in the acceptability of abortion. In Northern Ireland women were considerably less willing than men to condone abortion, in all but one of the situations. Older women were particularly conservative about abortion. Men's attitudes to abortion, however, were less influenced by age; in some circumstances the acceptability of abortion actually increased with age. This pattern is less evident in the British sample:

male and female attitudes are very similar, particularly with regard to abortion under circumstances where preference is not the motive (Table 7.9).

Finally, we turn to attitudes to pornography. Again, attitudes in Northern Ireland are less permissive. Slightly over half the sample thought that pornographic magazines and films should be banned altogether.

Respondents stating that pornographic magazines and films should be:

	Northern Ireland	Britain
	%	%
Banned altogether	55	39
Available in special adult shops but not displayed to the public	32	42
Available in special adult shops with public display permitted	7	10
Available in any shop for sale to adults only	5	7
Available in any shop for sale to anyone	1	1

As in Britain, attitudes to pornography are strongly influenced by age, gender and religious affiliation. In Northern Ireland, women were more censorious of pornography across all age groups. The proportion of young women who disapproved of pornography was particularly striking. Some 40% of women, compared to only 27% of men under 25, wished to see pornographic material banned altogether. In Britain, greater disapproval of pornography by women was also in evidence; though in the 18–24 age group women were more liberal than men (Table 7.10). A split in the feminist movement over attitudes to liberalisation may partly underlie this finding.

The attitudes reviewed in this section certainly provide support for the frequently expressed view that Northern Ireland is a more traditional society than Britain. The survey in Northern Ireland shows that attitudes are more conservative. Conservatism is particularly evident in relation to pre-marital sexual relationships and to abortion. Equally important, the survey has provided the opportunity to explore attitudes in Northern Ireland more fully. It has demonstrated a diversity of attitudes between younger and older respondents, between those stating different religious affiliations, and between men and women.

Conclusion

The extension of the Social Attitudes survey series from Britain to Northern Ireland provides a welcome opportunity to explore a range of themes relevant to an understanding of the contemporary position of women in Northern Ireland. It is important that direct comparisons can be made with the position of British women. It is hoped that this chapter has given a flavour of the kind of information on gender issues which can be obtained from the Social Attitudes surveys.

Differences in both the extent and type of participation in the labour-market of men and women, and differences in the structure of women's employment over the life-cycle in Northern Ireland and Britain have been discussed in terms of the striking differences in men's and women's contribution to domestic work, which remains very largely women's responsibility. By contrast, male and female attitudes to work in the Northern Ireland sample showed marked similarities. Most diversity occurred in attitudes to various social issues, both between Northern Ireland and Britain and within Northern Ireland. This was particularly influenced by religious affiliation and, in the case of women, by age.

The future interpretation of these findings is an open question. Using a rather different approach, other researchers have been struck by the greater liberalism of young women in Northern Ireland, as compared with their male counterparts, with regard to women's work roles (Kremer and Curry, 1986, p.51). But they found nothing to suggest the greater liberalism in younger women in relation to other social issues that was found in this survey.

Underlying this apparent discrepancy are at least two sets of issues. First, which research method is most likely to clarify our understanding of women's position? Kremer and Curry asked specifically about 'woman's place' at work and at home; the Social Attitudes survey asked the same questions about both women's and men's experiences, suggesting that one might draw inferences from the extent of similarity and difference in their answers. These two approaches and the relation between them have received insufficient critical comment.

The second, and more fundamental, issue relates to broader matters of interpretation. Some writers have questioned the status of the kinds of gender difference repeatedly found in attitude surveys (see, for example, Eagly, 1983; Lott, 1985). In the context of a critique of a scale of sexual attitudes, Howard (1988), for example, has rejected the conventional approach which treats gender as a property of individuals, and argues that gender differences may be better understood as indicators of differences in the position of women and men in society. Clearly such themes as these will need to be addressed in future work in this area. They are implicated in a more systematic examination of the traditionalism argument with which we opened the chapter.

References

ABBOTT, P. and WALLACE, C., *Introduction to Sociology: feminist perspectives*, Routledge, London (1990).

BEECHEY, V. and PERKINS, T., *A Matter of Hours: women, part-time work and the labour market*, Polity Press, Cambridge (1987).

COHEN, B., *Caring for Children: services and policies for children and equal opportunities in the United Kingdom*, Commission of the European Communities (1988).

DEX, S., *Women's Attitudes towards Work*, Macmillan, London (1988).

EAGLY, A. H., 'Gender and social influence: a social psychological analysis', *American Psychologist*, 38, 971–81 (1983).

EDGERTON, L., 'Public protest, domestic acquiescence: women in Northern Ireland', in Ridd, R. and Callaway, H. (eds), *Caught up in Conflict: women's responses to political strife*, Macmillan, London (1986).

EOCNI (EQUAL OPPORTUNITIES COMMISSION FOR NORTHERN IRELAND), *Where Do Women Figure?*, EOCNI, Belfast (1988).

FELDBERG, R. and GLENN, E., 'Male and female: job versus gender models in the sociology of work', *Social Problems*, 26(5), 524–38 (1979).

GRAHAM, H., 'Caring: a labour of love', in Finch, J. and Groves, D. (eds), *A Labour of Love: women, work and caring*, Routledge and Kegan Paul, London (1983).

GREEN, E., HEBRON, S. and WOODWARD, D., 'Women, leisure and social control', in Hamner, J. and Maynard, M. (eds), *Women, Violence and Social Control*, Macmillan, London (1987).

HOWARD, J. A., 'Gender difference in sexual attitudes: conservatism or powerlessness?', *Gender and Society*, 2(1), 103–14 (1988).

JOSHI, H., 'The changing form of women's economic dependency', in Joshi, H. (ed), *The Changing Population of Britain*, Basil Blackwell, Oxford (1989).

JOWELL, R., WITHERSPOON, S. and BROOK, L. (eds), *British Social Attitudes: the 5th report*, Gower, Aldershot (1989).

KREMER, J. and CURRY, C., *Attitudes towards Women in Northern Ireland*, EOCNI, Belfast (1986).

LAND, H. and ROSE, H., 'Compulsory altruism for some or an altruistic society for all?', in Bean, P., Ferris, J. and Whynes, D. (eds), *In Defence of Welfare*, Tavistock, London (1985).

LEWIS, J. and MEREDITH, B., *Daughters Who Care*, Routledge, London (1988).

LOTT, B., 'The potential enrichment of social/personality psychology through feminist research and vice-versa', *American Psychologist*, 40, 155–64 (1985).

McWILLIAMS, M., 'Women in Northern Ireland: an overview', *Ideas and Production: a journal of the history of ideas* (forthcoming).

MARTIN, J. and ROBERTS, C., *Women and Employment: a lifetime perspective*, HMSO, London (1984).

MORRIS, L., *The Workings of the Household: a US–UK comparison*, Polity Press, Cambridge (1990).

NORTHERN IRELAND ABORTION LAW REFORM ASSOCIATION, *Abortion in Northern Ireland: the report of an international tribunal*, Beyond the Pale Publications, Belfast (1989).

ROULSTON, C., 'Women on the margin: the women's movement in Northern Ireland 1973–1988', *Science and Society*, 53, 219–36 (1989).

TREWSDALE, J., *Womanpower No. 4: The Aftermath of Recession: changing patterns in female employment and unemployment in Northern Ireland*, EOCNI, Belfast (1987).

UNGERSON, C., *Policy is Personal*, Tavistock, London (1987).

WARD, M. and McGIVERN, M., 'Images of women in Northern Ireland', *The Cranebag Book of Irish Studies*, 4, 579–85 (1980).

WIMBUSH, E., 'Transitions: changing work, leisure and health experiences among mothers with young children', in Allatt, P., Keil, T., Bryman, A. and Blytheway, B. (eds), *Women and the Life Cycle: transitions and turning points*, Macmillan, London (1987).

WITHERSPOON, S., 'Sex roles and gender issues', in Jowell, R. and Witherspoon, S. (eds), *British Social Attitudes: the 1985 report*, Gower, Aldershot (1985).

WITHERSPOON, S., 'Interim report: a woman's work', in Jowell, R., Witherspoon, S. and Brook, L. (eds), *British Social Attitudes: the 5th report*, Gower, Aldershot (1989).

Table 7.1 Economic activity rates for women aged 18–59 in Northern Ireland and Britain (by age) (%)

	Northern Ireland					
	18–24	25–34	35–44	45–54	55–59	Total
Employed 30 hours or more	44	37	21	14	13	27
Self-employed full-time	1	–	3	–	4	1
Employed 29 hours or less	–	13	23	25	24	17
Self-employed part-time	–	–	2	–	–	1
Waiting to take up job	–	–	–	3	–	1
Unemployed	17	8	8	7	–	8
Total economically active	62	58	57	49	41	55
Looking after home	21	39	42	36	47	37
Retired	–	–	–	6	8	2
Other	4	1	1	10	4	3
Total economically inactive	25	40	43	52	59	42
Full-time students	13	1	–	–	–	2

Table 7.2 Occupations of women in the sample according to the compressed Goldthorpe Schema* (%)

Salariat (professional and managerial)	13
Routine non-manual (office and sales)	31
Petty bourgeoisie (self-employed including farmers with and without employees)	2
Manual foreman and supervisors	1
Working class (skilled, semi-skilled and unskilled, personal service and agricultural workers)	39
Unclassified (never had a job)	13

* For an explanation of this schema, see Jowell et al (1989), pp. 204–5

Table 7.3 Domestic division of labour (by sex and age) (%)

	Men							
Who is mainly responsible for:	18–24	25–34	35–44	45–54	55–59	60–64	65+	Total
General domestic duties								
mainly man	–	2	5	5	4	–	10	4
mainly woman	100	80	80	93	91	95	73	84
shared equally	–	17	13	2	4	5	14	10
not answered	–	2	2	–	–	–	3	1
General child-care duties								
mainly man	–	4	4	–	–	–	–	3
mainly woman	100	88	72	69	100	33	–	79
shared equally	–	8	24	31	–	67	–	18
not answered	–	–	–	–	–	–	–	–

Britain					
18–24	25–34	35–44	45–54	55–59	Total
48	35	31	31	24	34
2	3	4	2	1	3
4	15	29	27	24	21
–	1	4	3	1	2
1	1	1	1	–	1
10	7	2	3	3	5
65	62	71	67	53	66
16	36	27	29	26	28
–	–	–	2	10	1
4	1	2	3	11	3
20	37	29	34	47	32
14	1	–	–	–	3

Women								All							
18–24	25–34	35–44	45–54	55–59	60–64	65+	Total	18–24	25–34	35–44	45–54	55–59	60–64	65+	Total
–	3	–	4	–	–	11	3	–	2	2	4	2	–	10	4
76	85	96	88	96	91	85	89	85	83	89	91	94	93	77	87
23	12	3	7	4	9	4	8	15	14	7	5	4	2	10	8
–	–	1	–	–	–	–	–	–	1	1	–	–	5	3	1
–	–	–	–	–	–	–	–	–	2	2	–	–	–	–	1
69	90	89	95	100	100	–	89	80	89	81	81	100	50	–	84
31	10	11	5	–	–	–	11	20	9	17	19	–	50	–	15
–	–	–	–	–	–	–	–	–	–	–	–	–	–	–	–

Table 7.4 Domestic division of labour by women's employment status (%)

Who is mainly responsible for:	Employment status			
	Looking after home	Full-time employment	Part-time employment	Total
General domestic duties				
mainly man	2	2	4	3
mainly woman	92	82	92	89
shared equally	6	16	4	8
not answered	–	–	–	–
General child-care duties				
mainly man	–	–	–	–
mainly woman	92	75	97	89
shared equally	8	25	3	11
not answered	–	–	–	–

Table 7.6 Attitudes to sexual relationships (by sex and age) (%)

Northern Ireland

Views on:	Men								Women								All							
	18–24	25–34	35–44	45–54	55–59	60–64	65+	Total	18–24	25–34	35–44	45–54	55–59	60–64	65+	Total	18–24	25–34	35–44	45–54	55–59	60–64	65+	Total
Pre-marital sex																								
Always/mostly wrong	17	26	21	53	58	66	67	38	19	20	40	54	68	76	80	48	18	23	32	54	64	71	74	43
Sometimes wrong	24	22	23	12	8	9	2	16	15	21	18	13	13	11	6	14	21	22	20	12	11	11	4	15
Rarely/not at all wrong	52	43	41	28	32	19	14	35	54	49	27	22	17	7	13	29	52	46	33	25	23	12	14	32
Depends/varies	6	9	13	6	2	2	12	8	10	8	15	8	3	6	1	8	8	8	14	7	2	4	6	8
Not answered	–	–	1	–	–	2	4	1	2	1	–	3	–	–	1	1	1	1	1	2	–	2	2	1
Extra-marital sex																								
Always/mostly wrong	95	89	77	89	95	94	86	88	96	87	92	90	97	97	94	92	95	88	85	90	96	96	91	90
Sometimes wrong	4	6	10	9	5	–	4	6	2	7	2	5	3	3	1	3	3	7	6	7	4	2	3	5
Rarely/not at all wrong	1	2	4	–	–	2	2	2	1	1	1	–	–	–	4	1	1	1	2	–	–	1	3	1
Depends/varies	1	4	7	2	–	–	3	3	–	5	6	2	–	–	–	2	1	4	6	2	–	–	1	3
Not answered	–	–	1	–	–	4	4	1	2	–	–	3	–	–	2	1	–	–	1	1	–	1	2	1
Homosexual relationships																								
Always/mostly wrong	75	78	76	89	88	96	95	83	70	72	78	79	85	96	97	81	73	75	77	84	86	96	96	82
Sometimes wrong	18	4	3	2	3	–	–	5	7	7	8	5	–	1	1	5	14	5	6	3	1	1	1	5
Rarely/not at all wrong	2	13	13	3	8	–	1	7	15	16	7	2	9	3	–	7	7	14	10	3	4	2	1	7
Depends/varies	4	5	6	5	–	2	–	4	8	5	7	10	6	–	1	5	6	5	7	8	5	1	1	5
Not answered	–	–	2	–	–	2	4	1	–	1	–	3	–	–	1	1	–	1	1	2	4	1	1	1

Table 7.7 Attitudes to divorce (by sex and age) (%)

Northern Ireland

Divorce should be:	Men								Women								All							
	18–24	25–34	35–44	45–54	55–59	60–64	65+	Total	18–24	25–34	35–44	45–54	55–59	60–64	65+	Total	18–24	25–34	35–44	45–54	55–59	60–64	65+	Total
Easier to obtain	9	20	23	21	13	21	12	17	22	24	11	11	10	14	8	15	14	22	17	16	12	17	9	16
More difficult	23	24	26	31	40	36	36	29	39	20	33	34	46	44	47	36	29	22	30	32	43	41	42	32
Should remain same	61	51	48	45	43	40	40	48	39	50	46	48	42	34	34	43	52	50	47	47	43	37	37	46
Don't know	7	5	3	2	3	4	12	5	–	6	10	7	1	7	11	7	4	6	7	5	2	6	11	6

Table 7.5 Main reasons for women looking after home not having a paid job (by age) (%)

	18–34	35–59
Raising children	74	7
Prefer to look after home and family	11	52
Looking after dependent relative	–	14
Pregnancy or ill-health	7	2
Poverty trap	–	10
No jobs available	4	5
Unsuited for available jobs	–	2
Work unpaid in family business	–	2
Child-care cost	4	–
Work in paid job but less than 10 hours a week	–	5

Britain

Men								Women								All							
18–24	25–34	35–44	45–54	55–59	60–64	65+	Total	18–24	25–34	35–44	45–54	55–59	60–64	65+	Total	18–24	25–34	35–44	45–54	55–59	60–64	65+	Total
9	4	8	21	20	37	48	20	5	5	10	26	45	37	56	24	7	5	9	24	32	37	52	22
11	16	22	21	24	15	20	19	21	22	25	23	16	20	14	20	16	19	24	22	20	18	16	19
79	80	69	54	47	45	26	59	72	70	62	45	36	40	24	51	75	75	65	49	41	42	25	55
1	–	1	2	7	2	5	2	2	3	2	4	3	2	4	3	2	2	2	3	5	2	4	3
–	–	–	2	2	–	1	–	–	–	–	2	–	2	3	1	–	–	–	2	1	1	2	1
77	78	74	90	83	91	91	83	80	82	78	84	94	86	91	84	79	80	76	87	88	89	91	83
17	15	18	8	11	6	7	12	19	12	15	10	4	2	5	10	18	13	16	9	7	4	6	11
5	5	8	1	2	–	2	4	1	4	4	2	2	1	–	2	3	5	5	1	2	–	1	3
1	2	1	–	4	2	1	1	–	1	4	2	–	10	1	2	–	1	3	1	2	6	1	2
–	–	–	1	–	–	–	–	–	1	–	1	–	1	1	1	–	1	–	2	–	1	1	1
64	58	59	81	85	87	89	72	42	54	59	62	83	82	86	65	52	55	59	71	84	84	87	68
6	9	10	3	4	7	3	6	26	15	14	11	4	5	5	12	17	12	12	7	4	5	4	9
28	27	25	11	7	2	8	18	29	28	21	17	8	7	3	17	29	28	23	14	8	5	5	17
2	6	7	3	4	4	–	4	2	3	5	8	2	4	3	4	2	4	6	6	3	4	2	4
–	–	–	2	–	–	–	–	1	–	–	2	3	2	3	2	–	–	–	2	1	1	2	1

Britain

Men								Women								All							
18–24	25–34	35–44	45–54	55–59	60–64	65+	Total	18–24	25–34	35–44	45–54	55–59	60–64	65+	Total	18–24	25–34	35–44	45–54	55–59	60–64	65+	Total
21	14	19	9	7	8	9	13	27	12	14	9	7	4	11	13	24	13	16	9	7	6	10	13
20	24	19	21	29	27	41	26	29	24	24	41	45	40	40	33	25	24	22	32	37	34	40	30
55	56	60	64	59	61	47	57	41	60	58	50	44	54	41	50	48	58	59	56	52	57	43	53
4	6	2	6	5	4	3	4	3	4	4	–	4	2	9	4	3	5	3	3	5	3	6	4

Table 7.8 Attitudes to divorce (by sex and religion) (%)

	Northern Ireland											
	Men				Women				All			
Divorce should be:	Cath.	Prot.	Other	Total	Cath.	Prot.	Other	Total	Cath.	Prot.	Other	Total
Easier to obtain	15	13	29	17	17	11	24	15	16	12	27	16
More difficult	36	30	16	29	33	40	24	36	34	35	19	32
Should remain same	41	52	52	48	41	43	45	43	41	47	49	46
Don't know	8	5	3	5	8	6	6	7	8	5	4	6

Table 7.9 Attitudes to abortion (by sex and age) (%)

	Northern Ireland																							
	Men								Women								All							
Abortion should be allowed by law when:	18–24	25–34	35–44	45–54	55–59	60–64	65+	Total	18–24	25–34	35–44	45–54	55–59	60–64	65+	Total	18–24	25–34	35–44	45–54	55–59	60–64	65+	Total
Woman does not wish to have a child: Yes	30	29	31	36	33	37	31	32	23	36	23	29	31	14	19	26	27	33	27	32	32	24	24	29
No	70	69	65	64	67	50	62	65	72	60	75	65	65	76	73	69	71	65	71	64	66	64	69	67
Don't know	–	–	–	–	–	6	2	1	–	–	1	3	–	1	2	1	–	–	1	1	–	3	2	1
Not answered	–	2	4	–	–	8	4	2	5	3	1	3	4	9	5	4	2	2	2	2	2	8	5	3
Couple agree they do not want child: Yes	32	44	37	39	32	35	29	36	29	38	22	24	24	12	16	25	31	41	29	32	28	22	21	30
No	68	54	57	61	65	48	61	60	66	59	77	72	68	77	76	70	67	57	68	67	66	64	69	65
Don't know	–	–	–	–	–	6	3	1	–	–	–	–	–	1	2	1	–	–	–	–	–	3	2	1
Not answered	–	2	6	–	3	11	8	4	5	3	1	3	8	9	6	4	2	2	3	2	6	10	7	4
Woman is not married and doesn't wish to marry: Yes	30	36	26	32	45	31	22	31	28	35	21	22	30	17	21	25	29	36	23	27	37	23	22	28
No	70	62	66	68	55	52	66	65	67	62	78	77	66	73	69	70	70	62	73	72	61	64	68	68
Don't know	–	–	1	–	–	6	3	1	–	–	–	–	–	1	3	1	–	–	1	–	–	3	3	1
Not answered	–	2	6	–	–	11	8	3	3	3	1	2	4	9	6	3	1	2	3	1	2	10	7	3
Couple cannot afford more children: Yes	19	29	29	29	23	29	20	25	34	30	27	17	19	15	16	24	25	30	28	23	21	21	17	24
No	81	67	62	71	73	54	69	69	61	66	71	79	77	71	75	71	73	67	67	75	75	64	72	70
Don't know	–	–	1	–	–	6	4	1	–	–	–	–	–	1	3	1	–	–	1	–	–	3	3	1
Not answered	–	3	8	–	3	11	8	4	5	3	2	3	4	12	6	4	2	3	4	1	4	12	7	4
Strong chance of a defect in the baby: Yes	55	57	66	66	62	50	63	60	64	73	69	48	62	45	51	60	59	65	68	57	62	47	56	60
No	45	38	28	34	35	33	20	34	33	24	28	48	35	44	42	35	40	31	28	41	35	39	33	35
Don't know	–	1	1	–	–	6	8	2	–	–	2	–	–	1	3	1	–	1	2	–	–	3	5	1
Not answered	–	3	4	–	3	11	8	4	3	3	1	3	3	9	3	3	1	3	3	2	3	10	5	3
Woman's health endangered by pregnancy: Yes	79	87	83	90	70	54	71	79	72	87	78	71	76	53	63	73	76	87	80	80	73	53	66	76
No	21	10	10	10	23	33	14	15	23	11	19	23	24	33	27	22	22	10	15	17	24	33	22	19
Don't know	–	2	2	–	3	6	6	2	–	–	2	–	–	1	6	1	–	1	2	–	1	3	6	2
Not answered	–	1	4	–	3	7	8	3	5	2	1	6	–	12	4	4	2	2	3	3	1	10	6	3
Woman pregnant as result of rape: Yes	72	81	72	76	70	71	73	74	64	81	68	67	68	53	56	66	68	81	70	71	69	61	63	70
No	26	15	16	24	22	15	17	20	33	17	27	31	27	29	35	28	29	16	23	28	25	23	27	24
Don't know	–	–	5	–	–	6	7	2	–	–	2	–	3	4	6	2	–	–	4	–	1	5	6	2
Not answered	2	3	6	–	8	8	3	4	3	2	2	2	3	14	3	3	2	3	4	1	5	11	3	3

Britain

Men				Women				All			
Cath.	Prot.	Other	Total	Cath.	Prot.	Other	Total	Cath.	Prot.	Other	Total
6	10	18	13	16	9	17	13	11	9	17	13
46	27	19	26	42	35	26	33	44	32	23	30
44	61	56	57	40	51	52	50	42	55	54	53
4	2	6	4	2	4	5	4	3	3	5	4

Britain

Men								Women								All							
18–24	25–34	35–44	45–54	55–59	60–64	65+	Total	18–24	25–34	35–44	45–54	55–59	60–64	65+	Total	18–24	25–34	35–44	45–54	55–59	60–64	65+	Total
65	52	51	48	41	47	43	50	59	54	51	45	38	43	40	48	62	53	51	47	39	45	41	49
35	44	47	47	52	48	52	46	39	42	45	50	56	56	47	46	37	43	46	48	54	52	49	46
–	2	1	–	–	–	–	1	–	–	–	–	2	–	–	1	–	1	–	–	1	–	–	1
–	2	–	4	7	4	5	3	2	3	4	5	4	1	13	5	1	3	2	5	6	3	10	4
77	66	67	66	48	57	49	62	60	60	62	64	47	61	43	57	68	63	64	65	47	59	45	59
22	31	33	28	45	39	43	33	40	35	35	30	47	38	41	37	32	33	34	29	46	39	42	35
–	2	–	–	–	–	–	1	–	–	–	–	2	–	–	1	–	1	–	–	1	–	–	1
1	1	–	6	7	4	8	4	–	5	3	6	4	–	16	6	–	3	2	6	4	2	13	5
63	56	61	63	52	56	56	59	50	55	61	61	56	61	48	56	56	56	61	62	54	59	52	57
35	41	38	31	41	39	38	37	49	41	35	33	35	37	37	38	43	41	36	32	38	38	37	38
–	2	1	–	–	–	–	1	–	–	–	–	4	–	–	1	–	1	–	–	2	–	–	1
1	1	–	6	7	4	6	3	1	3	5	6	4	1	15	6	1	1	3	6	6	3	11	5
57	59	55	65	61	61	49	57	54	57	62	59	62	49	49	56	55	58	59	62	61	54	49	57
41	38	44	30	36	35	46	39	46	40	33	31	31	46	37	37	44	39	37	31	34	41	41	38
–	2	–	–	–	–	–	1	–	–	–	–	–	–	1	1	–	1	–	–	–	–	1	–
1	1	1	5	2	4	5	3	1	3	5	10	7	5	13	7	1	2	4	7	5	5	9	5
83	85	91	86	81	95	78	85	95	90	95	86	91	92	81	89	90	88	93	86	86	93	80	87
16	13	9	10	15	5	18	13	5	8	5	8	4	7	9	7	10	10	7	9	9	6	13	9
–	1	–	–	–	–	–	–	–	–	–	–	–	–	1	–	–	–	–	–	–	–	–	1
1	1	–	4	5	–	4	2	–	2	–	6	4	1	9	4	–	2	–	5	5	1	7	3
91	92	94	92	83	98	87	91	98	91	97	95	91	92	82	92	95	92	96	94	87	95	84	92
6	7	6	4	12	–	10	7	2	7	1	2	4	7	9	4	4	7	3	3	8	4	9	5
–	1	–	–	–	–	–	–	–	–	–	–	–	–	–	–	–	–	–	–	–	–	–	–
3	–	–	4	5	2	3	2	–	2	2	3	4	1	9	4	1	1	1	3	5	1	7	3
92	95	92	89	85	92	85	90	99	91	96	94	91	92	80	91	96	93	94	91	88	92	82	91
6	4	8	6	10	6	11	7	1	8	2	2	4	7	10	5	3	6	5	4	7	6	10	6
–	1	–	–	–	–	–	1	–	–	–	–	–	–	–	–	–	–	–	–	–	–	–	–
2	–	–	5	5	2	4	2	–	1	2	4	5	1	10	4	1	1	1	4	5	2	7	3

Table 7.10 Attitudes to pornography (by sex and age) (%)

| | Northern Ireland | | | | | | | | | | | | | | | | | | | | | | | |
| Pornographic material should be: | Men | | | | | | | | Women | | | | | | | | All | | | | | | | |
	18–24	25–34	35–44	45–54	55–59	60–64	65+	Total	18–24	25–34	35–44	45–54	55–59	60–64	65+	Total	18–24	25–34	35–44	45–54	55–59	60–64	65+	Total
Banned altogether	22	27	25	55	62	65	77	42	40	47	59	69	82	91	92	66	29	37	44	62	73	80	86	55
Available in special adult shops, not displayed	57	47	60	31	25	19	16	41	41	36	31	24	13	9	1	24	50	41	44	28	19	14	7	32
Available in special adult shops and displayed	15	11	9	7	3	10	2	9	7	9	3	6	–	–	3	5	12	10	6	7	1	4	3	7
Available in any shop for sale to adults	5	13	1	5	10	4	1	6	8	7	6	1	4	–	1	4	6	10	4	3	7	2	1	5
Available in any shop for sale to anyone	–	–	1	–	–	–	–	1	1	1	–	–	–	–	–	1	1	1	1	–	–	–	–	1
Not answered	1	1	3	1	–	1	3	2	3	1	1	–	–	–	3	2	2	1	2	1	–	'–	1	1

Britain

Men								Women								All							
18–24	25–34	35–44	45–54	55–59	60–64	65+	Total	18–24	25–34	35–44	45–54	55–59	60–64	65+	Total	18–24	25–34	35–44	45–54	55–59	60–64	65+	Total
19	9	25	26	50	34	64	31	13	21	33	54	75	67	83	45	16	16	30	40	63	52	75	39
46	56	57	56	36	47	20	46	59	57	51	34	13	30	9	39	53	57	53	45	24	38	14	42
24	16	11	14	4	8	4	12	16	12	11	6	2	1	1	8	20	14	11	10	3	4	2	10
11	17	8	2	7	8	6	9	10	9	4	5	8	–	5	6	10	12	6	4	7	4	5	7
–	–	–	–	–	3	1	1	–	–	–	–	–	2	–	1	–	–	–	–	–	2	1	1
–	2	–	2	2	–	5	2	1	1	–	1	2	1	3	1	1	1	–	1	2	–	4	1

8
Healthy eating:
attitudes and practice

Gillian Robinson and Mary Black

During the 1980s the issue of food and health has received more and more public attention and interest. This trend seems likely to continue into the 1990s, as good health increasingly becomes recognised as a resource for living. The controversies of the food debate – for example, discussions of intensive farming methods, the growth in prepared foods and the increase in notified cases of food-poisoning, have been accompanied by a marked change in attitudes towards healthier eating.

In this chapter, we will examine attitudes towards food, diet and health, and present eating habits and any data on changes in eating patterns that have occurred over the past two to three years. (These are based on reported eating behaviour and may not accurately reflect actual food consumption.) We will also examine any relationships that exist between these sets of attitudes and behaviours.

Background

Food has important implications for health. There is now strong evidence to suggest that the food we eat influences our risk of contracting various diseases, most notably ischemic heart disease (IHD), bowel and digestive disorders and obesity. In 1986, the Department of Health and Social Services launched its Change of Heart programme, which was aimed at preventing IHD in Northern Ireland. Along with Scotland, Northern Ireland has the unenviable position of being at the top of the world league table for deaths from IHD. It accounted for 33% of deaths in men and 25% of deaths in women (Coronary Prevention Group, 1988).

Trends in IHD in Northern Ireland are currently being monitored by the World Health Organisation MONICA project. The trends are being related to known risk factors and lifestyle habits such as diet, and to socio-economic factors. The work has highlighted a strong social-class gradient in the prevalence of IHD and in associated risk factors such as cigarette-smoking and lack of exercise (MONICA, 1990). Manual workers, as a group, experience more IHD than non-manual workers. There is also considerable evidence from elsewhere that there has been a decline in death rates from IHD in younger age groups by about 2% per annum, in both men and women

(Coronary Prevention Group, 1988). However, this decline reflects the same socio-economic bias.

Community-based preventive programmes in other countries, for example, in the United States of America and Finland, have managed to reduce the rates of IHD. The Change of Heart campaign is broadly similar to programmes carried out in other countries and concentrates attention on reducing the incidence of known risk factors for IHD, for example, cigarette-smoking, poor nutrition, lack of exercise and high blood-pressure. This is achieved by means of public education, the creation of health-promoting policies, education in schools and workplaces, and initiatives directed at key professions within the health services, such as general practitioners. A most important element in these programmes is the promotion of healthier eating.

There is now widespread agreement on the changes necessary if our national diet is to become more healthy. The NACNE report (NACNE, 1983) and the COMA report (COMA, 1984) set targets for the proportion that certain foods should contribute to our overall dietary energy requirements. Both the Household Food Consumption and Expenditure Survey (National Food Survey Committee, 1989) and other surveys (Barker et al, 1988; BMRB, 1989) report lower consumption of fruit and vegetables and higher consumption of fats than present dietary guidelines would recommend.

The health education messages are relatively straightforward:

1 *Reduce fat consumption, in particular saturated fat* (fat largely derived from animal sources). NACNE recommended that total fat consumption should form no more than 30% of total energy requirements and that no more than 10% should be saturated fat.

2 *Increase the amount of fibre in the diet.* NACNE recommended that fibre intake should be increased from 20 to 30 grams per day so that complex carbohydrates makes up 48% of total energy requirements.

3 *Cut down on sugar and sugary foods.* NACNE recommended that only 7% of total energy requirements should come from sugar.

4 *Cut down on salt.* Average consumption of salt is 10 grams per day. NACNE recommended that this be reduced to three grams per day.

5 *Eat a variety of foods and plenty of fresh fruit and vegetables.*

Attitudes towards food, diet and health.

From the answers to 11 general attitudinal questions in the survey (Tables 8.1a and 8.1b give full details) we computed a summed score for each respondent. This was based on allocating a score of one to five ('strongly agree' to 'strongly disagree') to each of the 11 answers. The maximum score was 55 (representing the most positive or health-conscious attitude towards food, diet and health) and the lowest score possible was 11 (the least positive attitude). Scores were calculated for the 756 people who answered all 11 questions. To simplify the subsequent discussion, we divided the respondents into two groups: positive (a score of between 34 and 55 points) and negative (scoring between 11 and 33 points).

A cut-off point of 34 was chosen because it represents the midpoint of the scale 11–55; and because to score 34 a respondent would have had to disagree with at least one of the statements indicating at least one 'healthy' attitude.

In addition, we found that this cut-off point split the sample into two groups of almost identical size.

	Positive attitude	Less positive attitude
	%	%
Total	51	49
Male		
18–34 years	47	53
35–54 years	61	39
55 years or more	34	66
Female		
18–34 years	54	46
35–54 years	60	40
55 years or more	39	61
Social class		
I/II	70	30
III non-manual	58	42
III manual	40	60
IV/V	33	67
Highest educational qualification		
Degree/professional	87	13
'A' level/'O' level	58	42
CSE/other	50	50
No qualifications	33	67
Household income (£)		
Less than 5000	30	70
5000–7999	40	60
8000–11999	52	48
12000–17999	71	29
18000 or more	71	29

The positive respondents tend to be from the higher social classes, be better educated, have a higher household income, and be in the 35–54 age group. Women tend to have a more positive attitude than men.

Five of the eleven questions concerned what Sheiham et al (1987) termed 'overt barriers to healthy eating'.

Overt barriers to healthy eating: % of sample who agree or disagree with each statement

	Agree strongly/ Just agree	Disagree strongly/ Just disagree
Food that is good for you:		
is usually more expensive	55	28
doesn't usually taste as nice as other food	36	35
generally takes too long to prepare	24	47
is hard to find in supermarkets	19	56
mothers would eat if the rest of their families would let them	29	40

Apart from the perceived expense of healthy food, which over half of our respondents report, none of the 'barriers' is regarded as such by the majority of our respondents. There is a more frequent perception of barriers in the lower socio-economic groups. Similarly, those with fewer or no educational qualifications tend to perceive more barriers to healthy eating. Both these groups are inclined to think that healthy food is more expensive, takes longer to prepare and does not taste as good as other food. Again, there are marked differences in attitudes by household income, with three-quarters of the poorer respondents believing that food that is good for you is usually more expensive.

Two other questions were designed to find out how far people saw good health as being outside their personal control. A minority of our respondents subscribe to these 'fatalistic' views of diet and health. As we might expect, older people tend to be more fatalistic than average, as are those with no educational qualifications, those from social classes III manual, IV and V, and those in the lowest income bands (see Tables 8.1a and 8.1b).

	Agree strongly/ Just agree %	Disagree strongly/ Just disagree %
Good health is just a matter of good luck	18	65
If heart disease is in your family, there is little you can do to reduce your chances of getting it	21	65

The final four questions looked at the importance of exercise and weight control, experts' views on diet and what constitutes a proper meal. Two-thirds of our respondents think that experts give conflicting advice. Once again, those from the lower social classes and those with no educational qualifications are more likely to agree with this statement. Some two-thirds of our respondents also hold to the more traditional view of a proper meal as having meat and vegetables. However, over half the sample do not believe that exercise can substitute for diet. More women than men agree that people worry too much about their weight.

	Agree strongly/ Just agree %	Disagree strongly/ Just disagree %
The experts contradict each other over what makes a healthy diet	66	17
A proper meal should include meat and vegetables	66	19
People worry too much about their weight	63	18
As long as you take enough exercise you can eat whatever foods you want	33	53

The population in general would appear to think that they have control over their health. However, there are differences in attitudes between sub-groups, with those in the lower social classes, those with fewer educational qualifications and those with lower household incomes having more traditional views about diet. They are also more inclined to see healthy food as expensive, taking longer to prepare and not tasting as nice as other food.

Eating habits

The frequency of consumption of the seven food groups referred to in the survey is shown in Figure 8.1. Data on bread consumption are presented below.

Reported bread consumption

	%
5 or more slices daily	24
3–4 slices daily	33
1–2 slices daily	32
4–6 slices weekly	7
Less often	3
Never eat bread	1

Half the respondents eat processed meats at least two to three days per week, and over 60% of respondents eat beef, lamb or pork as often. Eggs are eaten more than once a week by 44% of the sample. However, some 18% never eat eggs nowadays. Fish is the food least frequently eaten, with only 18% eating it more than once a week. Forty per cent eat chips or roast potatoes more than once a week. Fresh fruit and vegetables are eaten by the majority of respondents (78%) at least four to six days per week. Finally, just under half (46%) eat biscuits, pastries or cake every day.

Younger men and respondents on lower incomes tend to eat processed meats most frequently (see Tables 8.2a and 8.2b). For meat products, there is little difference between the sexes, although more females than males report that they never eat meat nowadays. Those with higher educational qualifications and those on higher incomes eat meat more often.

Respondents on lower incomes, those with fewer educational qualifications and those from the lower classes eat eggs more often. More females than males never eat eggs. Fish, as we have already noted, is eaten very little by our sample. However, those who do eat it tend to be from the higher social classes, be better educated and have higher incomes.

Chips or roast potatoes are eaten by males more frequently than females. Respondents from the lower social classes and those with lower incomes also tend to eat chips more frequently than other sub-groups.

Females eat fresh fruit and vegetables more frequently than males, as do respondents in the higher income brackets and those with higher educational qualifications. Bread is eaten in greater quantity by males, with a relatively high proportion (46%) eating five or more slices a day. Bread is also eaten in greater quantity by those in the lower socio-economic groupings, those with fewer educational qualifications and those with a lower income. Finally, there is little variation between sub-groups in the frequency of consumption of cakes, biscuits and pastries.

There is a difference between the eating habits of the positive and less

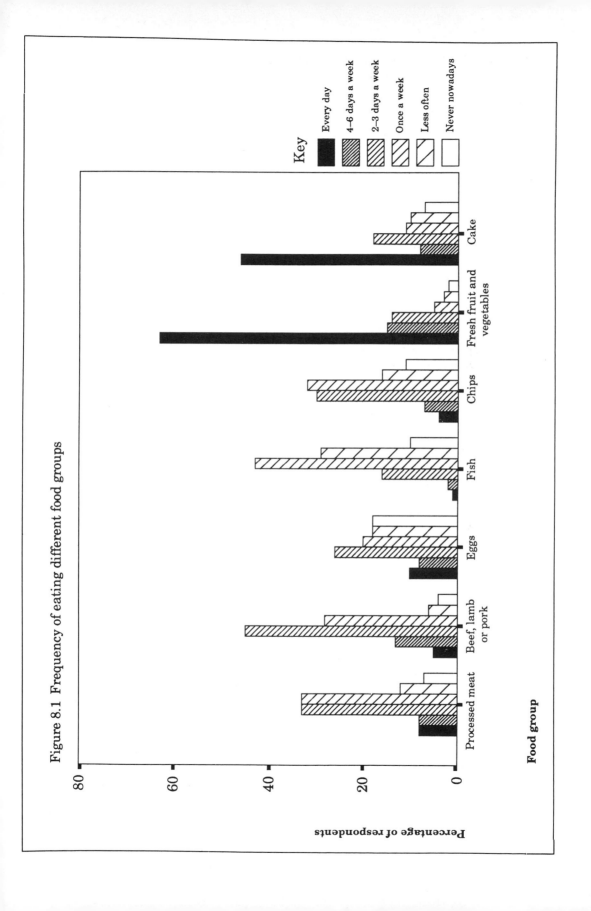

Figure 8.1 Frequency of eating different food groups

positive attitudinal groups. Those with a positive attitude to diet and health tend to eat foods like chips and processed meats less frequently than those with a less positive attitude. They also tend to eat more vegetables and fish. Statistical testing confirms that differences between the two groups are significant for all types of food. (Table 8.3 gives full details.)

Diet changes

From the questions asked in the survey it is possible to determine what changes, if any, the respondents have made to their diets over the last two or three years, and to ascertain the reasons for these changes.

This table shows the responses to a series of questions on dietary changes in the previous two or three years. Around two-thirds of our respondents have made healthy changes to their diet in the ways specified (with the exception of eating more fish and poultry and using more semi-skimmed or skimmed milk).

Compared with two or three years ago, would you say you are now:

	Answering 'yes' %
eating more grilled food instead of fried food	68
eating more wholemeal bread instead of white bread	61
using more low-fat spreads or soft margarine instead of butter	66
eating more fish and poultry instead of red meat	44
drinking or using more semi-skimmed or skimmed milk instead of full cream milk	38
eating more boiled or baked potatoes instead of chips or roast potatoes	67

Only 5% of respondents did not claim to have made any changes towards healthier eating in the last two or three years. The average number of changes made was 3.4.

Changes towards healthier eating

Number of changes made within the previous two or three years

	%
None	5
One	9
Two	17
Three	17
Four	21
Five	18
Six	13

Women (average change 3.6) appear to have made more recent changes to their diet than men (average change 3.2) (see Table 8.4). People in the middle age range (35–54) years are more likely to have changed; young men and older men are least likely to have done so. Those in the higher social classes are more likely to have changed than those in the lower social classes (average of 3.9 changes for social classes I/II compared with an average of 3.0 for those in social classes III/IV). However, it is in the educational sub-groups that the widest range is found: those with a degree or professional qualification made an average of 4.2 changes towards healthier eating, in comparison with those respondents holding the CSE qualification, who made an average of 2.9 changes. Similarly, it is those in the higher income brackets who have made the most changes.

Are the number of changes made linked to attitudes? As we might expect, they are. Respondents with a positive, or health-conscious, attitude made an average of 3.9 changes to their diet, while respondents with a less positive attitude made an average of 3.1 changes.

It is clear that the majority of people who are changing their food consumption are adopting more healthy eating habits, with more fish and more fruit and vegetables being consumed and less meat products, chips and cakes.

Respondents' changes in food consumption

	Healthy change	Unhealthy change	No change
	%	%	%
Processed meats	31 (less)	6 (more)	63
Beef, pork or lamb	21 (less)	5 (more)	73
Eggs	29 (less)	3 (more)	68
Fish	13 (more)	10 (less)	77
Chips/roast potatoes	23 (less)	6 (more)	71
Fresh fruit and vegetables	23 (more)	4 (less)	73
Cake, biscuits and pastries	20 (less)	5 (more)	72

For every food group the most frequently cited reason for change was to keep healthy (Table 8.5). Controlling weight was the second most often cited reason for respondents cutting down on their consumption of chips and cakes. Personal preference was given as a reason for several changes in dietary behaviour, and it was the second most frequently cited reason for cutting down on the intake of processed meats and eggs. One should note that the salmonella scare was headline news in late 1988, with news coverage continuing throughout the spring of 1989 when the survey was being conducted. This may have influenced respondents' eating habits and/or attitudes at the time. Poor value for money was the second most often cited reason for respondents having cut down their intake of beef, lamb or pork.

Discussion

The most striking feature to emerge from our work is the influence that socio-economic factors have on attitudes towards healthier eating, perceived barriers to improving diet, current eating practices, and dietary changes. In virtually every case it is the higher social classes, the better educated and those with higher household incomes whose attitudes and practice are the most healthy. These findings echo those of previous studies (BMRB, 1989; MONICA, 1990;

Sheiham et al, 1987; Barker et al, 1988). Another interesting finding is that women's attitudes and current practice is generally healthier than men's. Once again, this has been a common theme in the previous work.

A major perceived barrier to healthier eating for 55% of the sample was expense. Certain 'healthy' items of food are indeed more expensive: for example, wholemeal bread, lean meat and fish. Because poverty is widespread in Northern Ireland, with approximately two-fifths of the population living on low incomes (Evason, 1985), expense may be a real barrier for many households. Several studies have shown that income is the single biggest influence on the quality of a family's nutrition (Graham, 1986; WIN, 1988; HEA, 1989). Food is the largest item, and in some cases the only item, with which families can balance their budgets. When a family is managing on a very meagre income, differentials in the price of bread of up to 11p a loaf are very important, particularly since low income families rely very heavily on such 'filler' foods (Graham, 1986; WIN, 1988; HEA, 1989).

A small percentage of our sample subscribed to a 'fatalistic' view of diet and health. As in other studies (UMS, 1987; BMRB, 1989; Butler et al, 1989), it is the lower social groups that feel most fatalistic. This is important for two reasons. First, people's beliefs about their control over lifestyle are very closely linked to actual practice: those who believed that they could influence their health by their lifestyle were in fact already making changes. Those who did not hold this attitude were not making changes. Second, it is possible that so-called 'fatalistic' attitudes may reflect objective reality. Substantial constraints operate on those sub-groups among whom these attitudes are most prevalent, such as the effects of low income, unemployment and a poor educational level. These are all factors that would directly affect 'choice' of lifestyle (UMS, 1987; Butler et al, 1989).

The view that a 'proper meal' consists of meat and vegetables coincides with earlier findings (Charles and Kerr, 1985). Health education should take account of this and examine the practicalities of providing meals that are healthier and consistent with this view. People need to be reassured that meals that do not conform to this stereotype can also be nutritionally sound.

Almost 90% of respondents eat bread daily, with men eating larger quantities than women. Unfortunately, it is not possible to say what proportion of the bread is wholemeal. However, 61% of respondents report eating more wholemeal bread than two or three years ago, which is in line with current dietary guidelines.

Consumption of other foods follows the socio-economic pattern observed elsewhere, with lower income groups eating less meat and fish and relying more heavily on processed meat and eggs. Fish consumption, in general, is very low (18%) despite it being a 'healthy' alternative to meat.

Lower income groups are also eating more chips or roast potatoes than higher income groups. Barker et al (1988) found that lower income groups consumed more potatoes and that young unemployed men had the highest consumption of potatoes. In England (BMRB, 1989), it has also been found that these groups eat fried foods more regularly (using lard instead of polyunsaturated oil for frying), drink full-fat milk, eat white bread and consume low fibre cereals much more frequently than high income groups. This has important implications for the level of consumption of fat, which is a major risk factor in IHD.

Consumption of fresh fruit and vegetables is greatest amongst higher income groups and amongst women, confirming the finding of Barker et al (1988) in Northern Ireland. Interestingly, there is very little variation in the consumption of cakes, biscuits and pastries, though Barker et al found that women's consumption of these items was greater than men's.

There is a relationship between what people eat and their overall attitude. Those respondents who have a positive attitude to health and diet and who are also more socio-economically advantaged have a healthier diet. There is a wealth of evidence documenting health inequalities (Townsend, 1980; Graham, 1986 and Policy Research Institute, 1990). Are present health education approaches merely exacerbating these existing inequalities?

The dietary changes made by some two-thirds of respondents over the last two to three years are broadly in line with currrent recommendations. Only 5% reported having made no changes to their diet. Changes toward eating more fish and poultry are less common than others. Expense, cultural factors and practical considerations seem to be important determinants. Consumption of skimmed and semi-skimmed milk has increased for just over one-third of respondents. Health is one of the most often cited reasons for changes in diet. Women are making more changes to their diet than men; and, once again, socio-economic factors dominate the underlying pattern. Other studies have shown that women are more aware of messages about health than men (BMRB, 1989; Riddock, 1990).

Much needs to be done if changes to eating patterns, and thus to risk factors for IHD, are to be made throughout the population. Changes in the method and presentation of health education will not suffice. The wider agenda of health and the context in which health decisions are made must be a part of the approach. Otherwise, health education may only reinforce existing knowledge and do nothing to aid the application of this knowledge toward healthier practices by those groups who are most vulnerable.

Conclusions

The majority of the population is changing its eating habits towards healthier diets. However, this does not disguise the main finding of our survey that lower income groups experience a less healthy diet, feel less able to do anything to change their diet and are making fewer changes to their diet.

By and large women's attitudes and practice are healthier than their male counterpart.

The barriers to healthier eating are perceived as considerable in lower income groups. Health promotion and education must take full cognisance of these barriers when planning prevention programmes.

Attention should be given to political action such as lobbying for food subsidies. There now exists a considerable body of knowledge reinforcing our findings regarding socio-economic differences. New knowledge is required as to how to make health information have significance and practical application in low income groups. This can only be achieved by working with people in these sub-groups and together finding new approaches to these problems, that is, via a community development approach.

References

BARKER, M., McCLEAN, S. I., McKENNA, P. G., REID, N. G., STRAIN, J. J., THOMPSON, K. A., WILLIAMSON, A. P. and WRIGHT, M. E., *Diet, Lifestyle and Health in Northern Ireland*, University of Ulster, Coleraine (1988).

BMRB (BRITISH MARKET RESEARCH BUREAU), *Health and Lifestyle*, Health Education Authority, London, (1989).

BUTLER, J. R., FRENCH, J., LANCASTER, J. and LIPLAYD, P., *Lifestyle*, Department of Public Health, East Cumbria (1989).

CHARLES, N. and KERR, M., *Attitudes Towards the Feeding and Nutrition of Young Children*, Health Education Council, London (1985).

COMA (COMMITTEE ON MEDICAL ASPECTS OF FOOD POLICY), *Diet and Cardiovascular Disease*, HMSO, London (1984).

CORONARY PREVENTION GROUP, *Statistical Information on Coronary Heart Disease*, Coronary Prevention Group, London (1988).

EVASON, E., *On the Edge – A Study of Poverty and Long-term Unemployment in Northern Ireland*, Child Poverty Action Group, London (1985).

GRAHAM, H., *Caring for the Family: a short report of a study of the organisation of health resources and responsibilities in 102 families with pre-school children*, Health Education Council, London (1986).

HEA (HEALTH EDUCATION AUTHORITY), *Diet, Nutrition and Healthy Eating*, HEA, London (1989).

MONICA, Personal communication with Dr A. Evans (1990).

NACNE (NATIONAL ADVISORY COMMITTEE ON NUTRITION EDUCATION), *A Discussion Paper on Proposals for Health Educators in Britain*, Health Education Council, London (1983).

NATIONAL FOOD SURVEY COMMITTEE, MINISTRY OF AGRICULTURE, FISHERIES AND FOOD, *Household Food Consumption and Expenditure Survey*, HMSO, London (1989).

POLICY RESEARCH INSTITUTE, *Spatial and Social Variations in the Distribution of Health Indicators in Northern Ireland*, Policy Research Institute, Belfast (1990).

RIDDOCK, C., *The Fitness, Physical Activity and Lifestyles of Northern Ireland Post-primary School Children*, The Queen's University of Belfast, Belfast (1990).

SHEIHAM, A., MARMOT, M., RAWSON, D. and LUCK, N., 'Food values: health and diet', in Jowell, R., Witherspoon, S. and Brook, L. (eds), *British Social Attitudes: the 1987 report*, Gower, Aldershot (1987).

TOWNSEND, P., *Inequalities in Health – the Black Report*, Penguin, London (1980).

UMS (ULSTER MARKETING SURVEYS), *Change of Heart – Health Survey*, UMS, Belfast (1987).

WIN (WOMEN'S INFORMATION NETWORK), *Healthy Eating at What Price?*, WIN, Belfast (1988).

Table 8.1a Attitudes to food, health and diet, by age within sex, social class, highest educational qualification and household income (%)

| | | Age within sex | | | | | |
| | | Male | | | Female | | |
	Total	18–34	35–54	55+	18–34	35–54	55+
As long as you exercise you can eat whatever foods you want:							
Agree strongly/just agree	33	36	33	42	24	26	35
Neither agree nor disagree	14	18	14	12	18	10	11
Just disagree/disagree strongly	53	45	41	45	58	63	53
If heart disease is in your family, there is little you can do to reduce your chances of getting it:							
Agree strongly/just agree	21	23	19	28	14	15	28
Neither agree nor disagree	13	18	10	18	14	5	14
Just disagree/disagree strongly	65	59	68	53	72	78	56
The experts contradict each other over what makes a healthy diet:							
Agree strongly/just agree	66	57	66	78	56	68	73
Neither agree nor disagree	16	27	16	7	18	10	14
Just disagree/disagree strongly	17	15	16	13	24	21	10
People worry too much about their weight:							
Agree strongly/just agree	63	52	50	67	63	72	73
Neither agree nor disagree	18	28	19	19	19	11	11
Just disagree/disagree strongly	18	19	28	13	17	16	15
Good health is just a matter of good luck:							
Agree strongly/just agree	18	14	12	23	11	18	30
Neither agree nor disagree	16	20	12	18	16	10	18
Just disagree/disagree strongly	65	65	74	58	73	72	50
A proper meal should include meat and vegetables:							
Agree strongly/just agree	66	69	60	75	56	58	76
Neither agree nor disagree	15	13	17	13	21	15	11
Just disagree/disagree strongly	19	18	20	12	23	26	12

	Social class				Highest educational qualification				Household income (£)				
I/II	III Non-man.	III Man.	IV/V	Degree/ prof.	'A'/ 'O' level	CSE/ other	None	Less than 5000	5000– 7999	8000– 11999	12000– 17999	18000 or more
21	26	41	42	10	30	26	42	43	39	29	18	23
11	18	14	14	10	15	23	13	13	16	12	14	13
69	54	42	43	79	55	50	44	43	44	58	67	64
11	13	28	29	6	12	19	31	31	23	15	12	7
8	11	18	15	8	12	22	14	17	12	13	10	9
81	75	51	56	86	74	58	54	51	64	71	77	84
57	67	71	70	47	64	53	75	73	69	69	69	58
18	12	18	15	23	15	31	12	13	12	17	15	19
24	18	8	12	30	20	14	11	13	18	13	15	23
46	61	66	72	44	55	69	72	73	70	61	54	52
25	17	19	14	20	27	18	13	13	16	23	18	21
29	21	13	13	37	17	12	14	13	13	16	27	27
11	13	21	24	4	11	18	26	29	20	17	9	7
12	13	22	17	45	18	14	16	16	16	9	14	15
77	73	55	58	51	70	68	56	54	63	73	76	77
49	57	74	77	34	59	64	80	80	71	61	56	49
17	23	16	9	20	22	15	9	10	10	18	14	23
34	20	8	14	46	18	20	11	10	18	20	29	28

Table 8.1b Attitudes to food, health and diet, by age within sex, social class, highest educational qualification and household income (%)

| | | Age within sex | | | | | |
| | | Male | | | Female | | |
	Total	18–34	35–54	55+	18–34	35–54	55+
Healthy food doesn't usually taste as nice as other food:							
Agree strongly/just agree	36	34	41	39	30	27	43
Neither agree nor disagree	28	39	27	34	27	24	20
Just disagree/disagree strongly	35	26	29	25	44	48	34
Food that is good for you is usually more expensive:							
Agree strongly/just agree	55	53	46	65	52	48	66
Neither agree nor disagree	16	22	17	15	17	18	9
Just disagree/disagree strongly	28	24	35	18	31	34	23
Food that is good for you generally takes too long to prepare:							
Agree strongly/just agree	24	21	20	22	23	25	30
Neither agree nor disagree	28	41	25	40	28	13	20
Just disagree/disagree strongly	47	38	53	36	48	61	48
It is hard to find food that is good for you in supermarkets:							
Agree strongly/just agree	19	22	17	16	25	13	20
Neither agree nor disagree	25	33	29	28	26	16	16
Just disagree/disagree strongly	56	44	51	55	50	70	63
Mothers would eat healthier food if the rest of their families would let them:							
Agree strongly/just agree	29	24	29	31	26	31	37
Neither agree nor disagree	29	35	34	39	29	16	22
Just disagree/disagree strongly	40	41	35	28	45	52	39

	Social class				Highest educational qualification				Household income (£)				
I/II	III Non-man.	III Man.	IV/V	Degree/ prof.	'A'/ 'O' level	CSE/ other	None	Less than 5000	5000– 7999	8000– 11999	12000– 17999	18000 or more
19	33	45	40	13	29	44	44	42	43	32	31	27
28	30	29	31	29	31	29	27	27	21	35	14	34
52	36	24	28	58	39	27	27	29	36	32	52	39
42	49	61	67	30	49	50	66	75	59	61	40	37
18	17	18	13	23	18	21	12	10	11	17	15	24
39	34	18	19	46	31	27	20	14	29	22	43	39
11	19	28	31	10	17	28	30	32	26	23	16	15
28	25	33	28	23	35	25	26	26	26	31	21	27
61	55	36	39	66	47	45	42	41	48	45	62	57
12	12	23	28	9	18	22	22	23	22	25	11	13
26	23	29	26	26	28	21	23	20	24	20	23	25
62	64	45	45	64	53	55	54	56	54	55	65	62
19	30	30	39	18	24	25	36	38	35	33	22	21
29	24	40	24	26	35	35	26	30	21	27	31	27
51	45	28	34	56	39	39	37	31	43	39	46	51

Table 8.2a Frequency of eating various food groups, by attitude, age within sex, social class, highest educational qualification and household income (%)

| | | Attitude | | Age within sex | | | | | |
| | | | | Male | | | Female | | |
	Total	Positive	Less positive	18–34	35–54	55+	18–34	35–54	55+
Processed meat:									
Every day	8	4	9	14	12	7	6	3	4
4–6 days a week	8	6	9	17	6	5	9	6	2
2–3 days a week	33	28	39	45	36	30	34	27	26
Once a week	33	39	30	14	37	35	35	41	40
Less often	12	15	9	6	8	17	9	17	15
Never	6	8	5	5	2	6	8	7	12
Beef, lamb or pork:									
Every day	5	4	5	2	7	5	2	6	5
4–6 days a week	13	15	10	14	15	18	7	15	9
2–3 days a week	44	47	43	42	46	42	44	48	45
Once a week	28	23	32	36	27	21	33	22	28
Less often	6	5	8	4	4	12	8	4	5
Never	4	5	2	3	–	2	7	2	7
Eggs:									
Every day	10	8	13	13	9	17	8	6	10
4–6 days a week	8	6	8	14	8	12	7	3	4
2–3 days a week	26	28	25	23	33	23	22	29	26
Once a week	20	22	19	16	22	22	22	22	18
Less often	18	22	13	17	15	11	18	23	19
Never	18	14	21	17	12	15	24	17	21
Fish:									
Every day	1	1	1	2	–	–	1	–	1
4–6 days a week	2	3	1	1	3	2	1	1	1
2–3 days a week	15	19	13	12	18	17	10	17	20
Once a week	43	45	43	34	42	43	37	48	55
Less often	29	27	32	38	32	31	33	25	18
Never	10	7	11	13	6	7	18	9	6

Social class				Highest educational qualification				Household income (£)				
I/II	III Non-man.	III Man.	IV/V	Degree/ prof.	'A'/ 'O' level	CSE/ other	None	Less than 5000	5000– 7999	8000– 11999	12000– 17999	18000 or more
6	4	16	7	6	4	16	8	11	5	6	6	7
6	8	10	7	4	14	6	6	8	9	8	5	3
30	28	34	37	21	34	40	35	30	37	33	29	38
35	42	28	33	42	29	32	33	30	30	38	38	40
18	12	9	8	21	11	5	11	12	10	9	16	10
6	7	4	7	6	8	2	7	9	10	6	5	3
4	2	8	3	3	6	–	5	4	6	5	7	2
21	13	13	7	20	15	13	10	9	8	11	17	25
47	45	47	45	49	41	53	44	35	48	51	46	50
21	32	27	30	22	28	30	30	37	26	28	27	19
5	4	4	10	4	5	3	8	9	7	5	1	4
3	5	1	5	3	6	1	4	5	5	2	2	1
8	4	12	14	4	8	21	11	13	10	7	9	7
8	3	10	8	7	12	7	6	7	7	4	6	8
28	30	29	22	29	30	24	24	21	29	30	37	26
18	23	22	20	24	18	21	21	20	22	20	22	21
22	18	16	15	24	15	21	17	15	15	23	17	22
16	22	11	20	12	19	8	21	24	17	16	9	17
–	1	–	–	1	2	–	–	–	3	–	–	–
3	1	2	1	2	2	1	2	1	–	2	1	4
22	15	13	16	25	13	10	15	14	18	13	15	25
45	47	40	40	49	40	45	43	44	39	50	50	37
25	27	35	30	18	33	35	29	26	34	23	27	26
5	8	11	14	5	10	9	11	14	8	12	7	8

Table 8.2b Frequency of eating various food groups, by attitude, age within sex, social class, highest educational qualification and household income (%)

| | | Attitude | | Age within sex | | | | | |
| | | | | Male | | | Female | | |
	Total	Positive	Less positive	18–34	35–54	55+	18–34	35–54	55+
Chips or roast potatoes:									
Every day	4	1	6	7	3	1	1	4	4
4–6 days a week	7	4	10	17	5	2	12	6	–
2–3 days a week	30	34	27	43	37	25	37	26	12
Once a week	32	34	30	21	30	30	30	42	37
Less often	16	18	15	7	19	23	13	15	22
Never	11	10	12	5	6	18	5	7	26
Fresh fruit and vegetables:									
Every day	63	68	57	46	58	63	63	72	75
4–6 days a week	15	13	16	19	13	14	18	17	8
2–3 days a week	14	11	17	18	16	15	14	9	10
Once a week	5	4	5	8	9	5	2	2	3
Less often	3	2	4	6	3	2	3	–	3
Never	1	1	2	4	2	1	1	–	1
Cake, biscuits, pastries:									
Every day	46	45	49	44	39	52	48	51	45
4–6 days a week	8	10	6	16	6	6	8	6	7
2–3 days a week	18	16	20	17	21	11	17	16	23
Once a week	11	13	9	9	12	15	12	10	8
Less often	10	11	7	6	14	8	8	12	10
Never	7	5	9	8	8	9	7	5	8
Bread:									
5 or more slices a day	24	19	28	46	32	27	7	16	16
3–4 slices a day	33	31	34	24	34	36	29	34	42
1–2 slices a day	32	37	30	20	24	29	47	40	34
4–6 slices a week	7	8	5	8	5	6	8	9	4
Less often	3	3	3	1	2	1	5	2	5
Never	1	1	1	2	1	–	2	–	–

Social class				Highest educational qualification				Household income (£)				
I/II	III Non-man.	III Man.	IV/V	Degree/ prof.	'A'/ 'O' level	CSE/ other	None	Less than 5000	5000– 7999	8000– 11999	12000– 17999	18000 or more
1	1	4	7	1	4	2	5	4	7	3	1	1
5	5	5	12	4	9	6	8	7	5	11	6	7
23	36	36	31	24	36	49	25	26	35	37	26	33
33	31	33	29	34	32	22	33	29	29	29	41	30
28	17	13	11	28	12	17	15	16	14	11	21	22
10	10	9	10	10	8	3	15	18	10	9	6	8
68	65	54	61	73	62	59	61	56	66	59	67	63
19	16	12	14	13	18	18	13	15	12	12	15	21
7	11	20	15	7	11	16	16	17	13	21	11	4
3	4	8	5	4	5	2	6	7	4	4	4	7
1	4	5	3	2	3	4	3	4	4	3	3	3
1	1	2	2	2	2	1	1	2	2	2	–	2
42	49	53	45	45	45	55	46	41	50	62	46	44
12	6	7	6	13	10	8	6	10	7	2	12	10
20	15	16	18	18	16	12	20	16	22	14	17	22
11	10	9	11	12	11	13	10	12	6	10	9	10
10	11	10	11	8	12	10	9	10	10	10	11	8
5	8	5	10	4	7	2	9	11	5	3	6	6
17	15	37	29	8	23	37	27	22	27	22	21	12
34	31	31	34	34	33	24	35	40	37	27	36	32
36	40	24	32	39	33	32	31	30	28	42	36	42
6	9	7	3	11	6	7	5	5	6	6	5	8
5	3	1	2	5	3	1	2	3	3	4	2	4
2	2	–	–	3	2	–	–	1	–	–	–	2

Table 8.3 Frequency of eating each food group, by attitude (%)

	Every day		4–6 days a week		2–3 days a week		Once a week		Less often		Never	
	A*	B#	A	B	A	B	A	B	A	B	A	B
Processed meats	4	9	6	9	28	39	39	30	15	9	8	5
Beef, lamb or pork	4	5	15	10	47	43	23	32	5	8	5	2
Eggs	8	13	6	8	28	25	22	19	22	13	14	21
Fish	1	1	3	1	19	13	45	43	27	32	7	11
Chips or roast potatoes	1	6	4	10	34	27	34	30	18	15	10	12
Fresh fruit and vegetables	68	57	13	16	11	17	4	5	2	4	1	2
Cake, biscuits, pastries	45	49	10	6	16	20	13	9	11	7	5	9

*Positive attitude; #Less positive attitude

Table 8.4 Recent changes to healthier eating, by age within sex, social class, highest educational qualification and household income (%)

		Age within sex					
		Male			Female		
	Total	18–34	35–54	55+	18–34	35–54	55+
Compared with two or three years ago, would you say you are now							
eating more grilled food instead of fried food	68	65	67	56	74	78	66
eating more wholemeal bread instead of white bread	61	49	64	64	55	69	66
using more low fat spreads or soft margarine instead of butter	66	69	66	56	66	75	59
eating more fish and poultry instead of red meat	44	40	44	33	42	54	49
drinking or using more semi-skimmed or skimmed milk instead of full cream milk	38	32	36	31	39	56	32
eating more boiled or baked potatoes instead of chips or roast potatoes	67	52	64	72	60	77	76
Number of changes made:							
None	5	29	24	11	9	8	19
One	9	24	16	18	24	7	11
Two	17	18	15	19	17	11	21
Three	17	23	10	15	20	15	17
Four	21	20	13	13	16	19	19
Five	18	13	19	9	15	26	17
Six	13	11	15	10	17	28	19
Average change score	3.4	3.1	3.4	3.2	3.4	4.1	3.5

	Social class				Highest educational qualification				Household income (£)				
I/II	III Non-man.	III Man.	IV/V	Degree/ prof.	'A'/ 'O' level	CSE/ other	None	Less than 5000	5000– 7999	8000– 11999	12000– 17999	18000 or more
77	73	63	59	81	71	67	63	60	61	68	78	84
68	63	59	57	73	61	60	58	54	62	50	61	74
65	74	63	63	76	72	57	61	62	54	61	75	76
54	53	35	38	58	46	43	40	39	38	46	56	56
52	44	31	29	63	43	21	31	27	33	35	49	57
71	73	64	59	64	70	62	67	69	65	54	66	72
5	16	33	46	2	22	20	56	45	27	12	13	2
16	27	21	37	7	25	7	61	30	22	26	16	7
21	14	29	36	11	21	11	56	33	29	20	8	10
26	19	25	29	15	25	12	48	34	23	15	11	18
25	19	22	35	8	36	7	50	27	21	14	18	21
29	28	20	24	19	27	13	41	25	17	10	22	25
35	35	15	15	30	31	3	36	19	14	15	21	30
3.9	3.8	3.1	3.0	4.2	3.6	2.9	3.1	3.1	3.1	3.1	3.9	4.0

Table 8.5 Reasons for recent dietary changes (respondents were invited to give one or more reasons) (%)

Reasons for change:	Processed meat		Beef, lamb or pork		Eggs	
	Eating more now	Eating less now/ cut down/ cut out	Eating more now	Eating less now/ cut down/ cut out	Eating more now	Eating less now/ cut down/ cut out
To help control my weight	4	9	–	7	–	3
I was told to for medical reasons	4	11	5	10	–	11
It is good value for money	14	–	7	–	9	1
It is poor value for money	–	4	1	15	–	–
I wanted to keep healthy	7	45	16	38	12	39
I just like it more	38	–	34	–	51	2
I just don't like it as much	–	19	2	13	5	20
None of these reasons	39	14	31	19	16	20

Fish		Chips or roast potatoes		Fresh fruit and vegetables		Cake, biscuits, pastries	
Eating more now	Eating less now/ cut down/ cut out	Eating more now	Eating less now/ cut down/ cut out	Eating more now	Eating less now/ cut down/ cut out	Eating more now	Eating less now/ cut down/ cut out
5	2	1	20	8	–	–	32
18	3	2	11	13	5	–	15
9	–	13	–	2	–	–	1
–	10	–	–	–	8	–	4
47	14	–	51	67	–	–	34
27	–	41	–	11	–	70	1
–	39	–	11	–	39	2	9
5	31	40	8	3	48	27	7

9
AIDS and the moral climate

Ian Sneddon and John Kremer

Northern Ireland is a region that is unique in many respects, including its atypical profile in relation to the incidence and impact of Human Immuno-deficiency Virus (HIV) and Acquired Immune Deficiency Syndrome (AIDS). In comparison with the rest of the United Kingdom and with the Republic of Ireland, Northern Ireland is an area of low prevalence. By January 1990, there were only 14 AIDS cases reported in the Province, and 65 individuals were reported as HIV positive. For a population of one and a half million, these figures are well below incidence rates in other European countries.

Northern Ireland bears the hallmarks of a special case with regard to HIV and AIDS. The Social Attitudes survey throws new light on their impact on the people of Northern Ireland, and in particular on people's perception of their own risk. This chapter also reports on attitudes towards people with AIDS, and willingness to be tested for the virus.

Factors influencing HIV transmission

It is now well established that HIV is spread principally in one of three ways: during sexual intercourse (anal or vaginal); by infected blood (for example, through the sharing of needles and syringes by drug-users or through receiving infected blood by transfusion); or by transmission from an infected mother to her unborn baby. In terms of each of these sources of transmission, a number of factors may interact and establish hurdles that retard the spread of HIV within Northern Ireland.

Sexual activity

An appreciation of the sexual behaviour and attitudes of the people of Northern Ireland is relevant. Recent research confirms the general belief that rates of sexual activity are low in comparison with those in other European countries (Charlwood, Kerr and Maw, 1989). For example, data from an AIDS awareness questionnaire given to students at The Queen's University of Belfast and the University of Ulster at Coleraine indicated that only 38% of them were sexually active (Brown et al, 1987). Comparable studies outside Northern Ireland have found much higher levels of student sexual experience (for example, Clement et al, 1984). Our own research also has revealed that levels of sexual experience amongst students are relatively low (Sneddon and Kremer, forthcoming), with religiosity being one of the most important factors associated with a lack of sexual experience. Regular church attenders (of whom there were many in our study) rarely reported having had sexual intercourse.

Religion

The relationship between religion and sexual behaviour has been the subject of considerable research since the time of Kinsey et al (1948; 1953). A number of studies in the United States of America and Australia have indicated a positive correlation between religious commitment and conservative sexual behaviour and attitudes. In drawing this research together, Mol (1970) has suggested that strong religious beliefs contribute to a world-view that is capable of filtering out cues from the environment, including those which are sexually stimulating. More recent research (Martin and Westbrook, 1973), indicates that the relationship may be more complex and mediated by other cognitive and behavioural factors, as well as by cultural expectations that include traditional sex-role stereotypes.

In Northern Ireland, the considerable influence of the Churches, both Protestant and Catholic, is shown in many and varied ways. The high rates of church attendance (Curtice and Gallagher, 1990) bear ample testimony to this. In comparison with the rest of the United Kingdom, it is likely that religion in Northern Ireland plays a more significant role in the determination of people's attitudes and behaviour. Religious practice and its impact on sexual behaviour are the first of several factors that may characterise the epidemiology of HIV and AIDS in Northern Ireland.

Family

In Northern Ireland the family is still one of the most powerful social institutions (McShane and Pinkerton, 1986). Marriage is a more important context for sexual relations than in Britain (McLaughlin, forthcoming). Various religious and cultural traditions combine to imbue members of the community with a sense of the importance of family. The size of the Province is a contributory factor. It is impossible to move far from the parental home and its influence, without leaving Northern Ireland. More young adults than in Britain continue to live in the parental home.

The moral climate

The influences of religion and family combine to create a more conservative moral climate in Northern Ireland than in the rest of the United Kingdom. This was revealed in the survey in answers to questions dealing with attitudes towards sexual relationships. Respondents were asked for their views on premarital and extra-marital sexual relations. There are differences in attitudes across all age groups. Although there is a very strong feeling against extramarital sex in both samples, people in Northern Ireland take an even more disapproving stance than in Britain.

What would your general opinion be if:

	Northern Ireland				Britain			
a man and a woman had		Age				Age		
sexual relations before	Total	18–34	35–54	55+	Total	18–34	35–54	55+
marriage?	%	%	%	%	%	%	%	%
Always/mostly wrong	43	21	41	74	22	6	16	45
Sometimes wrong	15	21	16	7	20	18	23	18
Rarely/not at all wrong	32	49	30	13	55	75	58	32
Other/Don't know/No answer	9	9	13	5	3	2	2	5
a married person had								
sexual relations with someone								
other than his or her partner?								
Always/mostly wrong	91	91	88	95	84	79	81	91
Sometimes wrong	5	5	6	3	11	15	13	6
Rarely/not at all wrong	1	*	1	1	3	4	4	*
Other/Don't know/No answer	3	3	5	1	2	1	2	3

Attitudes towards homosexuality

Until 1982, homosexual acts between consenting adult males still constituted a criminal offence in Northern Ireland. There is general agreement that homosexual men are still obliged to maintain a lower profile than is the case in the rest of the United Kingdom. Previous research with student samples has found attitudes towards homosexuality to be more negative than in Britain (Brown et al, 1987; Sneddon and Kremer, forthcoming). This was confirmed by responses to questions in the present survey.

What would your general opinion be if:

	Northern Ireland				Britain			
two adults of the same sex		Age				Age		
had sexual relations	Total	18–34	35–54	55+	Total	18–34	35–54	55+
together?	%	%	%	%	%	%	%	%
Always/mostly wrong	82	75	81	95	69	54	65	86
Sometimes wrong	5	9	5	*	9	14	10	5
Rarely/not at all wrong	7	10	6	3	18	28	19	6
Other/Don't know/No answer	6	5	8	2	4	4	6	3

The great majority (82%) of Northern Ireland respondents believed that homosexual relations were always or mostly wrong, a considerably higher proportion than was found in Britain (69%). In the mid-1980s, there was a shift in attitudes in Britain towards a more censorious position on homosexuality (Airey and Brook, 1986). One hypothesis was that this was related to the connection between the male homosexual community and AIDS. This view, however, was not supported by the failure to find a similar shift in attitudes in the United States of America, where awareness of AIDS was assumed to be at least as high. During the 1980s, attitudes towards homosexuality in Northern Ireland seem generally to have been more negative than in Britain. This remains true in 1989. Indeed, the 1989 pattern of responses in Northern Ireland closely resembles that for 1985 in Britain (Airey and Brook, 1986).

Other factors

Moving beyond sex-related issues to other factors implicated in the spread of AIDS, three further points are relevant. In the first place, one consequence of the paramilitary presence in Northern Ireland has been the virtual exclusion of hard drugs. There is no evidence to suggest a significant drugs problem, either in the community at large, or in the prison population as is the case in the Irish Republic (O'Mahoney, 1989). Given the stance taken against drugs by paramilitaries, it is not likely that this situation will change in the short term. Drug offences are currently at 14 per 100,000 population, less than one-third of the United Kingdom figure.

A second issue, which is also related to the 'troubles', concerns population movement over the last 20 years. The influx of people into the Province from abroad, whether as tourists, students or long-term residents, has been limited. The likelihood of the disease being introduced is thereby decreased.

Finally, the Northern Ireland Blood Transfusion Service relies virtually exclusively on local sources for blood (and, more recently, blood products). The risk of using contaminated blood was always low, even before the routine testing and heat-treating of blood.

Perception of risk

The incidence of AIDS is relatively rare throughout Britain and Northern Ireland. Few people have knowingly met someone who is confirmed as being HIV positive.

As far as you know, have you ever met anyone who was confirmed as having the virus that causes AIDS?

	Northern Ireland	Britain
	%	%
Yes	3	5
No	97	95

At the beginning of 1990 there had been 10 confirmed deaths from AIDS in Northern Ireland and 65 cases of HIV positive infection. This should be compared with a total of 1612 deaths from AIDS and 11676 HIV positive cases across the United Kingdom. However, actual risk and perceived risk are not one and the same, as the following results demonstrate.

The majority of respondents in Northern Ireland were convinced of the serious threat posed by AIDS in Britain in the future. Indeed, their estimates surpassed those of people in Britain itself. Respondents were asked for their views on a statement predicting the scale of future deaths from AIDS.

Within five years AIDS will cause more deaths in Britain than any other single disease

	Northern Ireland	Britain
	%	%
Highly exaggerated	12	14
Slightly exaggerated	24	32
Approximately true	61	54
Don't know/Not answered	3	*

Only approximately one in three of the Britain and Northern Ireland samples agreed with a statement on the possibilities for a vaccine.

Within the next five years doctors will discover a vaccine against AIDS

	Northern Ireland	Britain
	%	%
Agree strongly	4	3
Agree	28	31
Neither agree nor disagree	47	46
Disagree	16	18
Disagree strongly	4	2
Don't know/Not answered	1	*

Over recent years the general public has been exposed to a wide range of messages about the threat of AIDS and the risks associated with unprotected sex and with contact with infected blood and other body fluids. The survey asked respondents how much they thought each of the following groups was at risk of AIDS: people who have sex with many different partners of the opposite sex; married couples who have sex only with each other; married couples who occasionally have sex with someone other than their regular partner; people who have a blood transfusion (see Table 9.1).

Nearly all respondents (95%) thought that sex with many partners put people at risk of AIDS. Over half (62%) thought that people were at risk if they occasionally slept with someone who was not their spouse. However, in both cases, males thought there was less risk than females; young adults of both sexes thought there was less risk than older people; and single females thought there was less risk than married females.

Those groups who are most likely to indulge in sex with multiple partners (Mahoney, 1978) were less likely to see such behaviour as risky. Most of the recent government information films have focussed on young, single and sexually active individuals. The present results suggest that they should continue to focus on this group; but they also cast doubt on the efficacy of the approaches that have so far been used. Early government campaigns contained very general messages about the threat of AIDS. This led to some concern that those groups who are not generally regarded as in any danger from HIV and AIDS, for example, older, married, monogamous couples, might be unnecessarily worried by the warnings. However, almost all the present respondents (97%) recognised that married couples who only sleep with each other are not at risk from AIDS.

Although there may not have been for a long time even a remote risk of infection from contaminated blood products, there was widespread concern about blood transfusions. More than one in three of respondents thought that people were greatly or quite a lot at risk from a blood transfusion. This indicates that attempts to reassure the public on this point have met with only limited success.

Certain groups of people were recognised as being particularly at risk (see Table 9.2 for details). Almost all respondents regarded male homosexuals (96%) and drug-users who share needles (99%) as at risk of AIDS. While these figures closely resembled those obtained in Britain, in Northern Ireland there was a greater tendency to see female homosexuals also as at risk.

How much at risk do you think female homosexuals are from AIDS?

	Northern Ireland			Britain		
	Total	Men	Women	Total	Men	Women
	%	%	%	%	%	%
Greatly at risk	56	51	60	43	42	44
Quite a lot at risk	17	18	16	22	22	22
Not very much at risk	12	15	10	19	20	18
Not at all at risk	6	7	5	9	10	9
Don't know/Not answered	10	10	10	7	5	8

However, only approximately one in three respondents (34%) saw doctors and nurses who treated AIDS patients as being at risk.

Attitudes towards people with AIDS

One of the worries that surrounds a new and devastating infectious illness like AIDS is that the resultant widespread fear may lead to stigmatisation of the victims. This process is more likely if minority groups are clearly identified as at risk. AIDS certainly fulfils this criterion. Both homosexuals and drug-users have been seen as constituting the majority of infected people in Western countries. However, AIDS has the added problem that it is seen by most people as a sexually transmitted disease – although it need not be transmitted in this way. Furthermore, the homosexual connection has meant that many people still perceive it as a 'gay disease', a disease that has been spread by 'perverted' sex.

This combination of circumstances surrounding HIV and AIDS makes it more likely that those who have the disease, and members of 'at risk' minority groups, may be the focus of discrimination and rejection. This has led to widespread concern over the rights and treatment of individuals who have either been diagnosed HIV positive or contracted AIDS. The survey considered a number of aspects of respondents' responses to people with AIDS.

Legal rights

Several questions were asked about the legal rights of people with AIDS (see Table 9.3 for details). A sizeable minority (41%) of respondents thought that employers 'probably' or 'definitely' should have the right to dismiss employees who contract AIDS. But less than one in three (30%) felt that doctors and nurses should have the legal right to refuse to treat AIDS patients. Most people (64%) felt that schools should not have the legal right to expel children who have AIDS; this was particularly true of unmarried respondents. Age had a strong influence on the responses to all three questions. As might be expected, the young were consistently more supportive of people with AIDS than were older people.

Caring for people with AIDS

A majority of respondents in Northern Ireland (60%) and in Britain (62%) agreed that people with AIDS get much less sympathy than they deserve. But around half did not agree that more money should be spent trying to find a cure for AIDS if it meant that research into other diseases was delayed. When the question of resources was raised, with reference to caring for patients who were dying from AIDS, there was a considerable difference in the responses from Northern Ireland and Britain. The former were more in favour of spending National Health Service resources on caring for AIDS patients.

The NHS should spend more of its resources on giving better care to people dying from AIDS.

	Northern Ireland %	Britain %
Agree strongly	9	6
Agree	48	34
Neither agree nor disagree	27	35
Disagree	13	21
Disagree strongly	2	4
Don't know/Not answered	*	*

Religion is one factor which influences responses to this question. Catholics were more likely than Protestants to agree that more funding should be allocated to AIDS patients (see Table 9.4).

Judgement of people with AIDS

The well-publicised history of the spread of HIV and AIDS in the homosexual community and the frequent warnings about promiscuity and unsafe sex have lent this disease a notoriety that can seldom have been matched. One aspect that some religious spokesmen have emphasised is the 'sinful' nature of the most frequent routes of transmission. Given the powerful role still played by religion in Northern Ireland, it is not surprising that respondents generally take a judgemental line on AIDS. However, aggregate data conceal the more subtle influences of religion on these attitudes. In the Northern Ireland survey, it was Protestants who took a more judgemental stand on AIDS, whereas in Britain it was Roman Catholics who adopted this position. Reasons for this difference are unclear. It may be that intra-denominational differences between Britain and Northern Ireland in religious observance and doctrine play their part.

	Northern Ireland				Britain			
		Religion				Religion		
People with AIDS only	Total	Cath.	Prot.	Other	Total	Cath.	Prot.	Other
have themselves to blame	%	%	%	%	%	%	%	%
Agree strongly	21	16	25	18	16	27	16	12
Agree	36	34	41	23	40	38	44	35
Neither	18	19	17	17	17	12	16	20
Disagree	21	27	15	30	23	17	21	27
Disagree strongly	4	3	2	10	4	5	3	6
Don't know/Not answered	*	1	*	–	–	–	–	–

Official warnings about AIDS should say that some sexual practices are morally wrong

Agree strongly	34	31	40	24	23	42	26	14
Agree	39	40	38	38	39	30	44	36
Neither	14	16	13	12	15	10	13	18
Disagree	10	10	8	18	18	15	14	25
Disagree strongly	2	1	*	8	4	3	3	6
Don't know/Not answered	1	2	*	–	–	–	*	–

AIDS is a way of punishing the world for its decline in moral standards

Agree strongly	14	12	18	7	7	15	8	4
Agree	26	28	25	23	20	22	23	16
Neither	24	24	24	20	23	15	24	23
Disagree	21	20	23	21	30	27	30	30
Disagree strongly	13	14	9	29	21	20	15	28
Don't know/Not answered	1	2	1	–	*	–	*	–

As might be expected, age had an important influence on responses to these questions. Younger respondents took a less censorious position than older people. Level of education was also an important factor (as measured by the age at which people left formal education, and by the highest educational qualification achieved). Those with a higher level of education were less judgemental in their attitudes (see Table 9.5).

Testing for the virus

There has been considerable debate over the suggestion that hospitals should be permitted randomly to test blood-samples that have been collected for other purposes. The advantage of such testing is that it gives epidemiologists a more accurate picture of the spread of HIV. At the same time, it raises a variety of ethical problems. Respondents were asked if they were in favour of such testing (see Table 9.6). The overwhelming majority expressed agreement with such a proposal (82% agreeing or agreeing strongly). One of the principal ethical problems that arises from such testing is whether the patient should be told of the test and, if so, in what circumstances. The majority of respondents (56%) thought that if someone had had their blood tested without their knowledge, they should be told about the test and given its result. A further 35% thought that the patient should be told of the test and given the choice of knowing the result or not. Only one in twenty believed that patients should not be told that they had been the subject of a random blood test for HIV.

Conclusion

The findings of this survey highlight a number of issues. In the first place, even though Northern Ireland is a relatively low-risk place in terms of actual incidence, the perception of risk was high. The single most important factor determining attitudes was age. Older respondents were more concerned about the risk of AIDS, and somewhat less tolerant of those with the disease. The implications of these results for the targeting of AIDS awareness campaigns are considerable. Greater selectivity may be needed to ensure that the message reaches those whom it is intended to reach.

Second, and as expected, both religion and religiosity play a part in determining attitudes to a number of issues. Whilst these two factors are significant, it is as yet unclear how they interrelate. Reference to other societies, for example Britain, may not always be illuminating in this analysis.

Third, attitudes towards those with AIDS remain negative. For example, 40% of the sample agreed that AIDS is a form of punishment for moral decadence, and 57% agreed that people with AIDS only have themselves to blame. When they are taken alongside evidence of low levels of acceptance of homosexuality, these data suggest that the climate of opinion towards AIDS and people with AIDS within Northern Ireland is far from tolerant.

References

AIREY, C. and BROOK, L., 'Interim report: social and moral issues', in Jowell, R., Witherspoon, S. and Brook, L. (eds), *British Social Attitudes: the 1986 report*, Gower, Aldershot (1986).

BROWN, J.S., IRWIN, W.G., STEELE, K. and HARLAND, R.W., 'AIDS – students' attitudes to and awareness of Acquired Immune Deficiency Syndrome', *Journal of the Royal College of General Practitioners*, 37, 457–8 (1987).

CHARLWOOD, G.P., KERR, S. and MAW, R.D., 'Sexual attitudes and practices of selected groups in Northern Ireland since the emergence of AIDS', *Ulster Medical Journal*, 58(2), 145–52 (1989).

CLEMENT, U., SCHMIDT, G. and KRUSE, M., 'Changes in sex differences in sexual behavior: a replication of a study on West German students (1966–1981)', *Archives of Sexual Behavior*, 13, 99–120 (1984).

CURTICE, J. and GALLAGHER, T., 'The Northern Irish dimension', in Jowell, R., Witherspoon, S. and Brook, L. (eds), *British Social Attitudes: the 7th report*, Gower, Aldershot (1990).

KINSEY, A., POMEROY, W. and MARTIN, C., *Sexual Behavior in the Human Male*, Saunders, Philadelphia (1948).

KINSEY, A., POMEROY, W., MARTIN, C. and GEBHARD, P., *Sexual Behavior in the Human Female*, Saunders, Philadelphia (1953).

McLAUGHLIN, E., 'A problem postponed', in Davies, C. and McLaughlin, E. (eds), *Women, Employment and Social Policy*, Policy Research Institute, Belfast (forthcoming).

McSHANE, L. and PINKERTON, J., 'The family in Northern Ireland', *Studies*, 167–76, Summer (1986).

MAHONEY, E.R., 'Age differences in attitude change toward premarital coitus', *Archives of Sexual Behavior*, 7, 493–501 (1978).

MARTIN, J. and WESTBROOK, M., 'Religion and sex in a university sample: data bearing on Mol's hypothesis', *Australian Journal of Psychology*, 25, 71–9 (1973).

MOL, H., 'Religion and sex in Australia', *Australian Journal of Psychology*, 22, 105–14 (1970).

O'MAHONEY, P., 'An investigation of attitudes and information on AIDS', *Irish Journal of Psychology*, 10(1), 21–38 (1989).

SNEDDON, I. and KREMER, J., 'Sexual behavior and attitudes of university students in Northern Ireland', *Archives of Sexual Behavior* (forthcoming).

Table 9.1 Risk from AIDS, by sex, age, religion, church attendance, highest educational qualification and marital status (%)

		Sex			Age			Religion	
	Total	Male	Female	18–34	35–54	55+	Cath.	Prot.	Other
People who have sex with many different partners of the opposite sex:									
Greatly at risk	71	66	75	65	71	76	77	67	70
Quite a lot at risk	24	28	21	32	25	16	21	27	25
Not very much at risk	2	4	1	3	2	–	*	2	4
Not at all at risk	–	–	–	–	–	–	–	–	–
Don't know/Not answered	3	3	2	–	*	7	1	4	–
Married couples who have sex only with each other:									
Greatly at risk	*	*	1	*	*	*	*	*	*
Quite a lot at risk	*	*	1	–	*	1	*	*	–
Not very much at risk	15	14	16	17	12	16	12	18	12
Not at all at risk	82	84	80	83	86	75	84	78	86
Don't know/Not answered	2	2	3	–	*	6	2	3	–
Married couples who occasionally have sex with someone other than their regular partner:									
Greatly at risk	13	11	15	11	9	19	14	13	11
Quite a lot at risk	49	45	54	45	51	52	53	47	47
Not very much at risk	32	38	26	39	36	19	29	32	37
Not at all at risk	2	2	1	2	1	1	*	2	2
Don't know/Not answered	4	5	4	2	2	8	4	5	1
People who have a blood transfusion:									
Greatly at risk	13	12	14	12	12	16	17	12	11
Quite a lot at risk	25	19	32	21	24	32	30	23	24
Not very much at risk	43	48	38	49	42	36	37	46	44
Not at all at risk	14	16	13	17	18	6	11	14	19
Don't know/Not answered	5	5	4	1	3	9	5	6	*

Church attendance		Highest educational qualification				Marital status		
Weekly+	Less than weekly	Degree	Professional	'A'/'O' level, CSE	Foreign/ None/ Don't know	Married now	Separated/ widowed/ divorced	Never married
76	63	54	64	67	77	74	72	61
20	31	35	33	32	16	22	23	33
*	4	10	1	1	2	3	–	2
–	–	–	–	–	–	–	–	–
2	1	–	1	–	5	1	6	4
*	*	–	–	*	*	*	*	–
*	–	–	–	–	*	*	–	*
15	15	13	15	15	15	13	11	23
81	83	88	84	85	78	85	83	71
2	2	–	–	–	5	*	6	5
14	11	–	7	9	18	14	10	11
53	45	56	60	45	50	51	50	43
26	39	42	29	40	25	31	32	35
*	2	4	3	1	1	2	*	1
6	2	–	–	3	6	2	8	8
15	11	–	4	11	18	13	20	9
29	21	19	27	21	30	25	25	26
38	49	60	48	48	35	44	35	45
12	17	21	21	18	9	15	13	13
6	3	–	–	2	8	3	8	6

Table 9.2 Risk from AIDS, by sex, age, religion, church attendance, highest educational qualification and marital status (%)

		Sex		Age			Religion		
	Total	Male	Female	18–34	35–54	55+	Cath.	Prot.	Other
Doctors and nurses who treat people who have AIDS:									
Greatly at risk	9	8	11	8	8	11	11	9	5
Quite a lot at risk	25	24	26	21	27	30	27	24	25
Not very much at risk	41	44	40	48	39	37	35	46	43
Not at all at risk	19	20	19	24	23	11	23	14	25
Don't know/Not answered	5	5	5	*	2	11	4	7	1
Male homosexuals:									
Greatly at risk	82	81	83	67	86	84	86	82	74
Quite a lot at risk	14	16	13	22	12	8	12	13	25
Not very much at risk	*	*	*	–	*	–	–	*	–
Not at all at risk	–	–	–	–	–	–	–	–	–
Don't know/Not answered	3	3	3	1	1	7	2	5	*
Female homosexuals:									
Greatly at risk	56	51	60	50	57	62	62	56	43
Quite a lot at risk	17	18	16	22	15	13	15	17	22
Not very much at risk	12	15	10	15	14	5	8	11	23
Not at all at risk	6	7	5	8	5	2	6	4	8
Don't know/Not answered	10	10	10	5	8	15	10	12	2
People who inject themselves with drugs using shared needles:									
Greatly at risk	91	89	92	91	93	88	88	91	93
Quite a lot at risk	8	9	6	9	7	6	10	6	7
Not very much at risk	–	–	–	–	–	–	–	–	–
Not at all at risk	–	–	–	–	–	–	–	–	–
Don't know/Not answered	2	2	2	*	–	5	2	3	–

Church attendance		Highest educational qualification				Marital status		
Weekly+	Less than weekly	Degree	Professional	'A'/'O' level, CSE	Foreign/ None/ Don't know	Married now	Separated/ widowed/ divorced	Never married
10	9	6	3	9	11	9	14	8
29	23	21	33	23	26	25	30	21
39	48	63	44	46	36	43	29	46
19	19	10	21	22	19	19	19	22
3	2	–	–	1	9	4	8	4
85	79	69	84	83	83	85	82	73
12	17	29	16	16	11	13	10	21
–	*	–	–	–	*	–	*	1
–	–	–	–	–	–	–	–	–
3	3	2	–	1	5	2	7	5
61	50	40	54	54	60	59	54	49
16	18	17	15	19	15	16	14	23
9	15	25	15	14	8	13	11	10
5	7	13	10	5	4	5	5	7
9	9	6	6	7	13	8	16	11
90	93	94	93	90	88	92	89	86
8	6	6	7	10	8	7	5	11
–	–	–	–	–	–	–	–	–
–	–	–	–	–	–	–	–	–
2	1	–	–	*	4	*	5	3

Table 9.3 Legal rights and AIDS, by sex, age, religion, church attendance, highest educational qualification and marital status (%)

	Total	Sex		Age			Religion		
		Male	Female	18–34	35–54	55+	Cath.	Prot.	Other
Employers should or should not have the legal right to dismiss people who have AIDS									
Definitely should	19	24	15	14	18	26	17	22	16
Probably should	22	23	22	22	20	26	25	21	21
Probably should not	28	26	31	30	29	25	26	30	29
Definitely should not	23	22	23	31	26	11	26	18	31
Don't know/Not answered	7	5	9	3	6	13	6	9	4
Doctors and nurses should or should not have the legal right to refuse to treat people who have AIDS									
Definitely should	12	10	13	9	13	14	8	15	10
Probably should	18	17	19	19	12	23	17	19	19
Probably should not	26	25	27	27	26	26	27	26	25
Definitely should not	39	43	35	43	46	27	45	33	43
Don't know/Not answered	5	5	6	1	3	10	4	7	2
Schools should or should not have the legal right to expel children who have AIDS									
Definitely should	9	11	7	6	8	14	7	10	10
Probably should	20	18	22	22	18	21	23	20	17
Probably should not	25	24	25	25	27	24	22	28	22
Definitely should not	39	39	38	45	43	27	42	33	47
Don't know/Not answered	7	7	8	3	4	15	6	9	4

Church attendance		Highest educational qualification				Marital status		
Weekly+	Less than weekly	Degree	Professional	'A'/'O' level, CSE	Foreign/ None/ Don't know	Married now	Separated/ widowed/ divorced	Never married
17	22	–	15	17	24	21	22	13
23	21	20	23	24	22	22	22	22
29	28	44	25	31	25	29	25	30
22	25	32	34	26	17	22	20	28
8	4	4	3	2	12	6	11	8
10	14	2	11	12	13	13	16	6
17	20	17	18	19	18	19	16	15
27	26	31	33	22	28	28	19	27
41	37	48	38	45	33	37	40	45
6	3	2	–	2	8	3	9	7
7	11	–	4	8	12	10	14	3
23	17	12	21	22	20	22	17	19
24	26	37	21	23	26	26	22	24
38	40	51	51	43	32	37	35	47
8	6	–	4	4	11	6	12	8

Table 9.4 Caring for people with AIDS, by sex, age, religion, church attendance, highest educational qualification and marital status (%)

		Sex			Age			Religion	
	Total	Male	Female	18–34	35–54	55+	Cath.	Prot.	Other
People who have AIDS get much less sympathy from society than they ought to get									
Agree strongly	27	25	29	28	31	23	23	18	29
Agree a little	33	32	34	36	30	32	28	24	29
Disagree a little	17	19	16	19	18	16	23	26	23
Disagree strongly	15	16	14	11	16	18	18	25	14
Don't know/Not answered	8	9	7	6	5	11	8	7	5
More money should be spent trying to find a cure for AIDS, even if it means that research into *other* serious diseases is delayed									
Agree strongly	22	27	18	25	24	18	26	17	31
Agree a little	24	27	21	27	21	23	27	20	28
Disagree a little	25	20	30	26	26	25	26	27	19
Disagree strongly	24	22	26	20	26	26	17	30	21
Don't know/Not answered	5	4	5	2	3	9	4	7	1
The NHS should spend more of its resources on giving better care to people dying from AIDS									
Agree strongly	9	9	9	13	6	8	12	8	9
Agree	48	47	49	45	54	48	55	41	58
Neither agree nor disagree	27	28	26	30	24	27	23	30	25
Disagree	13	12	13	13	14	11	8	18	8
Disagree strongly	2	2	2	–	2	4	1	3	*
Don't know/Not answered	*	2	*	*	*	2	2	*	–

Church attendance		Highest educational qualification				Marital status		
Weekly+	Less than weekly	Degree	Professional	'A'/'O' level, CSE	Foreign/ None/ Don't know	Married now	Separated/ widowed/ divorced	Never married
26	29	40	27	26	26	27	24	28
34	33	29	44	36	30	34	34	29
18	15	27	11	21	14	18	15	17
14	15	4	12	11	19	14	18	14
8	7	–	5	6	11	6	9	11
21	24	21	22	25	21	20	24	27
23	24	28	21	26	22	24	21	26
25	26	38	31	24	24	27	23	21
26	22	13	25	23	26	26	23	19
5	3	–	1	2	7	3	8	6
8	11	4	8	8	11	7	11	15
48	48	56	45	43	52	50	50	44
27	27	28	33	34	21	28	22	25
14	11	13	13	14	12	13	12	13
2	2	–	2	*	3	2	4	*
*	*	–	–	*	1	*	2	2

Table 9.5 Judgement of people with AIDS, by sex, age, religion, church attendance, highest educational qualification and marital status (%)

	Total	Male	Female	18–34	35–54	55+	Cath.	Prot.	Other
		Sex			**Age**			**Religion**	
Most people with AIDS only have themselves to blame									
Agree strongly	21	22	20	12	21	30	16	25	18
Agree	36	37	34	31	38	39	34	41	23
Neither agree nor disagree	18	16	19	22	15	17	19	17	17
Disagree	21	20	22	29	22	12	27	15	30
Disagree strongly	4	4	4	5	3	1	3	2	10
Don't know/Not answered	*	1	*	*	*	1	1	*	–
Official warnings about AIDS should say that some sexual practices are morally wrong									
Agree strongly	34	35	34	18	35	53	31	40	24
Agree	39	36	41	40	41	35	40	38	38
Neither agree nor disagree	14	15	13	22	12	6	16	13	12
Disagree	10	11	9	17	8	4	10	8	18
Disagree strongly	2	2	2	3	2	–	1	*	8
Don't know/Not answered	1	2	1	–	1	2	2	*	–
AIDS is a way of punishing the world for its decline in moral standards									
Agree strongly	14	13	16	3	16	26	12	18	7
Agree	26	27	25	23	27	29	28	25	23
Neither agree nor disagree	24	23	24	30	20	19	24	24	20
Disagree	21	21	22	26	22	15	20	23	21
Disagree strongly	13	16	11	18	13	8	14	9	29
Don't know/Not answered	1	1	2	–	*	3	2	1	–

| | Church attendance | | Highest educational qualification | | | | Marital status | | |
	Weekly+	Less than weekly	Degree	Professional	'A'/'O' level, CSE	Foreign/ None/ Don't know	Married now	Separated/ widowed/ divorced	Never married
	18	23	4	8	13	31	19	33	18
	41	31	36	44	36	34	39	36	27
	18	18	22	21	20	14	16	15	24
	20	24	27	22	25	19	22	12	28
	3	5	11	3	5	2	4	3	3
	*	*	–	2	*	*	*	2	*
	37	31	20	34	24	45	36	42	26
	42	35	15	31	44	39	40	38	38
	13	16	13	14	19	9	12	11	21
	6	14	43	17	10	6	9	5	13
	*	4	9	5	2	*	2	2	2
	1	*	–	–	1	1	*	2	*
	17	11	2	8	7	22	15	21	7
	29	22	17	12	26	29	28	26	21
	25	22	13	33	28	20	22	17	32
	18	25	30	26	23	19	21	25	22
	10	19	37	21	15	8	13	9	16
	2	*	–	–	*	2	*	3	*

Table 9.6 Testing for AIDS, by sex, age, religion, church attendance, highest educational qualification and marital status (%)

	Total	Sex		Age			Religion		
		Male	Female	18–34	35–54	55+	Cath.	Prot.	Other
As one way of getting to know how AIDS is spreading it has been suggested that hospitals should be allowed to test *any* patient's blood (that has been taken for *other* reasons) to see whether it contains the virus that causes AIDS									
Agree strongly	41	43	39	31	44	48	34	45	40
Agree	41	42	39	43	43	36	44	39	37
Neither agree nor disagree	9	7	12	15	6	6	11	9	8
Disagree	7	5	8	10	4	6	8	5	11
Disagree strongly	2	3	*	1	2	1	2	1	4
Don't know/Not answered	*	*	1	–	*	2	1	1	–
Should such patients:									
Not be told about the test	5	6	5	4	3	9	4	7	4
Be told about the test but *not* the result	2	3	1	3	2	2	2	2	2
Be told about the test and given choice about being told the result	35	38	32	43	32	29	33	34	42
Be told about the test and the result	56	52	59	50	62	57	60	55	53
Don't know/Not answered	2	2	2	*	2	4	2	2	–

Church attendance		Highest educational qualification				Marital status		
Weekly+	Less than weekly	Degree	Professional	'A'/'O' level, CSE	Foreign/ None/ Don't know	Married now	Separated/ widowed/ divorced	Never married
39	43	36	39	37	45	43	40	31
41	41	51	44	42	38	42	37	42
10	8	9	8	11	8	7	13	16
7	6	–	8	8	6	6	7	11
1	2	4	2	1	2	2	*	*
1	*	–	–	*	1	*	3	–
5	6	–	2	5	7	5	6	4
2	2	–	2	2	2	2	*	1
33	38	58	41	35	29	34	31	42
58	53	42	56	57	58	57	59	51
2	*	–	–	1	3	1	3	2

10

Is Northern Ireland
a conservative society?

Ed Cairns

There is general agreement among observers of the Northern Irish scene that 'above all else Ulster has been a religious region' (Akenson, 1973, p.25), indeed 'probably the most Christian society in the Western world except for the Republic of Ireland' (Rose, 1976, p.11). Most observers have assumed that this means that Northern Ireland is different from the rest of the United Kingdom, if not the rest of Europe. One corollary of this difference is that people in Northern Ireland hold more authoritarian attitudes and values. Within Northern Ireland, there may be differences in attitudes and values between the Catholic and Protestant communities that exacerbate their political conflict. According to many commentators, marked differences between Catholics and Protestants are peculiar to Northern Ireland, at least in the late twentieth century.

It is the aim of this chapter to examine these assumptions by using data from the Northern Ireland Social Attitudes survey and from the parallel survey carried out in Britain. Data on church attendance and church membership from the two surveys will be compared, to see whether Northern Ireland still deserves its label as a religious society. Whether people of Northern Ireland do indeed have more conservative attitudes and opinions will be examined by looking at their response to issues of welfare, law and order and political protest. Finally, the possible importance of denominational differences will be looked at. These analyses should show whether there are differences in opinion on social issues between the two communities in Northern Ireland and, if so, whether these differences are broadly doctrinal in nature or attributable to more local factors.

Church membership and church attendance

One measure of the religiosity of a society is the proportion of the population who claim a religious affiliation. According to the 1961 Northern Ireland Census of Population only 384 of the population of about 1.5 million described themselves as humanists, free-thinkers or atheists (Rose, 1971). This position has changed dramatically. In the Social Attitudes survey some 12% claim that they have no religious affiliation.

Comparison of Church membership in Britain and Northern Ireland in 1989

	Britain %	Northern Ireland %
Anglican/Church of Ireland	37	18
Catholic	11	36
Other Christian	16	33
Non-Christian	2	*
No religion	34	12
Not answered	*	2

In Britain, by comparison, those claiming no religious affiliation accounted for over one-third (34%) of those surveyed. Another measure of religiosity is frequency of church attendance. Again, Northern Ireland is outstanding in this respect. For example, according to the results of the survey carried out by Rose (1971), 95% of Catholics and 46% of Protestants in Northern Ireland attended church at least once a week in 1968. These rates, Rose claimed, were about four times those reported in predominantly Protestant countries such as England or Sweden, and three times higher than in Catholic countries such as France or Italy.

Since then, there has been some speculation that church attendance has been declining in Northern Ireland. This was the conclusion reached by Hickey (1984) on the basis of a small survey he conducted more than 10 years later in a small community in the northwest of the Province. More reliable information is available from a survey of the Northern Irish population carried out in 1978, in order to replicate Rose's 1968 work (Moxon-Browne, 1983). This survey found that 90% of Catholics and 39% of Protestants were attending church at least once a week.

These statistics can be brought up to date with data collected in the 1989 Social Attitudes survey. These reveal that church attendance by Catholics on a weekly basis has continued to decline, to 86%; but that the rate for Protestants has increased (to 44%) almost to the 1968 level reported by Rose (1971). Furthermore, the data from these three studies indicate that, while the proportion of Catholics attending church on a weekly basis is declining steadily, those who never attend remain a very small proportion of the total. The figures for Protestants, on the other hand, indicate that while weekly attendance may be increasing marginally, the proportion who never attend appears also to be increasing. In other words, if these trends continue, Protestants may divide into two categories: those who attend church weekly and those who never attend. Catholics, on the other hand, may be more likely to maintain their habit of attending church, even if on a less regular basis.

A comparison with equivalent data from Britain reveals that, despite the overall decline in weekly church attendance over the period 1968–89, people in Northern Ireland still attend church much more frequently. Some 50% of those surveyed in Britain reported that they never attended church; the corresponding figure for Northern Ireland is 10%.

Comparison of church attendance in Northern Ireland over three decades

		Catholic %	Protestant %
1968 (Rose, 1971)	Weekly	95	46
	Never	1	5
1978 (Moxon-Browne, 1983)	Weekly	90	39
	Never	3	10
1989	Weekly	86	44
	Never	3	15

Comparison of church attendance in Britain and Northern Ireland in 1989

	Britain %	Northern Ireland %
Apart from such special occasions as weddings, funerals and baptisms, how often nowadays do you attend services or meetings connected with your religion?		
Once a week	14	62
Once in two weeks	3	7
Once a month	6	10
Twice a year	13	6
Once a year in 1989	7	2
Less often	6	3
Never	51	10
Varies	1	*
Not answered	*	*

One possible explanation for this difference between Northern Ireland and Britain in the rate of church attendance can be ruled out. Because the Catholic Church lays much more stress on attending church, it could be argued that the greater proportion of Catholics in Northern Ireland (36% compared to 11% in Britain) has distorted the overall church attendance rates there. Indeed, a comparison of Protestant and Catholic attendance rates in Britain reveals that Catholics do attend church more regularly than Protestants. However, the proportion of Catholics attending on a weekly basis in Britain (42%) is much lower than in Northern Ireland (86%), and is actually closer to the rate of Protestants in Northern Ireland (44%). The rate for Protestants in Britain is extremely low, at 14%; two-fifths (41%) of those who could be classified as Protestant in Britain reported that they never attended church. The equivalent figure for Catholics was 18%. Frequent church attendance is probably a genuinely Northern Irish phenomenon, which influences both Catholics and Protestants equally. It is not simply attributable to the relatively greater proportion of Catholics in the Northern Irish population.

While there has undoubtedly been a decline in the religious nature of society in Northern Ireland, it still deserves its reputation as a religious society. Compared with the rest of the United Kingdom more of the population admits to a religious affiliation, and they attend church much more regularly.

Conservative attitudes in Northern Ireland and Britain

Studies of the psychology of religion have found that 'religionism' is associated with 'social stability, conservatism and authoritarianism' (Brown, 1987, p.142). Consistent with this finding is the suggestion of several writers that Irish social attitudes (including those in Northern Ireland) are more conservative than those in Britain. For example, according to Whyte (1971, p.23) 'deference to authority . . . has for long been a feature not just of Irish ecclesiastical life, but of Irish life in general' and has meant that the Irish are more amenable to authority than the British. As Rose (1971, p.248) notes, 'religion not only provides individuals with a way to orient themselves to another world, it can also influence their worldly outlooks'. More specifically, Heskin (1980, p.84) claims that people in Northern Ireland 'are raised with traditional and conservative political and religious values', making them rather more authoritarian in their outlook than, for example, people in England. Hickey (1984, p.116) suggests that this state of affairs is likely to continue for some time precisely because the importance of religion in Northern Ireland has hindered the modernising process and has delayed 'the development of a society which can be regarded as akin to the remainder of the United Kingdom'. Despite the widespread acceptance of this view – that norms and values prevalent in Northern Irish society are uniformly more conservative than those in Britain – there is little hard evidence to support it.

Greer (1980) provides some of the only relevant information that has been available to date. All the young people in his study, as well as being asked about their religious practices, were asked to comment on the morality of a number of issues such as 'capital punishment', 'suicide', and 'war'. He was able to compare the results of his 1968 survey with those of a comparable English survey carried out in 1970 by Wright and Cox (1971). On almost every issue, more of the young Protestant Northern Irish responded that it was 'always wrong' than the English sample. When Greer (1984) repeated his survey in 1978 he found that a similar group in Northern Ireland still adopted a more severe moral stance than the English young people of 10 years earlier.

What is not known is whether this conservative attitude is carried into adulthood. Nor do we know whether such conservative attitudes still hold sway in Northern Ireland. Finally, it must be remembered that Greer's survey was only of Protestants and did not sample them randomly.

The 1989 Social Attitudes survey is able to extend the picture because it included questions on issues similar to those in Greer's survey and addressed them to a random sample of the population both of Britain and of Northern Ireland. Questions were asked about general moral issues, including issues of authority, law and order and censorship. The Social Attitudes survey included a number of other questions to which the population of Northern

Ireland might be expected to respond in a conservative manner: for example, on the distribution of wealth, welfare, and political protest.

How adults in Northern Ireland responded to these issues is shown in Tables 10.1–10.6. The majority agree that wealth is unequally distributed and, on balance, accept the radical solution that the government should redistribute income to the less well-off (Table 10.1). These attitudes are echoed in Table 10.2: the majority do not agree that welfare is too generous or that the unemployed are malingerers. Only one question divides opinion: that which suggests that the majority of those on the dole are *fiddling in one way or another*. Despite the fact that the majority in Northern Ireland tend to hold what might be considered radical opinions on economic issues, the picture is very different for opinions on authority, the law and censorship (Tables 10.3–10.5). The majority of the population of Northern Ireland apparently hold rather conservative views: for example, favouring stiffer sentences for law-breakers and censorship of films and magazines. Finally, a majority, but not a clear majority, indicated that they supported peaceful forms of political protest – demonstrating, publishing leaflets and holding public meetings (Table 10.6).

Overall, this does not mirror the out-and-out authoritarian picture of Northern Irish society that might have been expected from the earlier information and commentary. Public opinion on economic issues in Northern Ireland has distinctly radical leanings and is somewhat divided as to the wisdom of allowing political protests. On moral issues, however, its overall tenor *is* distinctly conservative.

How do these opinions compare to those held in the rest of the United Kingdom? The data in Tables 10.1–10.6 indicate that there is very little difference. In Britain, according to the 1986 British Social Attitudes survey (Heath and Topf, 1987), the pattern is also one of 'economic radicalism and moral "traditionalism"'.

Why do people in Northern Ireland and Britain, despite very large differences in church membership and attendance, share the same opinions on general moral issues? And why have these opinions changed since Greer's (1980; 1984) surveys in the late 1960s and 1970s? Perhaps over this period people in Britain have become more authoritarian – that is, they have become more like people in Northern Ireland in their attitudes to general moral issues. This hypothesis receives some support if one compares British data gathered in 1986 and 1989 (Jowell et al, 1987; 1990). Opinion on economic issues in Britain is becoming more radical. For example, in 1986 some 43% agreed with the proposition that the government should redistribute income to the less well-off; this increased to 53% in 1989. In 1986, 50% thought that welfare benefits stifled individual attempts at economic independence, compared with only 30% in 1989.

Analyses indicate that opinion in Northern Ireland is not as uniformly authoritarian as some commentators have suggested. The picture is mixed, with a majority expressing relatively radical opinions on the redistribution of wealth and on welfare, and conservative opinions on issues relating to law and order, authority and censorship. Opinion in Northern Ireland is not so dramatically different from that in Britain as earlier research might have led one to believe. This is not to say that the two populations are entirely in agreement on all issues. In particular, people in Northern Ireland show more sympathy for the unemployed, less outright support for the death penalty and are somewhat less likely to support various forms of political protest.

Conservative attitudes among Catholics and Protestants in Northern Ireland

Opinion about the possibility that the two communities hold differing social attitudes is divided among Northern Ireland watchers. On the one hand, Heskin (1980, p.85) has suggested that, while 'authoritarian' Protestants and 'authoritarian' Catholics may hold diametrically opposed political views about Northern Ireland remaining in the United Kingdom, 'both, however, will probably have similar views on the appropriate treatment of (non-political) offenders, sex before marriage, the importance of religion and so forth'. According to Hickey, however, religious belief has a profound influence in Northern Ireland; as a result, differences in religious belief are of major social significance (Hickey, 1984).

Again, empirical evidence from Northern Ireland on this point is scant. Greer (1984) is the only investigator to have published relevant data. In 1981 he carried out a non-random survey of children, ranging in age from 14 to 16 years, who attended either Catholic or Protestant schools in Northern Ireland. In summary, his results suggested that Catholic attitudes were more strict on questions of sexual morality, the sacredness of life, violence and social justice. Protestants, on the other hand, were more strict where gambling or smoking was concerned. Finally, Catholic and Protestant children had similar views on the morality of such social issues as lying or stealing and the taking of alcohol or drugs.

The Northern Ireland Social Attitudes survey data suggest that more Catholics than Protestants hold radical views on questions concerning the distribution of wealth, welfare, law and order and support for political protest (Tables 10.7, 10.8, 10.10 and 10.12). These differences, however, should not be allowed to obscure the fact that the majority of Protestants (though only a bare majority) hold radical views on the distribution of wealth, while a large minority (40% plus) also do so in relation to welfare and political protests. On the other hand, on issues of law and order, the majority of Protestants take a much more conservative stance. This is especially true where the death penalty is concerned: 77% of Protestants as opposed to 30% of Catholics agree that *'for some crimes the death penalty is the most appropriate sentence'*.

On moral issues, especially censorship (Table 10.11), the majority of Catholics and Protestants in Northern Ireland are in agreement and take a conservative view. Such an attitude is also seen in response to other questions in the survey which dealt with sexual matters. For example, 94% of Catholics and 92% of Protestants view extra-marital sex as 'always' or 'mostly' wrong, and 81% and 87%, respectively, think that homosexuality is wrong.

Both groups in Northern Ireland are in agreement, too, over the role of schools in teaching children to obey authority (Table 10.9). However, the question that invited respondents to agree or disagree with the proposition

147

that *'young people today don't have enough respect for traditional British values'* showed a marked difference in attitude. Not surprisingly, given the inclusion of the word 'British', only a minority of Catholics (48%) agreed with the proposition, compared with a majority of Protestants (70%).

More interesting is the tendency for Protestant opinion on the distribution of wealth and on welfare and law and order (Tables 10.7, 10.8 and 10.10) to be in line with that of people in Britain (Tables 10.1, 10.2 and 10.4). This is what one would expect. Survey after survey has shown that the majority of Protestants in Northern Ireland think of themselves as 'British'. On the other hand, it is Catholic opinion in support of political protest (Table 10.12) that corresponds more closely with opinion in Britain (Table 10.6). For example, 65% of people in Britain agreed that *'people should be allowed to organise public meetings to protest against the government'*. In Northern Ireland, while 61% of Catholics agreed with this proposition, only 49% of Protestants did so.

These results suggest that, while the majority of people in Northern Ireland may hold radical views on the redistribution of wealth, welfare and political protest, more Catholics than Protestants hold such views. Where law and order is concerned, more conservative views are held by Protestants; on issues such as censorship and authority, both groups are equally conservative. Finally, and as expected, Protestant opinion is closer to that in Britain, except where support for political protest is concerned. On this issue, Catholics in Northern Ireland hold views more akin to those of the general population in Britain.

Conservative attitudes among British Catholics and Protestants

The data presented here suggest that Protestant public opinion in Northern Ireland tends to be less radical than that of Catholics. However, it is difficult to pin down the extent to which these differences are due to local circumstances. For example, are Catholics more in favour of welfare reform because they are over-represented among the unemployed in Northern Ireland? Or are they opposed to the death penalty because most members of the Provisional IRA are also Catholic? Or are these differences due solely to differences in religious belief, such as the teaching of the Catholic Church on the sacredness of human life?

According to research carried out by Greeley (1989), the latter explanation may be the most likely. He examined data from surveys carried out in seven countries. In all the countries, Catholics were more likely to emphasise 'fairness' and 'equality', were more likely to accept political extremists (of left or right) and were more likely to hold strong positions on issues of 'life ethics'. Greeley argues that this is evidence for the survival of what he calls 'the Catholic ethic' despite other changes in society. Protestants, on the other hand, were more likely to emphasise 'personal ethics' and to value thrift, industry, and individualism.

On the other hand, Alwin (1986) has recently reported that over the last 20 years or so, at least in the United States of America, Catholic–Protestant differences in child-rearing attitudes and values have diminished to a point at which they no longer exist. He claims that this is evidence in support of predictions that more general Catholic–Protestant differences in values will also gradually disappear.

One way to pursue this question further is to compare the opinions of Catholics and Protestants in Britain on the issues included in the Social Attitudes survey. This should make it possible to tease out the relative roles of religion and more local factors. The comparison shows that Catholics, both in Britain and Northern Ireland, hold a more radical attitude than Protestants toward the redistribution of wealth (Table 10.7). On this particular issue, differences between people of the same denomination are very small in comparison with those between people living in Britain and people living in Northern Ireland.

Northern Irish respondents are less likely to hold conservative opinions on welfare than are their co-religionists in Britain (Table 10.8). There are differences between the two denominations in Britain, but they are much smaller. The most striking result is that more Northern Irish Catholics hold 'radical' views than the other three groups. For example, in response to the proposition that most unemployed 'could find a job if they really wanted one', in Northern Ireland 47% of Protestants agreed, compared with only 19% of Catholics. In Britain, however, the corresponding figures were 56% of Protestants and 42% of Catholics.

As in Northern Ireland, British attitudes to the teaching of obedience to authority (Table 10.9) and to censorship (Table 10.11) do not show denominational differences. The fact that the majority of Northern Irish Catholics are alone in not agreeing that young people today lack respect for traditional British values probably hinges on the use of the word 'British'.

Law and order is another issue on which the interaction of the influence of denomination and place is apparent (Table 10.10). There are some differences between Catholics and Protestants in Britain: more Protestants favour absolute obedience to the law, and, where appropriate, the death penalty. However, these differences of up to 10 percentage points are much smaller than those that separate Protestants and Catholics in Northern Ireland on the same issues (Table 10.10). It is again Catholics in Northern Ireland who differ from the other three groups by being less likely to hold conservative views.

Finally, more Catholics than Protestants in Britain (Table 10.12), as in Northern Ireland, agree that peaceful forms of political protest should be allowed. However, fewer of both Catholics and Protestants in Northern Ireland agree with this form of behaviour than do their co-religionists in Britain. Northern Irish Protestants are the only one of the four groups who do not favour political protest.

On many of the social issues under examination here religious denomination per se does influence opinions. However, only in the case of the redistribution of wealth is the effect undiluted. More commonly, opinions are related both to religion and locality. Denominational differences are greater in Northern Ireland than in Britain.

Conclusions

The analyses reported here, as well as future analyses of the data, should make it more difficult for people writing about the society of Northern Ireland to generalise as they have done in the past. In particular, while it is the case that Northern Ireland is a religious society, it can no longer be argued that it is without qualification a conservative society. Nor can it any longer be claimed that, because Northern Ireland has a more religious society than Britain in terms of religious practice, public opinion there must, in all respects, be more conservative than in Britain. The reality is more complicated. At a more general level, the findings call into question the tendency in the psychological literature to link religiosity to conservatism or authoritarianism (see Argyle and Beit-Hallahmi, 1975 and Brown, 1987 for reviews). Finally, the data from the Social Attitudes survey show little evidence for a widespread secularisation of society in Northern Ireland. Nevertheless, there is evidence that, over the years, fewer people consider themselves to be members of a Church and fewer self-styled Church members attend church regularly.

Differences in religious affiliation are associated with differences in several areas of public opinion. Different attitudes toward the redistribution of wealth and to welfare, in particular, may relate to long-standing differences in Catholic and Protestant teaching on poverty, with Protestants being more likely to stress the role of personal responsibility in avoiding poverty. This is also borne out by the responses to a series of questions in the Continuous Household Survey, which has been carried out in Northern Ireland each year since 1983. For example, in 1985, in response to the question 'Why are there people in need in Northern Ireland?' the main reason given by Protestants was 'laziness or lack of will-power' (33%); while the major reason given by Catholics (34%) was 'injustice in society' (PPRU,1985). When the same question was asked in the present survey, the most frequent answer given by Catholics and by Protestants was *it's an inevitable part of modern life* (39% and 40% respectively). However, more Catholics (33%) than Protestants (17%) chose the social injustice response, and more Protestants (24%) than Catholics (10%) referred to laziness or lack of will-power.

The differences in attitudes to wealth and welfare are not always great and should not be exaggerated. However, the fact that they are to some extent mirrored in the British data increases the probability that they are real differences. Furthermore, the observation that Catholic–Protestant differences also exist in Britain, and that they involve issues very similar to those reported by Greeley (1989) in other countries, is of considerable general interest, beyond the confines of a study of society in Northern Ireland. In particular, it suggests that sectarian differences in Northern Ireland in attitudes towards wealth and welfare may not only be due to the fact that Catholics in Northern Ireland are more likely to have experienced unemployment or that they are over-represented in the lower economic strata (PPRU, 1985). Rather, it suggests that differences may be due to fundamentally different religious value systems. These are differences that are likely to persist, even if Catholics cease to occupy their present unfavourable economic position.

Catholics in Northern Ireland are more likely to be frequent attenders at church. One may infer from this that more Catholics in Northern Ireland are committed to their religious beliefs. If this is the case, perhaps it explains the greater differences between Protestants and Catholics in Northern Ireland than in Britain on, for example, law and order issues, with Catholics being less punitive. Yet one would also expect to find corresponding denominational differences on other issues. Their absence suggests that the present political climate in Northern Ireland may exaggerate denominational differences in public opinion on specific issues – particularly those related to law and order.

Such a conclusion would accord well with that reached by Greeley (1989). He noted an attitude towards the role of government on the part of Catholics that he described as 'paradoxical'. On the one hand, they favoured 'liberal' policies, involving government intervention and egalitarianism on economic issues; on the other hand, they expressed support for 'violent resistance' when 'flaws in government become intolerable'.

The data presented here reinforce the view of Hickey (1984) that 'religion and the world view based upon it, particularly the political expression of that world view' are likely to become 'more sharply identified as the point of difference between the two groups', as other differences fade in significance.

References

AKENSON. D.H., *Education and Enmity: the control of schooling in Northern Ireland 1920–50*, David and Charles, Newton Abbot (1973).

ALWIN, D.F., 'Religion and parental child-rearing orientations: evidence of a Catholic–Protestant convergence', *American Journal of Sociology*, 92(2), 412–40 (1986).

ARGYLE, M. and BEIT-HALLAHMI, B., *The Social Psychology of Religion*, Routledge and Kegan Paul, London (1975).

BROWN, L.B., *The Psychology of Religious Belief*, Academic Press, London (1987).

GREELEY, A., 'Protestant and Catholic: is the analogical imagination extinct?', *American Sociological Review*, 54, 485–502 (1989).

GREER, J., 'The persistence of religion in Northern Ireland', *Character Potential*, 9, 139–49 (1980).

GREER, J., 'Moral cultures in Northern Ireland', *Journal of Social Psychology*, 123, 63–70 (1984).

HEATH, A. and TOPF, R., 'Political culture', in Jowell, R., Witherspoon, S. and Brook, L. (eds), *British Social Attitudes: the 1987 report*, Gower, Aldershot (1987).

HESKIN, K., *Northern Ireland: a psychological analysis*, Gill and Macmillan, Dublin (1980).

HICKEY, J., *Religion and the Northern Ireland Problem*, Gill and Macmillan, Dublin (1984).

JOWELL, R., WITHERSPOON, S. and BROOK, L. (eds), *British Social Attitudes: the 1987 report*, Gower, Aldershot (1987).

JOWELL, R., WITHERSPOON, S. and BROOK, L. (eds), *British Social Attitudes: the 7th report*, Gower, Aldershot (1990).

MOXON-BROWNE, E., *Nation, Class and Creed in Northern Ireland*, Gower, Aldershot (1983).

PPRU (POLICY PLANNING and RESEARCH UNIT), 'Continuous Household Survey: Religion', *PPRU Monitor*, 2, June (1985).

ROSE, R., *Governing Without Consensus: an Irish perspective*, Faber and Faber, London (1971).

ROSE, R., *Northern Ireland: a time of choice*, Macmillan, London (1976).

WHYTE, J., *Church and State in Modern Ireland 1923–1970*, Gill and Macmillan, Dublin (1971).

WRIGHT, D. and COX, E., 'Changes in moral beliefs among sixth-form boys and girls over a seven-year period in relation to religious belief, age and sex differences', *British Journal of Social and Clinical Psychology*, 10(4), 332–41 (1971).

Table 10.1 Comparison of attitudes in Britain and Northern Ireland in 1989: Redistribution of Wealth

	Britain			Northern Ireland		
	Agree	Neither	Disagree	Agree	Neither	Disagree
	%	%	%	%	%	%
Government should redistribute income to less well off	53	24	21	55	18	24
Ordinary people don't get fair share of nation's wealth	65	18	16	68	16	14
There is one law for the rich and one for the poor	69	14	16	65	16	16

Table 10.2 Comparison of attitudes in Britain and Northern Ireland in 1989: Welfare

	Britain			Northern Ireland		
	Agree	Neither	Disagree	Agree	Neither	Disagree
	%	%	%	%	%	%
Government should spend more on welfare benefits even if it leads to higher taxes	61	23	15	67	20	12
Around here, most unemployed people could find a job if they really wanted one	52	19	28	35	18	45
Many people who get social security don't really deserve any help	28	27	45	22	22	54
Most people on the dole are fiddling in one way or another	31	31	37	34	29	36
If welfare benefits weren't so generous people would learn to stand on their own two feet	30	23	46	32	21	45

Table 10.3 Comparison of attitudes in Britain and Northern Ireland in 1989: Authority

	Britain			Northern Ireland		
	Agree	Neither	Disagree	Agree	Neither	Disagree
	%	%	%	%	%	%
Young people today don't have enough respect for traditional British values	58	21	19	60	27	11
School should teach children to obey authority	84	10	5	89	6	4

Table 10.4 Comparison of attitudes in Britain and Northern Ireland in 1989: Law and Order

	Britain			Northern Ireland		
	Agree	Neither	Disagree	Agree	Neither	Disagree
	%	%	%	%	%	%
People who break the law should be given stiffer sentences	77	15	6	77	17	4
The law should always be obeyed even if a particular law is wrong	44	26	29	39	24	34
For some crimes the death penalty is the most appropriate sentence	74	7	18	59	8	31

Table 10.5 Comparison of attitudes in Britain and Northern Ireland in 1989: Censorship

	Britain			Northern Ireland		
	Agree	Neither	Disagree	Agree	Neither	Disagree
	%	%	%	%	%	%
Censorship of films is necessary to uphold moral standards	69	15	15	73	15	11

Table 10.6 Comparison of attitudes in Britain and Northern Ireland in 1989: Political Protest

	Britain			Northern Ireland		
	Agree	Neither	Disagree	Agree	Neither	Disagree
	%	%	%	%	%	%
People should be allowed to publish leaflets in protest against government	63	26	10	54	31	13
People should be allowed to organise protest marches and demonstrations	56	28	14	49	28	22
People should be allowed to organise public meetings to protest against government	65	25	9	55	28	16

Table 10.7 Comparison of Catholics and Protestants: Britain and Northern Ireland in 1989: Redistribution of Wealth

	Catholics			Protestants		
	Agree	Neither	Disagree	Agree	Neither	Disagree
	%	%	%	%	%	%
Government should redistribute income to less well off						
NI	68	20	11	48	17	33
GB	65	14	21	46	22	32
Ordinary people don't get fair share of nation's wealth						
NI	75	13	12	63	18	17
GB	78	12	10	62	18	19
There is one law for the rich and one for the poor						
NI	73	13	12	58	16	24
GB	77	12	11	67	14	19

Table 10.8 Comparison of Catholics and Protestants: Britain and Northern Ireland in 1989: Welfare

	Catholics			Protestants		
	Agree	Neither	Disagree	Agree	Neither	Disagree
	%	%	%	%	%	%
Government should spend more on welfare benefits even if it leads to higher taxes						
NI	79	14	6	60	24	15
GB	72	19	9	62	23	15
Around here, most unemployed people could find a job if they really wanted one						
NI	19	16	64	47	21	30
GB	42	20	37	56	20	24
Many people who get social security don't really deserve any help						
NI	11	15	71	29	27	42
GB	23	23	54	31	28	41

continued

Table 10.8 *continued*

	Catholics			Protestants		
	Agree	**Neither**	**Disagree**	**Agree**	**Neither**	**Disagree**
	%	%	%	%	%	%
Most people on the dole are fiddling in one way or another						
NI	21	27	50	43	31	24
GB	28	27	45	32	34	34
If welfare benefits weren't so generous people would learn to stand on their own two feet						
NI	17	18	64	45	24	29
GB	27	16	57	35	24	42

Table 10.9 Comparison of Catholics and Protestants: Britain and Northern Ireland in 1989: Authority

	Catholics			Protestants		
	Agree	**Neither**	**Disagree**	**Agree**	**Neither**	**Disagree**
	%	%	%	%	%	%
Young people today don't have enough respect for traditional British values						
NI	48	33	17	70	21	7
GB	64	17	19	67	20	13
Schools should teach children to obey authority						
NI	86	7	6	93	4	3
GB	85	11	4	89	7	3

Table 10.10 Comparison of Catholics and Protestants: Britain and Northern Ireland in 1989: Law and Order

	Catholics			Protestants		
	Agree	**Neither**	**Disagree**	**Agree**	**Neither**	**Disagree**
	%	%	%	%	%	%
People who break the law should be given stiffer sentences						
NI	66	25	7	85	12	2
GB	79	15	6	81	13	5
The law should always be obeyed even if a particular law is wrong						
NI	28	22	48	49	25	24
GB	42	22	36	49	26	25

continued

Table 10.10 *continued*

	Catholics			Protestants		
	Agree	Neither	Disagree	Agree	Neither	Disagree
	%	%	%	%	%	%
For some crimes the death penalty is the most appropriate sentence						
NI	30	11	56	77	6	18
GB	68	8	24	78	7	15

Table 10.11 Comparison of Catholics and Protestants: Britain and Northern Ireland in 1989: Censorship

	Catholics			Protestants		
	Agree	Neither	Disagree	Agree	Neither	Disagree
	%	%	%	%	%	%
Censorship of films and magazines is necessary to uphold moral standards						
NI	74	15	9	78	13	7
GB	78	9	13	73	15	12

Table 10.12 Comparison of Catholics and Protestants: Britain and Northern Ireland in 1989: Political Protest

	Catholics			Protestants		
	Agree	Neither	Disagree	Agree	Neither	Disagree
	%	%	%	%	%	%
People should be allowed to publish leaflets to protest against government						
NI	60	28	10	47	35	16
GB	68	20	12	60	28	12
People should be allowed to organise protest marches and demonstrations						
NI	56	22	20	41	32	25
GB	64	23	14	53	30	17
People should be allowed to organise public meetings to protest against government						
NI	61	25	12	49	31	19
GB	72	19	9	62	27	11

Appendix 1
Technical details of the survey

Kevin Sweeney

Development of the questionnaire

In late 1988, an advisory panel was formed to undertake the task of defining the overall structure and content of the survey questionnaire, and the Northern Ireland module in particular. The panel, consisting of representatives of Social and Community Planning Research (SCPR), Policy Planning and Research Unit (PPRU), Central Community Relations Unit (CCRU), Policy Research Institute (PRI) and the academic community, planned the Northern Ireland module and advised on which modules from the British questionnaire might be included in the Northern Ireland version. They also assessed the outcome of a number of pilot studies.

The panel concentrated initially on outlining the areas of interest and relevance to community relations, which was to be the subject of the special module. Aware of the value of exploiting opportunities for trend analysis, it also reviewed previous research as a source of suitable questions (see for example, Rose, 1971; Moxon-Browne, 1983; Smith and Chambers, 1987). The scope of the questionnaire was constrained by the need to keep within the limits of a face-to-face interview of about one hour in length. Final responsibility for the detailed wording, structure and content of the questionnaire remained with SCPR.

Two pilot surveys were completed in the early weeks of 1989. Questionnaire content was reviewed and revised in the light of the outcome of the pilot surveys.

Content of the questionnaire

The basic schema of the Northern Ireland Social Attitudes questionnaire mirrored that of the British survey. It had two components. The first was a questionnaire administered by interviewers and lasting, on average, a little over an hour. The second component was a self-completion supplement which was filled in by respondents after the interview, and was either collected by interviewers or returned by post.

Each year, the British questionnaire includes a number of 'core' questions, covering areas such as defence, the economy and labour-market participation, as well as a range of background and classificatory questions. The questionnaire also contains sets of questions (or modules) on attitudes to other issues, such as public and private morality, the environment or health. These are repeated less frequently – on a two- or three-year cycle, or at longer intervals. The Northern Ireland questionnaire included the 'core' questions and a selection of modules from the 1989 British survey.

The views of the advisory panel guided SCPR in its choice of modules for Northern Ireland. The choice was difficult, given that the British sample size permits two versions of the questionnaire to be fielded, each with some different modules. All British modules could not be included in an interview lasting an hour. On the other hand, some questions from the Northern Ireland module on community relations were included in the British questionnaire.

The self-completion supplement consisted principally of the International Social Survey Programme (ISSP) module (for further details of the ISSP see Jowell et al, 1989); and also of those items from the British questionnaire and the Northern Ireland module that were most appropriately asked in this format.

An outline of the content of the Northern Ireland Social Attitudes survey questionnaire in 1989 is given below.

Content of the Northern Ireland Social Attitudes survey questionnaire

Core
(Common to both versions of the British questionnaire – except that marked**)

Newspaper readership
Defence
International relations
Economic issues and policies
Household income
Economic activity
Labour-market participation
Social class
Religion
Poverty**

Modules
(Included in only one version of the British questionnaire)

Moral issues
Diet and health
Housing
AIDS

Northern Ireland module
(*Selected items included in one version of the British questionnaire)

Community relations
Perceptions of religious prejudice*
Protestant–Catholic relations*
Segregation and integration
Even-handedness of institutions
Equality of opportunity in employment
Education*
Political partisanship
Community/national identity
Trust in government structures*
Constitutional questions*

ISSP module

Work orientations

The sample

The British Social Attitudes survey is designed to yield a representative sample of adults aged 18 and over, living in private households. The Northern Ireland survey aimed to sample the same population in Northern Ireland.

For practical reasons, the electoral registers are used as the sampling-frame in Britain, and a multi-stage sample design is employed. The sample in Northern Ireland was drawn using the sampling-frame and methods that are normally employed for government surveys in Northern Ireland.

The sampling-frame was the rating list, a copy of which is maintained by PPRU for such purposes. This copy, in computer-readable form, is provided by the Rating Division of the Department of Environment (NI). The PPRU list is limited to those addresses that have a domestic-rated portion. This provides a very good sampling-frame for private households. It excludes people living in institutions (but not those living in private households at such institutions).

The PPRU list is updated twice yearly, following the rate-billing periods in April and September. It represents both an up-to-date and complete list of all private addresses in Northern Ireland. The list misses only those new-build properties that have not been added before the previous update or occupied since the last update. As currently implemented, however, the list does contain a proportion of non-viable addresses (vacant, demolished, etc.). An adjustment of the size of the selected sample is necessary to compensate for this.

The sample for the 1989 survey was drawn in February of that year from the list updated in the previous November. Since the sampling-frame is of addresses, a further sampling is required to select individual adults for interview. Subsequently, weighting of the achieved sample is required to compensate for the effect of household size on the probability of selection of individual respondents.

Sample design and selection of addresses

It is normal practice for household surveys conducted by PPRU to use an unclustered, simple random-sample design. A combination of the small geographical size of Northern Ireland, the generally low population density (outside the Greater Belfast area), and the extent of coverage of PPRU's field-force makes this design no less efficient in terms of cost than a clustered sample-design. The design has a high utility in generating representative samples of the population for multi-purpose surveys. It increases the precision of survey estimates, over those of a clustered design, at any given sample-size.

Addresses are selected from a computer-based copy of the rating/valuation list using a NAG random number generation routine. The addresses selected for all surveys conducted by PPRU are excluded from further sampling for a period of two years. Before addresses were selected, Northern Ireland was stratified into three geographical areas (Figure 1). This stratification, based on district council boundaries, consists of: Belfast – Belfast District Council; East – broadly the remaining district council areas east of the River Bann, excluding Moyle, and Newry and Mourne; West – the remaining district council areas. Within each of these strata a simple random-sample of addresses was selected from the rating list, with probability proportionate to the number of addresses in that stratum. Proportions in Figure 1 show the distribution of addresses on the rating list, the distribution of selected addresses and the distribution of addresses at which interviews were achieved. A higher response rate in the West than the East resulted in a small distortion in the balance of addresses between these two strata.

Figure 1 Geographical distribution of the sample

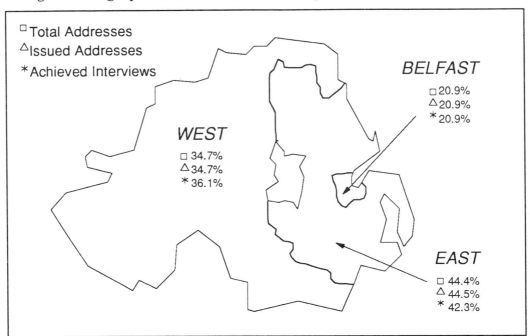

Selection of individuals

One individual was selected for interview at each address at which interviewers were successful in achieving initial co-operation. Interviewers were instructed first to list all people at the address who were eligible for inclusion in the sample: that is, all adults currently aged 18 or over who were resident at that address. Interviewers then referred to a 'Kish' grid to select one respondent from those listed. (The 'Kish' grid consisted of only a single, computer-generated line, based on the last digit of the identity number allocated to the address by PPRU. This represented a considerable simplification in administration over a normal printed grid and was greatly appreciated by interviewers.)

Because the selection of an individual respondent at each address could not be conducted with probability proportionate to household size, the sample needed to be weighted before analysis.

Weighting of the achieved sample

The computation of weights for the achieved sample was carried out by SCPR and included in the data-set. Individuals in large households had a lower probability of selection as respondents than those in small households. Accordingly, the data were weighted in inverse proportion to the number of eligible adults at the address, derived from the details of household structure recorded by interviewers on the questionnaire.

The weights applied to the Northern Ireland sample were, in general, larger than those applied to the British sample. The average weight was 2.06. In order to retain the actual number of interviews, the weighted sample was scaled back to the originally achieved size, yielding a total of 866 interviews and an average weight of 1.

Weight	No.	%	Scaled weight
1	229	26.4	0.484
2	448	51.7	0.967
3	125	14.4	1.450
4	40	4.6	1.934
5	16	1.8	2.418
6	5	0.6	2.901
7	3	0.3	3.385

Fieldwork

Fieldwork in Northern Ireland began in late February, about one month before the British survey went into the field. This was for logistic reasons. Full details and copies of all field documents are published in Brook et al (1990).

Pilot surveys

A pre-pilot exercise was conducted between 13 and 19 January 1989, and a full-scale pilot survey between 27 January and 2 February 1989.

For both pilot surveys, electoral wards were chosen to represent the range of respondents expected in the final survey and to ensure the inclusion of as wide a range of views as possible. In this way questionnaire structure and wording were likely to be fully tested. The pre-pilot questionnaire included only the Northern Ireland module and some background material. The full-scale pilot tested the whole questionnaire proposed for Northern Ireland.

Six electoral wards were selected for both pilot surveys, to represent both urban and rural locations, working and middle-class backgrounds and predominantly Protestant and predominantly Catholic areas. The sample-size chosen for each selected ward reflected both the need to achieve 10 completed interviews over a one-week period with a minimum of call-backs, and also the likelihood of contacting respondents with the required characteristics in each area. The wards were selected using available Census information.

One interviewer was assigned to each ward. All interviewers achieved very close to their target of completed interviews. The interviewers were fully briefed by SCPR before each pilot. They themselves provided considerable feedback during a full de-briefing session after each pilot. Interviewers were somewhat apprehensive about the content of the questionnaire before the first pilot, but they experienced very few problems in the field.

Electoral wards selected for pilot surveys

	Type	% Cath. 1981 (enumerated population)	% Cath. 1981 (revised)	Sample size no.
Greater Belfast				
New Lodge	Working class	65	81	15
Carrowreagh	Working class	*	4	15
Clandeboye	Middle class	4	2	15
Finaghy	Middle class	29	38	40
Rural				
Derrynoose		57	66	20
Ballinamalard		14	20	20

The second pilot was run under the same conditions. Refinements that were identified were included in the final draft of the questionnaire for the main-stage survey. The same interviewers were used on both pilot surveys.

The pilot surveys were invaluable, not only in generating useful feedback on the content and length of the questionnaire, but also in allaying any apprehension that interviewers might have had about the project. At least one of the pilot-survey interviewers was present at each of the main-survey briefing sessions.

Main-stage survey

The main-stage fieldwork was conducted by 62 interviewers from PPRU's panel. They were fully briefed and familiarised with the survey procedures by SCPR. Fieldwork began on 27 February 1989. All but six interviews were completed by the end of April.

The survey was conducted as an SCPR survey, with all survey documents clearly identifying that research organisation. Interviewers, however, carried and presented their normal PPRU identity cards. To avoid any confusion on the part of respondents, they also carried, and left with respondents, a letter of introduction from the research team at SCPR. The letter clearly identified the relationship between PPRU and SCPR in the context of the survey. Respondents were given the London telephone number of the Social Attitudes research team at SCPR, as well as a Belfast telephone number, in case they had any queries or uncertainties about the survey or the interviewer. The Belfast telephone number was a direct telephone line manned by PPRU field-staff during office hours, and otherwise covered by an answering machine. Only a very small number of respondents used either method of contact. In some instances this was to reschedule an appointment with an interviewer; on a few occasions it was to indicate unwillingness to participate in the survey.

A total of 1400 addresses was selected initially; and 1398 were allocated to interviewers by PPRU's normal allocation procedures, which ensure minimum travelling distances for each interviewer. The fieldwork was supervised by PPRU using the standard quality control methods employed on all government surveys in Northern Ireland. Interviewers were required to make at least three calls (normal procedure allows for additional calls to be made should the interviewer be passing the address while working in the area) at an address before declaring it a non-contact and returning the allocation sheet to headquarters. The timing of the initial contact calls is left to the discretion of the interviewer, based on knowledge of the area, to maximise the likelihood of finding someone at home. Before declaring an address to be a non-contact, at least one call must have been made in the morning, afternoon and evening or weekend. Non-contact addresses were returned to headquarters and, if possible, were re-issued before the end of the field period for (up to) three more calls. Field-staff at PPRU monitored the return of work and completed preliminary checks on questionnaires. Coding staff at PPRU maintained telephone contact with all interviewers. Quality problems were dealt with initially by this means.

An overall response rate of 66% was achieved, based on the total number of issued addresses that were within the scope of the survey (that is, occupied private addresses).

Main-stage survey responses

| | Northern Ireland | | Belfast | | East | | West | |
	No.	%	No.	%	No.	%	No.	%
Addresses issued	1398		292		622		484	
Vacant, derelict	94		13		40		41	
In scope	1304	100	279	100	582	100	443	100
Interview achieved	866	66	181	65	373	64	312	70
Interview not achieved	438	34	98	35	209	36	131	30
Refused	264	20	54	19	131	23	79	18
Non-contact	103	8	28	10	46	8	29	7
Other non-response	71	5	16	6	32	5	23	5

The response rate achieved in the West (70%) was higher than in the rest of Northern Ireland. Overall, refusals were obtained at 20% of the effective addresses, the greater part of which resulted from a refusal on the part of the selected individual to take part in the survey (Figure 2). Approximately one-third of refusals resulted from a reluctance, at initial contact, to provide the information necessary for respondent selection at the address. At some 8% of addresses, the interviewer could not contact either the household or the selected respondent within the field period.

The interview took, on average, 75 minutes to complete.

163

Figure 2 Summary of response to the survey

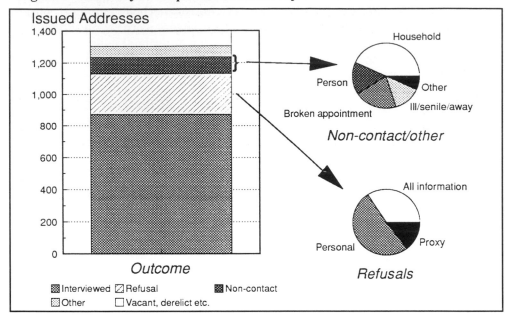

Self-completion questionnaire

The self-completion questionnaire was either collected by the interviewer at the time of interview or at a later time when working in the area, or was returned by the respondent by post. Respondents were given an addressed and post-paid envelope in which to return the self-completion questionnaire. This envelope was addressed to SCPR at a Post Office box in Belfast, from which they were forwarded to SCPR.

The return of self-completion questionnaires was monitored by PPRU field-staff. Up to two reminder letters were sent at two-weekly intervals after the initial interview. In all, 90% of the self-completion questionnaires were returned.

Self-completion questionnaire responses

		%	%
Achieved interviews	866	100	
Self-completion returned	780	90	100
returned with questionnaire	507		65
collected by interviewer	73		9
posted by respondent	200		26
Not returned	86	10	

Data preparation and coding

As questionnaires were returned from the field, they were checked against the issued sample by PPRU's field section. After preliminary checking, the results of which were fed back to the interviewers, the completed

164

questionnaires were sent to SCPR for checking, editing, coding, keying and computer editing. The same procedures were used by SCPR as for the British Social Attitudes data-set. Full details of these procedures may be found in Brook et al (1990).

Analysis variables

The analysis variables in the Northern Ireland data-set are the same as those in the British survey. However, region is not coded in the Northern Ireland data, and the questions on party identification use Northern Irish political parties. A number of analysis variables were coded, by SCPR, from the current or last job held by the respondent (and spouse or partner). Summary variables derived from these and some further derived variables are included in the data-set. The principal analysis variables available in the data-set are listed below.

Coded analysis variables

Occupation code (KOS)
Employment status
Socio-economic group (SEG)
Social class (I to V)
Goldthorpe class schema (1 to 5)
Standard industrial classification (SIC)

Derived analysis variables

Age within sex   Highest educational qualification
Household type   Accommodation tenure
Party political identification   Marital status
Current economic position   Religion

Sampling errors

No sample is likely to reflect precisely the characteristics of the population it is drawn from, because of both sampling and non-sampling errors. An estimate of the amount of error due to the sampling process can be calculated. For a simple random-sample design, in which every member of the sampled population has an equal and independent chance of inclusion in the sample, the sampling error of any percentage, p, can be calculated by the formula

$$\text{s.e. (p)} = \sqrt{\frac{p(100-p)}{n}}$$

where n is the number of respondents on which the percentage is based. The sample for the Northern Ireland Social Attitudes survey is drawn as a simple random-sample, and thus this formula can be used to calculate the sampling error of any percentage estimate from the survey. A confidence interval for the population percentage can be calculated by the formula

$$\text{95\% confidence interval} = p \pm 1.96 \times \text{s.e.(p)}$$

If 100 similar, independent samples were chosen from the same population, 95 of them would be expected to yield an estimate for the percentage, p, within this confidence interval.

The sample for the British Social Attitudes survey is clustered according to a stratified multi-stage design. It requires the calculation of complex standard errors, taking into account the spread of percentage response between clusters. This procedure has generally yielded design factors (DEFTs) ranging between 1.2 and 1.8 in surveys before 1989 (the 1989 survey used a different method for the calculation of complex standard error, which does not result in the computation of DEFTs). These DEFTs represent a measure of the efficiency of the sample against that obtained using simple random sampling. They can be used to scale-up the standard error which is calculated by the formula above.

The absence of design effects in the Northern Ireland survey, and therefore, of the need to calculate complex standard errors, means that the standard error and confidence intervals for percentage estimates from the survey are only slightly greater than for the British survey, despite the smaller sample-size. It also means that standard statistical tests of significance (which assume random sampling) can be applied directly to the data.

A percentage estimate of 10% (or 90%) from the Northern Ireland survey has a standard error of 1.02% and a 95% confidence interval of ±2%. A percentage estimate of 50% has a standard error of 1.7% and a 95% confidence interval of ±3.3%.

The table below gives examples of the sampling errors and confidence intervals for typical percentage estimates from the Northern Ireland Social Attitudes survey.

		% (p)	Standard error of p (%)	95% confidence interval
Classification variables				
Q65	**Religion**			
	Protestant	50.6	1.7	47.3–53.9
	Catholic	35.8	1.6	32.8–39.2
	No religion	11.8	1.1	10.9–13.1
Q100	**Housing tenure**[1]			
	Owns	62.6	1.6	59.4–65.8
	Rents from NIHE	30.7	1.6	27.7–33.8
Q20	**Economic activity**			
	Working	48.2	1.7	44.7–51.3
	Unemployed	10.1	1.0	9.1–11.1
Attitudinal variables				
Q9	**Expects inflation to go up**	86.7	1.2	84.4–89.0
Q12	**Expects unemployment to rise**	41.5	1.7	38.2–44.8
Q84	**Both parents same religion**	95.0	0.7	94.3–95.7
Q90b	**Supports fair employment law**	50.7	1.7	47.4–54.0
Q17a	**Pre-marital sex always wrong**	30.0	1.6	28.4–31.6

[1]Unweighted data

Representativeness of the sample

In any survey, there is a possibility of non-response bias. Non-response bias arises if the characteristics of non-respondents differ significantly from those of respondents, in such a way that they are reflected in the responses given in the survey. Accurate estimates of non-response bias can only be obtained by comparing characteristics of the achieved sample with the distribution of the same characteristics in the population at the time of sampling. Such comparisons can usually only be made with current Census of Population data.

Demographic characteristics

It is not possible to estimate accurately whether any non-response bias exists in the Northern Ireland Social Attitudes survey. However, Tables 1 and 2 compare the characteristics of both the households and individuals sampled with those sampled in the Continuous Household Survey (CHS) of the same year. The CHS has a much larger sample (over 3000 households are interviewed) and uses the same simple random-sample design. All adults aged 16 or over are interviewed. No weighting is required to compensate for the effect of household size on probability of selection. The CHS has been running for seven years and produces consistent estimates from year to year.

The characteristics of the two samples are very similar. Most differences are within the range of sampling error. Household characteristics are based on unweighted estimates from the Social Attitudes survey, because the probability of household selection is independent of household size. The only substantive difference is in the distribution of the socio-economic group (SEG) of respondents. This may have resulted from slight differences in the way SEG is coded and summarised in the two surveys.

Religious denomination

The religious denomination stated by respondents aged 18 and over in the two surveys has a somewhat different pattern (Table 3). The most striking difference is that 12% of respondents in the Social Attitudes survey gave a 'No religion' response, compared with only 2% of respondents in the CHS.

It is possible that the context of the questions in the two surveys influenced the propensity of respondents to state their religious denomination. The CHS is principally a factual survey, in which a question on religious denomination may have a more 'matter of fact' context. Recording respondents' views on social, economic and political issues may place the same question in a more sensitive context. However, it is equally possible that the question asked in the CHS receives a factual answer that is related to the respondent's background, whilst in the context of the Social Attitudes survey the response represents a statement of the respondent's current religious 'persuasion'.

It is difficult to disentangle these possibilities from the survey data. However, respondents to the Social Attitudes survey who gave 'No religion' as a response to the initial question were then asked in which religion they were brought up. When the religious denomination of all respondents is examined, using *either* their stated denomination *or* that in which they were brought up,

167

all but a small number of respondents can be assigned to a denomination and the distribution matches closely that of the CHS (Table 4). Of the people who initially said that they had no denomination, three-quarters had been brought up as Protestants and a quarter as Catholics.

Since the CHS attempts to interview all adults at selected addresses, a second level of non-co-operation in the survey is introduced. Thirteen per cent of adults aged 18 and over could not be directly assigned a religious denomination (Table 3), since they had not been asked the question. However, all of them can in principle be assigned a denomination, based on that of other members of their household. This has been done in the figures presented in Table 4. Of those assigned a denomination in this way, 45% were in Catholic households and 51% in Protestant households. These proportions probably reflect a slight bias toward younger persons (a greater proportion of whom are Catholic) being among those who could not be contacted to participate in the survey.

The figures given in Tables 3 and 4 suggest that the distribution of religious denomination among those sampled in the two surveys is similar, despite any difference in the denomination stated in response to an initial question.

References

BROOK, L., TAYLOR, B. and PRIOR, G. (eds), *British Social Attitudes 1989 Survey: technical report*, SCPR, London (1990).

JOWELL, R., WITHERSPOON, S. and BROOK, L. (eds), *British Social Attitudes: special international report*, Gower, Aldershot (1989).

MOXON-BROWNE, E., *Nation, Class and Creed in Northern Ireland*, Gower, Aldershot (1983).

ROSE, R., *Governing Without Consensus: an Irish perspective*, Faber and Faber, London (1971).

SMITH, D. J. and CHAMBERS, G., *Equality and Inequality in Northern Ireland, III Perceptions and Views*, PSI Occasional Paper 39 (1987).

Table 1 Comparison of Social Attitudes survey sample with Continuous Household Survey 1989

Characteristics of sampled households		Social Attitudes survey (1989)[1]	Continuous Household Survey (1989)
		%	%
Household type[2]	1 adult 18–59	7	7
	2 adults 18–59	10	9
	Youngest 0–4	20	19
	Youngest 5–17	25	19
	3 or more adults	12	15
	2 adults 60 or over	13	15
	1 adult 60 or over	14	16
Tenure	Owner-occupied	63	60
	Rented, NIHE	31	32
	Rented, housing association	2	1
	Rented, other	4	6
	Rent-free	1	1
	Other	–	–
Type of accommodation	Detached	32	30
	Semi-detached	24	23
	Terraced	39	38
	Purpose-built flat	5	6
	Converted flat	1	1
	Other	–	1
Household income (£)	Less than 5000	35	36
	5000–7999	18	17
	8000–11999	13	13
	12000 or over	27	25
	Unknown	8	10
Base = 100%		866	3064

[1]Household characteristics are based on unweighted data from the Social Attitudes survey.

[2]Household type in the Continuous Household Survey is based on adults aged 16 and over.

Table 2 Comparison of Social Attitudes survey sample with the Continuous Household Survey 1989

Characteristics of sampled individuals aged 18 and over		Social Attitudes survey (1989) %	Continuous Household Survey (1989) %
Sex	Male	48	47
	Female	52	53
Age	18–24	16	15
	25–34	20	21
	35–44	18	18
	45–54	14	14
	55–59	8	6
	60–64	7	7
	65 and over	17	20
Marital status	Single	21	24
	Married/cohabiting	65	62
	Widowed	10	9
	Divorced/separated	4	5
Economic activity	Working	48	48
	Unemployed	10	8
	Inactive	42	41
	Not answered	–	4
SEG	Professional/managerial	11	10
	Intermediate/Junior non-manual	30	24
	Skilled manual	22	20
	Semi-skilled manual	22	27
	Unskilled manual	6	6
	Other	10	13
Base = 100%		866	6182

Table 3 Stated religious denomination

Religious denomination of persons aged 18 years and over	Social Attitudes survey (1989) %	Continuous Household Survey (1989) %
Protestant	50	61
Catholic	36	36
Non-Christian	–	1
No religion	12	2
Unwilling to say	2	1
Base= 100%	866	5384
(Undefined CHS)[1]		(13%)

[1]Religion is undefined in CHS for individuals who do not fully co-operate in the survey and are, therefore, not asked their denomination. The base for this percentage is the total number of adults aged 18 and over in the sampled households (6146).

Table 4 Redefined religious denomination

Religious denomination[1] of persons aged 18 years and over	Social Attitudes survey (1989) %	Continuous Household Survey (1989) %
Protestant	59	60
Catholic	38	37
Non-Christian	–	1
No religion	1	1
Unwilling to say	2	1
Base = 100%	866	6146

[1]Religious denomination has been redefined, in both surveys, for all those who stated 'No religion' or were unwilling to specify their denomination. In the Social Attitudes survey denomination was calculated from the religion in which the respondent was brought up. In CHS, denomination was redefined using the denomination specified by other members of the household.

Appendix 2
Notes on the tabulations

1. Figures in the tables are from the 1989 survey unless otherwise indicated.
2. Tables are percentaged as indicated.
3. In tables, and asterisk (*) indicates less than 0.5 but greater than zero, and a dash (–) indicates zero.
5. Percentages equal to or greater than 0.5% have been rounded up in all tables (for example, 0.5% = 1%).
6. Tables are all based on weighted data.
7. In many tables the proportions of respondents answering 'Don't know' or not giving an answer are omitted. This, together with the effects of rounding and weighting, means that percentages will not always add to 100%.
8. The self-completion questionnaire was not completed by 10% of respondents in Northern Ireland and 14% of respondents in Britain. Percentage responses to the self-completion questionnaire are based on all those who completed it.

Appendix 3
The questionnaire

The Northern Ireland questionnaires are reproduced on the following pages. The keying codes have been removed and the percentage distribution of answers to each question inserted instead. Percentages in the main questionnaire are based on the total sample (866 weighted and unweighted). In the self-completion questionnaire they are based on the 784 (weighted) who returned it.

For further details on the questionnaires readers are referred to Jowell et al (1990).

Reference

JOWELL, R., WITHERSPOON, S. and BROOK, L. (eds), *British Social Attitudes: the 7th report,* Gower, Aldershot (1990)

SCPR
SOCIAL & COMMUNITY PLANNING RESEARCH

Head Office: 35 NORTHAMPTON SQUARE, LONDON EC1V 0AX
TELEPHONE 01-250 1866

Northern Field Office: CHARAZEL HOUSE, GAINFORD, DARLINGTON
CO. DURHAM DL2 3EG. TELEPHONE 0325-730888

P.1005

March 1989

NORTHERN IRELAND SOCIAL ATTITUDES:

1989 SURVEY

Serial
Number

Area
Number

CARD 02

Version A = 1
B = 2
N1 = 3

3

Time inter-
view started

24 hr. clock

Interviewer
Number

0

OUO:
Batch
Code

SECTION ONE

N = 866
Qs. 1-20

NI

			Skip to
1.a)	Do you normally read any daily morning newspaper at least 3 times a week?	Yes 57.2	b)
		No 42.8	Q.2

IF YES

b) Which one do you normally read?
IF MORE THAN ONE ASK: Which one do you read most frequently?
ONE CODE ONLY

(Scottish) Daily Express	2.7
Daily Mail	2.7
Daily Mirror/Record	12.9
Daily Star	3.1
The Sun	12.9
Today	1.3
Daily Telegraph	1.6
Financial Times	0.6
The Guardian	1.1
The Independent	1.0
The Times	0.3
Morning Star	0.1
The News Letter	6.1
The Irish News	8.8
The Irish Times	0.2
Other Irish/Northern Irish/Scottish/regional or local daily morning paper (WRITE IN:)	1.9
More than one	—

Other (WRITE IN:)

2.a) Now a few questions about the UK's relationships with other countries.
Do you think the UK should continue to be a member of the EEC - the Common Market - or should it withdraw? RECORD IN COL a)

b) And do you think the UK should continue to be a member of NATO - the North Atlantic Treaty Organisation - or should it withdraw? RECORD IN COL b)

	(a) EEC	(b) NATO
Continue	70.2	65.6
Withdraw	17.4	12.5
Don't know	10.7	19.4

3. On the whole, do you think that the UK's interests are better served by ... READ OUT ...

... closer links with Western Europe,	36.4
or - closer links with America?	16.6
(Both equally)	31.5
(Neither)	3.0
(Don't know)	12.5

2

NI

4.a) Do you think that the siting of American nuclear missiles in Britain makes Britain a safer or a less safe place to live? RECORD IN COL a)

b) And do you think that having its own independent nuclear missiles makes Britain a safer or a less safe place to live? RECORD IN COL b)

	(a) American nuclear missiles	(b) Own nuclear missiles
Safer	25.6	39.7
Less safe	61.0	47.5
No difference	0.8	0.5
Don't know	12.3	11.7

5. CARD A
Which, if either, of these two statements comes closest to your own opinion on UK nuclear policy?

The UK should rid itself of nuclear weapons while persuading others to do the same	37.1
The UK should keep its nuclear weapons until it can persuade others to reduce theirs	58.3
(Neither of these)	2.6
Don't know	1.9

6. Which political party's views on defence would you say comes closest to your own views?
CODE ONE ONLY

Conservative	42.2
Labour	18.6

ONLY CODE ALLIANCE AFTER PROBE:
Social and Liberal Democrats or SDP (Owen)?

Social and Liberal Democrat/Liberal/SLD	2.0
SDP/Social Democrat	0.9
Mainland or Northern Ireland? (Mainland - Alliance)	0.3
Other (WRITE IN:)	0.4
Don't know	26.1
None	9.3

7. CARD B
Which of the phrases on this card is closest to your opinion about threats to world peace?

America is a greater threat to world peace than Russia	9.8
Russia is a greater threat to world peace than America	23.7
Russia and America are equally great threats to world peace	49.3
Neither is a threat to world peace	11.7
(Don't know)	5.4

SECTION TWO

Now I would like to ask you about two economic problems - inflation and unemployment.

9. First, inflation: in a year from now, do you expect prices generally to have gone up, to have stayed the same, or to have gone down?

   IF GONE UP OR GONE DOWN:
   By a lot or a little?

To have gone up by a lot	42.9
To have gone up by a little	43.8
To have stayed the same	7.9
To have gone down by a little	3.5
To have gone down by a lot	0.6
(Don't know)	1.2

10. Second, unemployment: in a year from now, do you expect unemployment to have gone up, to have stayed the same, or to have gone down?

    IF GONE UP OR GONE DOWN:
    By a lot or a little?

To have gone up by a lot	19.7
To have gone up by a little	21.8
To have stayed the same	33.4
To have gone down by a little	20.0
To have gone down by a lot	2.3
(Don't know)	2.8

11.a) If the government had to choose between keeping down inflation or keeping down unemployment, to which do you think it should give highest priority?

Keeping down inflation	32.9
Keeping down unemployment	64.0
Both equally	1.6
Others	-
Don't know	0.7

b) Which do you think is of most concern to you and your family ... READ OUT ...

... inflation,	55.1
or - unemployment?	41.7
Both equally	0.8
Neither	-
Others	0.2
Don't know	1.3

12. Looking ahead over the next year, do you think the UK's general industrial performance will improve, stay much the same, or decline?

    IF IMPROVE OR DECLINE:
    By a lot or a little?

Improve a lot	2.9
Improve a little	20.9
Stay much the same	47.5
Decline a little	17.1
Decline a lot	3.4
(Don't know)	8.1

8.a) Do you think the long term policy for Northern Ireland should be for it ... READ OUT ...

		Skip to
... to remain part of the United Kingdom,	69.4	
or - to reunify with the rest of Ireland?	23.6	
NI independent state	0.6	
NI split into two	-	
Irish to decide	0.4	
Don't know	3.7	

b) Some people think that government policy towards Northern Ireland should include a complete withdrawal of British troops. Would you personally support or oppose such a policy? PROBE: strongly or a little?

		Skip to
Support strongly	19.0	
Support a little	13.5	
Oppose strongly	46.9	
Oppose a little	14.1	NOW GO TO Q.9, PAGE 4
Withdraw in long term	1.5	
Let Irish decide	0.2	
Others	0.4	
Don't know	4.1	

GO TO Q.9, PAGE 4

NI

ASK ALL

16. Thinking of income levels generally in Britain today, would you say that the gap between those with high incomes and those with low incomes is ... **READ OUT** ...

... too large,	86.0
about right,	10.4
or - too small?	2.0
Don't know	1.5

17. Generally, how would you describe levels of taxation?

CARD C

a) Firstly for those with high incomes? Please choose a phrase from this card. **RECORD ANSWER IN COL a) BELOW**

b) Next for those with middle incomes? Please choose a phrase from this card. **RECORD ANSWER IN COL b) BELOW**

c) And lastly for those with low incomes? Please choose a phrase from this card. **RECORD ANSWER IN COL c) BELOW**

	(a) High incomes	(b) Middle incomes	(c) Low incomes
Taxes are: Much too high	4.2	5.4	46.0
Too high	9.4	32.4	37.5
About right	31.5	55.2	12.7
Too low	36.1	4.5	1.6
Much too low	15.9	0.4	0.3

18.a) Among which group would you place yourself ... **READ OUT** ...

... high income,	2.0
middle income,	47.4
or - low income?	50.4
Don't know	0.2

CARD D

b) Which of the phrases on this card would you say comes closest to your feelings about your household's income these days?

Living comfortably on present income	21.9
Coping on present income	50.1
Finding it difficult on present income	19.7
Finding it very difficult on present income	8.3
Other (WRITE IN:) _____	-

NI

13. Here are a number of policies which might help the UK's economic problems. As I read them out, will you tell me whether you would support such a policy or oppose it?
READ OUT ITEMS i)-x) AND CODE FOR EACH

	Support	Oppose	D/K
i) Control of wages by law	35.7	60.1	3.9
ii) Control of prices by law	66.9	30.5	2.6
iii) Reducing the level of government spending on health and education	7.3	91.2	1.3
iv) Government controls to cut down goods from abroad	69.8	25.5	4.6
v) Increasing government subsidies for private industry	65.5	27.0	7.0
vi) Reducing government spending on defence	56.4	36.6	6.6
vii) Government schemes to encourage job sharing	76.4	19.4	3.6
viii) Government to set up construction projects to create more jobs	90.1	7.7	1.9
ix) Government action to cut interest rates	86.8	8.3	4.7
x) Government controls on hire purchase and credit	81.9	13.0	4.9

14. On the whole, would you like to see more or less state ownership of industry, or about the same amount as now?

More	15.1
Less	22.4
About the same amount	51.4
(Don't know)	11.0

15.a) It is said that many people manage to avoid paying their full income tax. Do you think that they should not be allowed to get away with it - or do you think good luck to them if they can get away with it?

		Skip to
Good luck if they can get away with it	70.7	b)
Should not be allowed	28.6	Q.16
Don't know	0.7	

IF 'SHOULD NOT BE ALLOWED' (CODE 1 AT a)

b) If you knew of somebody who wasn't paying their full income tax, would you be inclined to report him or her?

Yes	7.1
No	61.6
Don't know	0.7
Other answer (WRITE IN.) _____	1.2

178

- 7 -

NI

19.a) Looking back over the last year or so, would you say your household's income has ... **READ OUT** ...

		Skip to
... fallen behind prices,	52.0	
kept up with prices,	39.3	
or - gone up by more than prices?	6.4	
(Don't know)	2.3	

b) And looking forward to the year ahead, do you expect your household's income will ... **READ OUT** ...

... fall behind prices,	51.5	
keep up with prices,	37.3	
or - go up by more than prices?	5.8	
(Don't know)	4.7	

CARD E

20. Which of these descriptions applies to what you were doing last week, that is, in the seven days ending last Sunday? **PROBE:** Any others? **CODE ALL THAT APPLY IN COLUMN I**

IF ONLY ONE CODE AT I, TRANSFER IT TO COLUMN II
IF MORE THAN ONE AT I, TRANSFER HIGHEST ON LIST TO II

	COL I	COL II ECONOMIC POSITION	Skip to
In full-time education (not paid for by employer, including on vacation)	A	2.3	Q.50
On government training/employment scheme (e.g. Employment Training, Youth Training Programme, etc)	B	0.1	Q.39
In paid work (or away temporarily) for at least 10 hours in the week	C	48.0	Q.21
Waiting to take up paid work already accepted	D	0.2	Q.39
Unemployed and registered at a benefit office	E	7.8	
Unemployed, not registered, but actively looking for a job	F	1.5	Q.40
Unemployed, wanting a job (of at least 10 hrs per week), but not actively looking for a job	G	0.8	
Permanently sick or disabled	H	4.1	Q.50
Wholly retired from work	J	15.3	Q.45
Looking after the home	K	19.9	Q.46
Doing something else (WRITE IN:)	L	-	Q.50

21. IF IN PAID WORK OR AWAY TEMPORARILY (CODE 03 AT Q.20) [N=380]
In your (main) job are you ... **READ OUT** ...

... an employee,	82.5	Q.22
or - self-employed?	17.5	Q.34

- 8 -

NI

N = 316
Qs. 22-33

22. ALL EMPLOYEES (CODE 1 AT Q.21) ASK Qs.22-33
How many hours a week do you normally work in your (main) job?

(IF RESPONDENT CANNOT ANSWER, ASK ABOUT LAST WEEK)

MEDIAN: 39 HOURS

AND CODE:		Skip to
10-15 hours a week	7.3	
16-23 hours a week	9.0	
24-29 hours a week	3.7	
30 or more hours a week	80.0	

23.a) How would you describe the wages or salary you are paid for the job you do - on the low side, reasonable, or on the high side? **IF LOW:** Very low or a bit low?

Very low	12.1	
A bit low	27.6	
Reasonable	56.8	
On the high side	3.4	
Other answer (WRITE IN)		

CARD F

b) Thinking of the highest and the lowest paid people at your place of work, how would you describe the gap between their pay, as far as you know? Please choose a phrase from this card.

Much too big a gap	21.2	
Too big	24.4	
About right	44.3	
Too small	1.1	
Much too small a gap	0.6	
(Don't know)	7.5	

24.a) If you stay in this job would you expect your wages or salary over the coming year to ... **READ OUT** ...

... rise by more than the cost of living,	14.8	
rise by the same as the cost of living,	46.8	
rise by less than the cost of living,	27.2	
or - not to rise at all?	8.9	
(Will not stay in job)	0.8	
(Don't know)	1.4	

b) Over the coming year do you expect your workplace will be ... **READ OUT** ...

... increasing its number of employees,	18.5	
reducing its number of employees,	24.3	
or - will the number of employees stay about the same?	56.6	
	-	
Other answer (WRITE IN) Don't know	0.7	

179

- 9 -

NI

		Skip to
25.a) Thinking now about your own job. How likely or unlikely is it that you will leave this employer over the next year for any reason? Is it ... **READ OUT** ...		
... very likely,	12.1	b)
quite likely,	13.1	
not very likely,	29.8	Q.26
or - not at all likely?	44.6	
Don't know	-	

IF VERY OR QUITE LIKELY AT a)
CARD G

b) Why do you think you will leave? Please choose a phrase from this card or tell me what other reason there is.

MORE THAN ONE CODE MAY BE RINGED

Firm will close down	0.7
I will be declared redundant	4.9
I will reach normal retirement age	0.1
My contract of employment will expire	3.0
I will take early retirement	0.1
I will decide to leave and work for another employer	15.4
I will decide to leave and work for myself, as self-employed	0.8
I will leave to look after home/children/relative	1.7
Other answer (WRITE IN)	-

ASK ALL EMPLOYEES

26.a) Suppose you lost your job for one reason or another - would you start looking for another job, would you wait for several months or longer before you started looking, or would you decide __not__ to look for another job?

		Skip to
Start looking	87.3	b)
Wait several months or longer	3.7	
Decide not to look	8.2	Q.27
Don't know	0.8	

IF START LOOKING

b) How long do you think it would take you to find an acceptable replacement job?

MEDIAN: 2
OR CODE:

Never	6.2
Don't know	15.4

ASK ALL EMPLOYEES

27. If without having to work, you had what you would regard as a reasonable living income, do you think you would still prefer to have a paid job or wouldn't you bother?

Still prefer paid job	82.8	b)
Wouldn't bother	16.6	
Don't know	0.6	

Other answer (WRITE IN) | -

28.a) During the last five years - that is since March 1984 - have you been unemployed and seeking work for any period?

Yes	23.9	b)
No	76.1	Q.29

IF YES

b) For how many months in total during the last five years?

MEDIAN: 9 **MONTHS**

- 10 -

NI

ASK ALL EMPLOYEES

		Skip to
29.a) For any period during the last five years have you worked as a self-employed person as your main job?		
Yes	4.1	b)
No	95.9	c)

IF YES AT a).

b) In total, for how many months during the last five years have you been self-employed?

WRITE IN: MONTHS OR YEARS

Median not calculated

IF NO AT a)

c) How seriously in the last five years have you considered working as a self-employed person ... **READOUT** ...

... very seriously,	7.6
quite seriously,	10.2
not very seriously,	11.1
or - not at all seriously?	66.8

ASK ALL EMPLOYEES

30.a) As far as you know, does your employer keep any records of your religious background?

Yes	37.7
No	48.4
Don't know	13.7

CARD H

b) Thinking about the people at your workplace - as far as you know, about how many are the same religion as you - or have you no idea at all? Please choose your answer from this card.

All	15.9
Most	24.5
Half	26.9
Less than half	16.9
None	0.3
(Don't know - no idea)	15.4

31.a) Aside from your main job, do you have any other paid jobs, like a second job or other paid work?
IF YES: Is that regular work or do you only do it sometimes?

Yes - regularly	4.8	b)
Yes - sometimes	2.3	
No, no other paid work	92.9	Q.32

IF YES (CODE 1 OR 2 AT a)

b) How many hours a week do you normally work in these __other__ jobs, not including time spent travelling to work?

DO NOT COUNT MAIN JOB

WRITE IN: Hours per week

Median not calculated

ASK ALL EMPLOYEES

32.a) At your place of work are there unions, staff associations, or groups of unions recognised by the management for negotiating pay and conditions of employment?

		Skip to
Yes	62.8	
No	36.7	b)
Don't know	0.6	

IF YES

b) On the whole, do you think these unions or staff associations do their job well or not?

Yes	31.0
No	28.6
Don't know	2.8

ASK ALL EMPLOYEES

33.a) In general how would you describe relations between management and other employees at your workplace ... **READ OUT** ...

... very good,	38.2
quite good,	42.6
not very good,	13.1
or - not at all good?	5.5
Don't know	

	Skip to
NOW GO TO SECTION 3 (p.16)	Q.50

b) And in general, would you say your workplace was ... **READ OUT** ...

... very well managed,	34.0
quite well managed,	48.9
or - not well managed?	15.7
Don't know	

ALL SELF-EMPLOYED (CODE 2 AT Q.21): ASK Qs.34-38

34.a) How many hours a week do you normally work in your (main) job?
(IF RESPONDENT CANNOT ANSWER, ASK ABOUT 'LAST WEEK')

N = 64   Qs. 34-38   MEDIAN 45 HOURS

AND CODE:

10-15 hours a week	4.6
16-23 hours a week	-
24-29 hours a week	4.0
30 or more hours a week	91.4

b) During the last 5 years - that is since March 1984 - have you been unemployed and seeking work for any period?

Yes	18.5
No	79.5

35. If without having to work, you had what you would regard as a reasonable living income, do you think you would still prefer to do work, or wouldn't you bother?

Still prefer paid work	91.4
Wouldn't bother	8.6
Don't know	-
Other answer (WRITE IN:)	-

36. Have you, for any period in the last five years, worked as an employee as your main job rather than as self-employed?

Yes	23.2
No	76.8

37.a) Compared with a year ago, would you say your business is doing ... **READ OUT** ...

		Skip to
... very well,	9.3	
quite well,	21.2	
about the same,	46.4	
not very well,	15.2	
or - not at all well?	1.3	
(Business not in existence then)	5.3	

b) And over the coming year, do you think your business will do ... **READ OUT** ...

... better,	23.2
about the same,	57.6
or - worse than this year?	15.2
(Don't know)	2.6
Other: (WRITE IN:)	

38.a) In your work or business, do you have any partners or other self-employed colleagues?

		Skip to
Yes, have partner(s)	34.4	
No	65.6	Q.50

NOTE: DOES NOT INCLUDE EMPLOYEES

b) And in your work or business do you have any employees, or not?

Yes, has employee(s)	39.1
No	60.9

N.B. FAMILY MEMBERS MAY BE EMPLOYEES ONLY IF THEY RECEIVE A REGULAR WAGE OR SALARY.

NOW GO TO SECTION 3 (p.16)

ALL ON GOVERNMENT SCHEMES OR WAITING TO TAKE UP PAID WORK
(CODES 02 OR 04 AT Q.201): ASK Q.39

39.a) During the last five years - that is since March 1984 - have you been unemployed and seeking work for any period?

Yes	No
No	(3)
	(0)

b) If without having to work, you had what you would regard as a reasonable living income, do you think you would still prefer to have a paid job or wouldn't you bother?

		Skip to
Still prefer paid job	(3)	
Wouldn't bother	(0)	
Don't know	(0)	Q.50
Other answer (WRITE IN:)	(0)	

NOW GO TO SECTION 3 (p.16)

181

NI

ALL UNEMPLOYED (CODES 05, 06, 07 AT Q.20): ASK Qs.40-44

40.a) In total how many months in the last five years - that is, since March 1984 - have you been unemployed and seeking work?
MEDIAN: MONTHS 30

b) How long has this present period of unemployment and seeking work lasted so far?
MEDIAN: MONTHS 12

c) How confident are you that you will find a job to match your qualifications ... **READ OUT** ...

... very confident,	6.1
quite confident,	19.9
not very confident,	41.4
or - not at all confident?	32.6

d) Although it may be difficult to judge, how long from now do you think it will be before you find an acceptable job?
MEDIAN: MONTHS 4

		Skip to
		Q.42
Never	15.5	b)
Don't know	47.5	

41.a) INTERVIEWER CHECK:

Respondent answered 01-02 months at Q.40d (above)	8.0	
Respondent answered anything else	92.0	

IF CODE 2 AT a)

b) How willing do you think you would be in these circumstances to retrain for a different job ... **READ OUT** ...

... very willing,	30.4
quite willing,	31.5
or - not very willing?	19.3
(Don't know?)	7.2

c) How willing would you be to move to a different area to find an acceptable job ... **READ OUT** ...

... very willing,	15.5
quite willing,	12.7
or - not very willing?	59.7
(Don't know?)	0.6

d) And how willing do you think you would be in these circumstances to take what you now consider to be an unacceptable job. ... **READ OUT** ...

... very willing,	7.7
quite willing,	19.3
or - not very willing?	56.4
(Don't know?)	5.0

ASK ALL UNEMPLOYED

42. If without having to work, you had what you would regard as a reasonable living income, do you think you would still prefer to have a paid job or wouldn't you bother?

Still prefer paid job	85.1
Wouldn't bother	14.4
Other answer (**WRITE IN**)	-
Don't know	0.6

NI

43.a) Have you ever actually considered moving to a different area - an area other than the one you live in now - to try to find work?

		Skip to
Yes - Northern Ireland	11.0	b)
Yes - Mainland Britain	24.3	
No	64.6	Q.44

IF YES: In Northern Ireland or mainland Britain?

IF YES AT a)

b) Why did you not move to a different area? Any other reasons? **PROBE FULLY. RECORD VERBATIM.**

	(No.)
Moved in past	(5)
No housing available	(5)
Too much upheaval	(5)
No jobs anywhere	(2)
Waiting to move	(1)
Other answers	(ii)

ASK ALL UNEMPLOYED

44. Do you think that there is a real chance nowadays that you will get a job in this area, or is there no real chance nowadays?

		Skip to
Real chance	38.7	
No real chance	60.2	Q.50

NOW GO TO SECTION 3 (p.16)

ALL WHOLLY RETIRED FROM WORK (CODE 09 AT Q.20): ASK Q.45

45.a) Do you (or does your husband/wife) receive a pension from any past employer?   N = 166

		Skip to
Yes	35.4	c)
No	63.1	e)

b) (Can I just check) are you over (MEN:) 65 (WOMEN:) 60?

Yes	90.9
No	9.1

IF YES AT b)

c) On the whole would you say the present state pension is on the low side, reasonable, or on the high side? IF **'ON THE LOW SIDE'**: Very low or a bit low?

Very low	47.4
A bit low	22.6
Reasonable	19.7
On the high side	-

d) Do you expect your state pension in a year's time to purchase more than it does now, less, or about the same?

		Skip to
More	2.2	
Less	63.9	
About the same	19.7	Q.50
Don't know	4.0	

IF NO AT b)

e) At what age did you retire from work?
WRITE IN: YEARS

		Skip to
Median nor calculated		
Never worked	-	Q.50

NOW GO TO SECTION 3 (p.16)

SECTION THREE

NI N = 866
Qs.50-922

ASK ALL

CARD I

50. Here are some items of government spending. Which of them, if any, would be your highest priority for extra spending? And which next? Please read through the whole list before deciding.

ONE CODE ONLY IN EACH COLUMN

	1st Priority	2nd Priority
Education	15.0	28.5
Defence	1.1	0.8
Health	56.4	22.0
Housing	5.4	13.3
Public transport	0.6	0.9
Roads	2.1	3.9
Police and prisons	1.1	2.8
Social security benefits	12.3	14.9
Help for industry	4.8	9.8
Overseas aid	0.1	1.1
(NONE OF THESE)	0.3	0.4
(Don't know)	0.8	1.3

CARD J

51. Thinking now only of the government's spending on social benefits like those on the card. Which, if any, of these would be your highest priority for extra spending? And which next?

ONE CODE ONLY IN EACH COLUMN

	1st Priority	2nd Priority
Retirement pensions	43.4	16.7
Child benefits	11.8	19.0
Benefits for the unemployed	14.0	18.3
Benefits for disabled people	24.5	33.7
Benefits for single parents	6.1	11.5
(NONE OF THESE)	0.1	0.2
(Don't know)	0.1	0.6

52. I will read two statements. For each one please say whether you agree or disagree. Strongly or slightly?

	(a) Falsely claim	(b) Fail to claim
a) Large numbers of people these days falsely claim benefits.		
Agree strongly	40.8	40.1
Agree slightly	26.5	33.6
Disagree slightly	10.8	11.5
Disagree strongly	13.5	8.1
(Don't know)	8.3	6.4
b) Large numbers of people who are eligible for benefits these days fail to claim them.		

NI Qs. 46-49 N = 184

			Skip to
46.a) ALL LOOKING AFTER HOME (CODE 10 AT Q.20): ASK Qs.46-49			
Do you currently have a paid job of less than 10 hours a week?	Yes	4.8	
	No	94.7	

INCLUDE THOSE TEMPORARILY AWAY FROM A PAID JOB OF LESS THAN 10 HOURS A WEEK

b) What are the main reasons you do not have a paid job (of more than 10 hours a week) outside the home?
PROBE FULLY FOR MAIN REASONS AND RECORD VERBATIM.

Raising children	14.0	Pregnant/ill health	2.9
Retired/too old	7.0	Dependent relative	5.8
Prefer looking after home/family	19.8	Poverty trap	2.9
No jobs available	5.8	Already works less than 10 hours per week	1.2
Unsuitable for available jobs	1.2	Childcare costs	1.2
		Unpaid work/family business	0.6

			Skip to
47.a) Have you, during the last five years, ever had a full or part time job of 10 hours per week or more?	Yes	19.1	b)
	No	79.5	Q.48

IF YES AT a)
b) How long ago was it that you left that job?

WRITE IN: [NO. OF MONTHS AGO] OR [NO. OF YEARS AGO] → Q.49

Median not calculated

			Skip to
48.a) IF NO AT Q.47a)			
How seriously in the past five years have you considered getting a full-time job? ... READ OUT ...	... very seriously,	1.7	
	quite seriously,	3.7	
	not very seriously,	6.7	
	or - not at all seriously?	67.4	Q.49

PROMPT, IF NECESSARY: FULL-TIME IS 30 HRS+ PER WEEK

IF NOT VERY OR NOT AT ALL SERIOUSLY, ASK b)

b) How seriously, in the past five years, have you considered getting a part-time job? ... READ OUT ...	... very seriously,	2.0	
	quite seriously,	6.5	
	not very seriously,	8.4	
	or - not at all seriously?	56.7	

			Skip to
49. ASK ALL LOOKING AFTER THE HOME			
Do you think you are likely to look for a paid job in the next 5 years?	Yes - full-time	9.3	
IF YES: Full-time or part-time?	Yes - part-time	27.8	
	No	59.3	Q.50
	Don't know	0.3	
Other (WRITE IN) _____		2.0	

17

NI

53. Opinions differ about the level of benefits for the unemployed. Which of these two statements comes closest to your own ... READ OUT ...

... benefits for the unemployed are too low and cause hardship,	56.3
OR - benefits for the unemployed are too high and discourage people from finding jobs?	27.2
(Neither)	6.6
Both because wages are low	0.7
Both, it varies	3.3
About right	0.6
Other answer	1.1
Don't know	4.1

CARD K

54. Suppose the government had to choose between the three options on this card. Which do you think it should choose?

Reduce taxes and spend less on health, education and social benefits	5.0
Keep taxes and spending on these services at the same level as now	37.3
Increase taxes and spend more on health, education and social benefits	50.7
(None)	3.0
(Don't know)	4.0

CARD L

55. All in all, how satisfied or dissatisfied would you say you are with the way in which the National Health Service runs nowadays? Choose a phrase from this card.

Very satisfied	6.1
Quite satisfied	38.8
Neither satisfied nor dissatisfied	17.4
Quite dissatisfied	20.3
Very dissatisfied	17.4
Don't know	0.1

CARD L AGAIN

56. From your own experience, or from what you have heard, please say how satisfied or dissatisfied you are with the way in which each of these parts of the National Health Service runs nowadays?
READ OUT i-vi BELOW AND RING ONE CODE FOR EACH

	Very satisfied	Quite satisfied	Neither satisfied nor dis- satisfied	Quite dis- satisfied	Very dis- satisfied	D/K
i) First, local doctors/ GPs?	30.9	48.9	7.7	7.8	4.7	0.0
ii) National Health Service dentists?	20.0	55.4	12.1	7.9	2.7	1.7
iii) Health visitors?	17.5	39.7	21.9	6.1	2.2	12.2
iv) District nurses?	23.1	42.5	20.5	2.8	0.9	10.0
v) Being in hospital as an inpatient?	33.6	42.0	12.5	5.5	2.5	3.9
vi) Attending hospital as an outpatient?	22.7	42.1	9.9	15.6	7.0	2.6

18

NI

57.a) Are you covered by a private health insurance scheme, that is an insurance scheme that allows you ro get private medical treatment? FOR EXAMPLE: BUPA and PPP

		Skip to
Yes	6.2	b)
No	93.7	Q.58

IF YES AT a)

b) Does your employer (or your husband's/wife's employer) pay the majority of the cost of membership of this scheme?

Yes	2.7
No	3.1
Don't know	0.2

ASK ALL

58.a) Do you think that the existence of private medical treatment in National Health Service hospitals is a good or bad thing for the National Health Service, or doesn't it make any difference to the NHS?

Good thing	21.1
Bad thing	44.5
No difference	28.9
Don't know	5.5

b) And do you think the existence of private medical treatment in private hospitals is a good thing or bad thing for the National Health Service, or doesn't it make any difference to the NHS?

Good thing	33.6
Bad thing	18.9
No difference	39.4
Don't know	7.1

CARD M

59. Which of the views on this card comes closest to your own views about private medical treatment in hospitals?

Private medical treatment in all hospitals should be abolished	13.2
Private medical treatment should be allowed in private hospitals, but not in National Health Service hospitals	45.6
Private medical treatment should be allowed in both private and National Health Service hospitals	37.0
(Don't know)	3.9

60.a) Now thinking of GPs and dentists.
Do you think that National Health Service GPs should or should not be free to take on private patients?

	Should	Should not	(Don't know)
	54.7	40.8	4.4

b) And do you think that National Health Service dentists should or should not be free to give private treatment?

	Should	Should not	
	60.8	33.7	5.4

61. It has been suggested that the National Health Service should be available only to those with lower incomes. This would mean that contributions and taxes could be lower and most people would then take out medical insurance or pay for health care. Do you support or oppose this idea?

Support	26.5
Oppose	66.9
(Don't know)	6.6

NI

ASK ALL

65.a) Do you regard yourself as belonging to any particular religion?
IF YES: Which?
CODE ONE ONLY - DO NOT PROMPT

	%	Skip to
No religion	11.8	b)
Christian - no denomination	1.7	
Roman Catholic	35.8	
Church of Ireland/Anglican	17.5	
Baptist	1.6	
Methodist	4.0	
Presbyterian	22.2	c)
Free Presbyterian	0.8	
Brethren	0.4	
Other Protestant (**WRITE IN:**)	1.5	
Other Christian (**WRITE IN:**)	0.6	
Hindu	-	
Jewish	-	
Muslim	-	
Sikh	-	
Buddhist	0.1	
United Reformed/Congregational	0.3	
Other non-Christian (**WRITE IN:**)		
Refused/unwilling to say	1.8	Q.66

IF NO RELIGION (CODE 01 AT a)   N = 110

b) In what religion were you brought up?
PROBE IF NECESSARY: What was your family's religion?

	%	Skip to
No religion	4.9	Q.66
Christian - no denomination	2.0	
Roman Catholic	22.5	
Church of Ireland/Anglican	30.4	
Baptist	0.0	
Methodist	7.8	
Presbyterian	30.4	c)
Free Presbyterian	0.0	
Brethren	0.0	
Hindu	-	
Jewish	-	
Muslim	-	
Sikh	-	
Buddhist	-	
Other non-Christian (**WRITE IN:**)		
Other Protestant (**WRITE IN:**)		
Other Christian (**WRITE IN:**)		
Refused/unwilling to say	1.0	Q.66

IF ANY RELIGION AT a) OR b) ASK c) - OTHERS SKIP TO Q.66   N = 860

c) Apart from such special occasions as weddings, funerals and baptisms, how often nowadays do you attend services or meetings connected with your religion?
PROBE AS NECESSARY

	%
Once a week or more	54.2
Less often but at least once in two weeks	6.3
Less often but at least once a month	8.5
Less often but at least twice a year	6.0
Less often but at least once a year	2.1
Less often	3.2
Never or practically never	16.4
Varies too much to say	0.4
Refused/unwilling to answer	2.3

NI

62. Some people think it is best for secondary schoolchildren to be separated into grammar and secondary intermediate schools according to how well they have done when they leave primary school. Others think it is best for secondary schoolchildren not to be separated in this way, and to attend comprehensive schools.

On balance, which system do you think provides the best all-round education for secondary schoolchildren ... **READ OUT** ...

	%
... a system of grammar and secondary intermediate schools,	51.9
or - a system of comprehensive schools?	40.3
Other (**WRITE IN**)	0.7
(Don't know)	7.0

SECTION FOUR

63.a) Now moving on to the subject of social class.
To what extent do you think a person's social class affects his or her opportunities today ... **READ OUT** ...

	%
... a great deal,	29.6
quite a lot,	34.3
not very much,	27.4
or - not at all?	5.9
Other answer (**WRITE IN**)	0.2
Don't know	2.6

b) Do you think social class is more or less important now in affecting a person's opportunities than it was 10 years ago, or has there been no real change?

	%
More important now	28.6
Less important now	30.4
No change	38.0
Don't know	2.9

c) Do you think that in 10 years' time social class will be more or less important than it is now in affecting a person's opportunities, or will there be no real change?

	%
More important in 10 years' time	25.1
Less important in 10 years' time	27.5
No change	44.1
Don't know	3.2

CARD N

64.a) Most people see themselves as belonging to a particular social class. Please look at this card and tell me which social class you would say you belong to? **RECORD ANSWER IN COL a)**

b) And which social class would you say your parents belonged to when you started at primary school? **RECORD ANSWER IN COL b)**

	(a) Self	(b) Parents
Upper middle	1.2	1.6
Middle	23.4	18.7
Upper working	17.3	11.9
Working	51.9	58.4
Poor	4.2	7.9
(Don't know)	1.9	1.2

21

NI

ASK ALL

66.a) Some people say there is very little real poverty in the U.K. today. Others say there is quite a lot. Which comes closest to your view ... **READ OUT** ...

... that there is very little real poverty in the U.K. 35.5
or - that there is quite a lot? 62.7
(Don't know) 1.8

b) Over the last ten years, do you think that poverty in the U.K. has been increasing, decreasing or staying at about the same level?

Increasing 49.0
Decreasing 19.6
Staying at same level 28.6
(Don't know) 2.3

c) And over the next ten years, do you think that poverty in the U.K. will ... **READ OUT** ...

... increase, 47.5
decrease, 16.7
or - stay at about the same level? 29.7
(Don't know) 5.6

67. Would you say someone in the U.K. was or was not in poverty ... **READ OUT EACH STATEMENT BELOW AND CODE FOR EACH** ...

	Was	Was not	(Don't know)
a) ... they had enough to buy the things they really needed, but not enough to buy the things most people take for granted?	27.9	69.3	2.8
b) ... they had enough to eat and live, but not enough to buy other things they needed?	62.1	35.6	2.3
c) ... they had not got enough to eat and live without getting into debt?	92.6	6.0	1.5

CARD O

68. Why do you think there are people who live in need? Of the four views on this card, which one comes closest to your own?

CODE ONE ONLY

Because they have been unlucky 11.9
Because of laziness or lack of willpower 17.7
Because of injustice in our society 24.8
It's an inevitable part of modern life 39.5
(None of these) 1.2
Other (**WRITE IN**) _____ 2.2
(Don't know) 2.3

69. How often do you and your household feel poor nowadays ... **READ OUT** ...

... never, 38.0
every now and then, 45.8
often, 8.3
or - almost all the time? 7.2
(Don't know) 0.7

NI

SECTION FIVE

70. Do you think that divorce in Northern Ireland should be ... **READ OUT** ...

... easier to obtain than it is now, 15.7
more difficult, 32.5
or - should things remain as they are? 45.6
(Don't know) 6.3

CARD P

71. Now I would like to ask you some questions about sexual relationships.

a) If a man and a woman have sexual relations before marriage, what would your general opinion be? Please choose a phrase from this card. **RECORD IN COL a)**

b) What about a married person having sexual relations with someone other than his or her partner? Please choose a phrase from this card. **RECORD IN COL b)**

c) What about sexual relations between two adults of the same sex? Please choose a phrase from this card. **RECORD IN COL c)**

	(a) BEFORE MARRIAGE	(b) EXTRA MARITAL	(c) SAME SEX
Always wrong	30.0	77.1	76.0
Mostly wrong	13.3	13.3	6.0
Sometimes wrong	15.4	4.6	5.1
Rarely wrong	7.8	0.7	2.0
Not wrong at all	24.4	0.7	5.1
Depends/varies	8.0	2.6	4.7
Don't know	0.2	0.2	0.3

72.a) Now I would like you to tell me whether, in your opinion, it is acceptable for a homosexual person ... **READ OUT EACH ITEM AND CODE FOR EACH**

	Yes	No	Other answer	Don't know
i) ... to be a teacher in a school?	35.1	54.9	6.3	2.7
ii) ... to be a teacher in a college or university?	44.2	49.0	4.1	2.3
iii) ... to hold a responsible position in public life?	47.8	44.7	2.6	3.7

b) What did you understand the word "homosexual" to mean at this question: ... **READ OUT** ...

... men only - that is, gays 30.9
women only - that is, lesbians 0.1
or - either? 67.8
Don't know 0.5

c) Do you think female homosexual couples - that is, lesbians - should be allowed to adopt a baby under the same conditions as other couples?

Yes 11.1
No 85.6
Others 0.6
Don't know 1.9

d) And do you think male homosexual couples - that is, gays - should be allowed to adopt a baby under the same conditions as other couples?

Yes 5.4
No 92.1
Others 0.7
Don't know 1.1

NI

SECTION SIX

73. Now some questions on food.

ASK a) to e) ABOUT EACH LISTED FOOD BEFORE GOING TO ASK ABOUT THE NEXT.

IF NAMED FOOD EATEN AT ALL (CODES 1-5 AT a), SKIP TO c).	IF NAMED FOOD NEVER EATEN, (CODE 1 AT b), ASK ABOUT NEXT FOOD.

CARD Q OR R

a) How often do you eat _____ (FOOD) nowadays?

ALL OTHERS: ASK b)

b) Have you never eaten _____, or have you cut it/them out in the last 2 or 3 years or longer ago?

IF FOOD CUT OUT AT b) (CODES 2 OR 3 AT b), SKIP TO e).

ALL OTHERS: ASK c)

c) Are you eating about the same amount as you did 2 or 3 years ago, or more _____, or less _____?

RECORD UNDER a) BELOW   RECORD UNDER b) BELOW   RECORD UNDER c) BELOW

CARD Q	(a)						(b)			(c)		
	EVERY DAY	4-6 DAYS A WEEK	2-3 DAYS A WEEK	ABOUT ONCE A WEEK	LESS OFTEN	NEVER NOWADAYS	NEVER EATEN	CUT OUT IN LAST 2 OR 3 YEARS	CUT OUT LONGER AGO	ABOUT THE SAME AMOUNT	MORE	LESS
PROCESSED MEAT LIKE SAUSAGES, HAM OR TINNED MEAT	7.5	7.8	33.0	33.3	11.8	6.6	27.7	29.4	39.5	63.4	6.0	30.5
BEEF, LAMB OR PORK	4.5	12.9	44.5	28.3	5.9	3.6	3.7	46.4	27.5	73.1	4.8	21.4
EGGS	10.3	7.8	26.1	20.2	17.5	17.8	23.6	55.6	11.1	66.0	2.9	26.9
FISH	0.7	1.5	15.5	43.2	29.2	9.6	54.2	19.0	18.4	76.5	12.2	10.3
CHIPS OR ROAST POTATOES	3.6	7.3	30.0	31.7	16.3	11.1	33.9	34.8	16.7	71.2	5.5	22.9
FRESH FRUIT AND VEGETABLE	62.6	14.6	13.6	4.7	2.8	1.5	51.7	31.0	6.9	73.2	22.8	3.5
BISCUITS, PASTRIES & CAKES	46.2	8.4	17.6	10.7	9.7	7.4	27.6	39.8	24.8	72.2	5.8	21.2

CARD R	5 OR MORE SLICES A DAY	3-4 SLICES A DAY	1-2 SLICES A DAY	4-6 SLICES A WEEK	LESS OFTEN	NEVER NOWADAYS	NEVER EATEN	CUT OUT IN LAST 2 OR 3 YEARS	CUT OUT LONGER AGO	ABOUT THE SAME AMOUNT	MORE	LESS
BREAD	22.9	31.4	31.2	6.4	2.6	0.8	3.3	3.8	4.4	72.7	4.1	18.7

N.B. For Qs.73 b-e, responses are percentaged on all those asked each question.

187

NI

d) (Is)/(Are) _____ good for people, bad for people or neither?

IF EATEN MORE OR LESS (CODES 2 OR 3 AT c), SKIP TO e).	

ALL OTHERS: ASK d), THEN GO TO NEXT FOOD.

ASK e) ABOUT ANY FOOD CUT OUT (CODE 2 OR 3 AT b) OR EATEN MORE OR LESS (CODE 2 OR 3 AT c)

CARD S

e) You said that you had changed the amount of _____ you eat. Have you changed for any of these reasons? PROBE UNTIL 'NO': Any other of these reasons?

RECORD UNDER d) BELOW   RECORD UNDER e) BELOW

	(d)			(e)								
	GOOD FOR PEOPLE	BAD FOR PEOPLE	NEITHER	TO HELP CONTROL MY WEIGHT	I WAS TOLD TO FOR MEDICAL REASONS	IT IS GOOD VALUE FOR MONEY	IT IS POOR VALUE FOR MONEY	I WANTED TO KEEP HEALTHY	I JUST LIKE IT MORE	I JUST DON'T LIKE IT AS MUCH	NONE OF THESE REASONS	
PROCESSED MEAT LIKE SAUSAGES, HAM OR TINNED MEAT	24.7	19.3	52.1	7.7	10.2	2.6	3.0	37.5	6.6	17.0	10.3	
BEEF, LAMB OR PORK	55.3	7.1	32.3	5.0	9.2	1.7	11.5	31.7	5.3	12.4	20.2	
EGGS	63.0	5.5	21.2	1.5	10.2	1.0	-	34.1	4.8	15.6	18.6	
FISH	87.8	0.1	6.9	2.9	9.2	3.7	4.2	27.0	11.9	19.1	19.8	
CHIPS OR ROAST POTATOES	17.4	49.2	28.0	14.5	11.8	9.2	-	39.6	6.6	9.9	11.8	
FRESH FRUIT AND VEGETABLE	92.9	1.4	5.7	6.8	11.6	1.2	1.0	55.4	8.9	5.8	8.9	
BISCUITS, PASTRIES & CAKES	14.5	52.7	27.4	25.7	12.9	0.4	4.0	24.3	12.8	11.2	10.4	

	GOOD FOR PEOPLE	BAD FOR PEOPLE	NEITHER	TO HELP CONTROL MY WEIGHT	I WAS TOLD TO FOR MEDICAL REASONS	IT IS GOOD VALUE FOR MONEY	IT IS POOR VALUE FOR MONEY	I WANTED TO KEEP HEALTHY	I JUST LIKE IT MORE	I JUST DON'T LIKE IT AS MUCH	NONE OF THESE REASONS	
BREAD	56.8	2.5	27.5	22.5	7.4	0.4	0.4	18.3	6.4	12.1	17.9	

N.B. For Qs.A73 b-e, responses are percentaged on all those asked each question.

NI

ASK ALL

74.a) Do you ever take sugar in hot drinks nowadays?			Skip to
	Yes	44.8	b)
	No	55.2	Q.75

IF YES AT a)

b) Are you taking about the same amount as you did two or three years ago, or more sugar in hot drinks, or less?

About the same amount	30.6	
More	1.2	
Less	12.7	

ASK ALL

75.a) Do you ever eat sweets or chocolates nowadays?			Skip to
	Yes	79.7	b)
	No	20.3	Q.76

IF YES AT a)

b) Are you eating about the same amount as you did two or three years ago, or more sweets and chocolates or less?

About the same amount	38.0
More	5.6
Less	35.2

ASK ALL

76. Compared with two or three years ago, would you say you are now ...

READ OUT EACH STATEMENT IN TURN

	Yes	No	(Don't know)
a) ... using more low fat spreads or soft margarine instead of butter, or not?	65.6	34.1	0.0
b) ... eating more grilled food instead of fried food, or not?	68.1	31.4	0.2
c) ... eating more fish and poultry instead of red meat, or not?	44.2	55.6	0.2
d) ... drinking or using more semi-skimmed or skimmed milk instead of full cream milk, or not?	37.8	61.6	0.3
e) ... eating more wholemeal bread instead of white bread, or not?	61.0	38.7	0.1
f) ... eating more boiled or baked potatoes instead of chips or roast potatoes, or not?	66.7	33.2	0.1

26

NI

SECTION SEVEN

77. Now I would like to ask some questions about religious prejudice against both Catholics and Protestants in Northern Ireland.

a) First thinking of Catholics - do you think there is a lot of prejudice against them in Northern Ireland nowadays, a little, or hardly any?

A lot	32.6
A little	39.7
Hardly any	21.3
(Don't know)	5.8

b) Do you think there is generally more religious prejudice against Catholics now than there was 5 years ago, less, or about the same amount?

More now	20.4
Less now	24.9
About the same	50.0
Other	0.1
Don't know	3.4

c) Do you think there will be more, less, or about the same amount of religious prejudice against Catholics in 5 years time compared with now?

More in 5 years	15.0
Less	25.8
About the same	51.8
Other	0.4
Don't know	4.9

78.a) And now, thinking of Protestants - do you think there is a lot of prejudice against them in Northern Ireland nowadays, a little, or hardly any?

A lot	23.0
A little	43.6
Hardly any	26.6
(Don't know)	-

b) Do you think there is generally more religious prejudice against Protestants now than there was 5 years ago, less, or about the same amount?

More now	21.3
Less now	11.1
About the same	59.1
Other	-
Don't know	4.0

c) Do you think there will be more, less or about the same amount of religious prejudice against Protestants in 5 years time compared with now?

More in 5 years	17.2
Less	15.5
About the same	59.6
Other	0.8
Don't know	4.8

79. How would you describe yourself:
... READ OUT ...

... as very prejudiced against people of other religions,	1.8
A little prejudiced,	16.0
or - not prejudiced at all?	81.3
Other	0.1
Don't know	0.1

NI

32.a) And do you think most people in Northern Ireland would mind or not mind if one of their close relatives were to marry someone of a different religion? IF WOULD MIND: A lot or a little?

Would mind a lot	34.3
Would mind a little	32.7
Would not mind	28.3
(Don't know/can't say)	4.3

b) And you personally? Would you mind or not mind? IF WOULD MIND: A lot or a little?

Would mind a lot	15.5
Would mind a little	14.6
Would not mind	66.8
(Don't know/can't say)	1.8

CARD T

83.a) About how many of your friends would you say are the same religion as you - that is, Protestant or Catholic? Please choose an answer from this card.

PROBE AS NECESSARY: As far as you know?

All	16.1
Most	47.2
Half	26.0
Less than half	6.8
None	0.8
(Don't know)	0.6

CARD T AGAIN

b) What about your relatives, including relatives by marriage?

All	42.2
Most	41.2
Half	9.3
Less than half	5.4
None	1.1
(Don't know)	0.4

CARD T AGAIN

c) And what about your neighbours? As far as you know?

PROBE AS NECESSARY: As far as you know?

All	30.8
Most	31.0
Half	21.7
Less than half	7.5
None	1.2
(Don't know)	7.3

84. Were both your parents of the same religion, for instance both Catholic or both Protestant?

Yes	95.0
No	4.6
(Refused)	-
(Don't know)	0.1

NI

80.a) What about relations between Protestants and Catholics? Would you say they are better than they were 5 years ago, worse, or about the same now as then?

IF 'IT DEPENDS', PROBE BEFORE CODING

Better	21.8
Worse	27.4
About the same	47.0
Other answer (WRITE IN)	1.5
(Don't know)	2.0

b) And what about in 5 years time? Do you think relations between Protestants and Catholics will be better than now, worse than now, or about the same as now?

IF 'IT DEPENDS', PROBE BEFORE CODING

Better than now	25.9
Worse than now	16.1
About the same	52.7
Other answer (WRITE IN)	0.3
(Don't know)	4.6

c) Do you think that religion will always make a difference to the way people feel about each other in Northern Ireland?

Yes	86.7
No	3.4
Other answer (WRITE IN)	0.6
(Don't know)	3.7

81.a) Do you think most people in Northern Ireland would mind or not mind if a suitably qualified person of a different religion were appointed as their boss? IF WOULD MIND: A lot or a little?

Would mind a lot	11.5
Would mind a little	22.8
Would not mind	57.6
(Don't know/can't say)	7.7

b) And you personally? Would you mind or not mind? IF WOULD MIND: A lot or a little?

Would mind a lot	2.7
Would mind a little	4.0
Would not mind	91.9
(Don't know/can't say)	1.0

		Skip to

86.a) If you had a choice, would you prefer to live in a neighbourhood with people of _only your own religion_, or in a _mixed-religion neighbourhood?_

PROBE IF NECESSARY: Say if you were moving ...

Own religion only ...	22.7
Mixed religion neighbourhood	71.2
(Don't know)	5.1

b) And if you were working and had to change your job, would you prefer a workplace with people of only your own religion, or a mixed-religion workplace?

PROBE IF NECESSARY: Say if you _did have a job_ ...

Own religion only	10.4
Mixed-religion workplace	84.0
(Don't know)	4.5

c) And if you were deciding where to send your children to school, would you prefer a school with children of _only_ your own religion, or a _mixed-religion school?_

PROBE IF NECESSARY: Say if you did have school-age children ...

Own religion only ...	36.9
Mixed-religion school	55.3
(Don't know)	7.3

87.a) On the whole, do you think the Protestants and Catholics in Northern Ireland who apply for the same jobs have the _same_ chance of getting a job or are their chances of getting a job different?

IF 'IT DEPENDS': On the whole ...

		Skip to
Same chance	47.7	
Different chance	41.8	
(Don't know/Can't say)	10.0	Q.88 b)

IF 'DIFFERENT' OR 'DON'T KNOW' AT a)

b) Which group is _more_ likely to get a job - Protestants or Catholics?

IF 'IT DEPENDS': On the whole ...

Protestants	31.3
Catholics	9.1
It depends	4.0
Don't know	4.2

c) Are they _much_ more likely or just _a bit_ more likely to get a job?

Much more	14.3
Bit more	25.6
(Don't know/Can't say)	9.0

CARD U

For each of the next questions, please use this card to say whether you think _Catholics_ are treated better than Protestants in Northern Ireland, or whether _Protestants_ are treated better than Catholics, or whether both are treated equally.

READ OUT EACH ITEM AND CODE ONE FOR EACH

	Catholics treated much better	Catholics treated a bit better	Both treated equally	Protestants treated a bit better	Protestants treated much better	It depends/ Don't know/ Can't say	Skip to
a) First, the National Health Service in Northern Ireland. How does it treat Catholic and Protestant patients?	2.3	2.7	89.3	1.3	0.1	3.7	
b) What about the Northern Ireland Housing executive - how does it treat Catholics and Protestants who apply for a home?	3.9	7.6	67.0	6.2	1.9	13.0	
c) What about your local district council - how does it treat Catholics and Protestants who apply for jobs?	2.5	5.4	50.0	14.0	6.0	21.5	
d) And what about central government in Stormont - how do they treat Catholics and Protestants who apply for jobs?	2.6	8.7	51.7	11.5	5.1	19.5	
e) What about government schemes for the unemployed - how do they treat Catholics and Protestants who apply for places?	2.8	5.4	74.7	2.3	0.7	13.4	
f) And the RUC - how do they treat Catholic and Protestant members of the public?	0.5	2.0	56.3	19.4	11.7	9.6	
g) What about the army - how do they treat Catholic and Protestant members of the public?	-	0.8	60.7	18.4	8.4	11.2	
h) And the Ulster Defence Regiment - how do they treat Catholic and Protestant members of the public?	0.1	0.1	44.4	25.1	16.8	12.9	
i) And the courts - how do they treat Catholics and Protestants accused of committing non-terrorist offences?	0.2	1.6	82.1	4.5	2.6	8.4	
j) And how do the courts treat Catholics and Protestants accused of committing terrorist offences?	1.3	4.3	71.1	6.7	8.3	7.8	

ASK ALL

Now I'm going to ask separately about employment chances of Protestants and Catholics.

8.a) Some people think that many employers are <u>more</u> likely to give jobs to Protestants than to Catholics. Do you think this happens
... **READ OUT** ...

		Skip to
... a lot,	14.4	} b)
a little,	47.9	
or - hardly at all?	28.9	Q.89
(Don't know)	8.3	

IF 'IT DEPENDS': In <u>general</u>, what would you say?

IF 'A LOT' OR 'A LITTLE' AT a)

b) Why do you think this happens? Do you think it is <u>mainly</u> because employers discriminate against Catholics or mainly because Catholics are not as well qualified as Protestants?

IF 'BOTH', PROBE BEFORE CODING

Mainly because employers discriminate	48.4
Mainly because Catholics aren't qualified	4.7
Both (AFTER PROBE)	3.6
(Don't know/Can't say)	5.5

ASK ALL

89.a) Some people think that many employers are <u>more</u> likely to give jobs to Catholics than to Protestants. Do you think this happens
... **READ OUT** ...

		Skip to
... a lot,	9.5	} b)
a little,	44.5	
or - hardly at all?	35.5	Q.90
(Don't know)	10.1	

IF 'IT DEPENDS': In <u>general</u>, what would you say?

IF 'A LOT' OR 'A LITTLE' AT a)

b) Why do you think this happens? Do you think it is <u>mainly</u> because employers discriminate against Protestants, or mainly because Protestants are not as well qualified as Catholics?

IF 'BOTH', PROBE BEFORE CODING

Mainly because employers discriminate	42.9
Mainly because Protestants aren't qualified	2.6
Both (AFTER PROBE)	3.1
(Don't kno-/Can't say)	5.1

90.a) Some people say that all employers should keep records on the religion of their employees to make sure there is no discrimination. Other people say this is not necessary. What about you - do you think employers <u>should</u> or <u>should not</u> keep records about their employees' religion?

		Skip to
Should	25.8	b)
Should <u>not</u>	68.6	
(Don't know/Can't say)	5.1	c)

IF SHOULD OR SHOULD NOT AT a)

b) Do you feel this way strongly or just a bit?

		Skip to
Strongly	59.7	
Just a bit	13.3	} c)

ASK ALL

c) Do you generally support or oppose a <u>fair employment law</u> in Northern Ireland, that is a law which <u>requires</u> employers to keep records on the religion of their employees and make sure there is no discrimination?

		Skip to
Support	50.7	} d)
Oppose	39.6	
(Don't know/Can't say)	9.2	Q.91

IF SUPPORT OR OPPOSE AT c)

d) Do you (support/oppose) it strongly, or just a bit?

Strongly	56.4
Just a bit	31.4

ASK ALL

91. And thinking about education ...

First, about mixed or integrated schooling - that is, schools with fairly large numbers of both Catholic and Protestant children: do you think the government should <u>encourage</u> mixed schooling, <u>discourage</u> mixed schooling or leave things as they are?

Encourage it	63.5
Discourage it	6.2
Leave things as they are	29.3
Don't know	0.3

NI
ASK ALL

94.a) Generally speaking, do you think of yourself as a supporter of any one political party?

		Skip to
Yes	34.9	d)
No	64.6	b)

IF NOT AT a)
b) Do you think of yourself as a little closer to one political party than to the others?

		Skip to
Yes	23.6	d)
No	41.0	c)

IF NO AT b)
c) If there were a general election tomorrow, which political party do you think you would be most likely to support? **CODE ONE ONLY UNDER c & d)**
IF MAINLAND ALLIANCE, PROBE: Social and Liberal Democrat or SDP (Owen)?

IF YES AT a) OR b)
d) Which one? **CODE ONE ONLY UNDER c & d)**
IF MAINLAND ALLIANCE, PROBE: Social and Liberal Democrat or SDP (Owen)?

IF MAINLAND PARTY NAMED AT c) OR d)
e) If there were a general election in which only Northern Ireland parties were standing, which one do you think you would be most likely to support?

CODE ONE ONLY UNDER e)

	c & d)	e)	Skip to
Conservative	18.6	e)	
Labour	6.8	e)	
Social and Liberal Democrat/Liberal/SLD	0.7	e)	
SDP/Social Democrat	0.6	e)	
(Mainland) Alliance (AFTER PROBE)	0.3	e)	
Alliance (NI)	4.6	9.3	
DUP/Democratic Unionist Party	7.0	10.8	
OUP/Official Unionist Party/Ulster Unionist Party	17.5	27.2	
Other Unionist	0.7	1.2	
Sinn Fein	2.7	2.7	f)
SDLP	14.9	16.8	
Workers Party	2.2	3.1	
Campaign for Equal Citizenship	0.4	0.4	
Other party (WRITE IN)	0.1	0.3	
Other answer (WRITE IN)	0.3	0.3	
None	17.3	19.6	Q.95
Refused/unwilling to say	4.4	5.6	Q.95
D/K	0.5	0.8	

IF ANY NORTHERN IRELAND PARTY CODED AT c) & d) OR e)
f) Would you call yourself very strong ... (QUOTE PARTY NAMED) ... fairly strong, or not very strong?

Very strong	7.9
Fairly strong	22.2
Not very strong	41.2
Don't know	0.3

NI
CARD W

92 Please use this card to say whether you think that Protestants or Catholics in Northern Ireland have a better chance ...

READ OUT EACH ITEM AND CODE FOR EACH

	Catholics have a much better chance	Catholics have a slightly better chance	Both groups have equal chances	Protestants have a slightly better chance	Protestants have a much better chance	(Don't know/can't say)	Skip to
a) ... to go to a good primary school?	0.8	2.7	89.9	3.0	0.3	2.3	
b) ... how about chances to go to a good secondary intermediate school?	0.7	2.7	88.5	4.5	1.1	2.1	
c) ... and chances to go to a good grammar school?	0.8	2.7	85.4	6.9	1.7	2.1	
d) ... and chances to go to university?	1.6	2.8	89.1	2.7	1.1	2.3	

NI
CARD X

91 All pupils in state secondary schools study certain subjects - like English and maths. For each subject I read out, please tell me whether you agree or disagree that all secondary school pupils should have to study it ...

READ a)-g) AND CODE ONE FOR EACH

	Strongly agree	Agree	Neither agree nor disagree	Disagree	Strongly disagree	(Don't know)	Skip to
a) ... the history of Northern Ireland?	25.9	45.4	9.7	14.5	2.5	1.5	
b) ... British history?	18.4	54.8	11.2	12.0	1.6	1.6	
c) ... the history of the Republic of Ireland?	14.6	43.3	11.9	21.9	5.8	1.8	
d) ... Irish language and culture?	7.8	23.4	15.5	35.6	14.1	3.1	
e) ... Protestant religious beliefs?	7.0	34.5	16.9	30.4	6.5	3.2	
f) ... Catholic religious beliefs?	7.0	33.8	15.9	31.5	8.3	2.8	
g) ... non-denominational religious beliefs - not specifically Catholic or Protestant?	7.4	38.7	19.1	25.8	4.7	3.9	

35

NI
ASK ALL
CARD Y

95. a) Which of these best describes the way you usually think of yourself?

British	44.3
Irish	25.0
Ulster	6.9
Northern Irish	20.0
(Sometimes British, sometimes Irish) Other	3.1
Other	0.1
Don't know	0.2

b) When there is an argument between Britain and the Republic of Ireland, do you generally find yourself on the side of the British or of the Irish governments? IF 'IT DEPENDS', PROBE BEFORE CODING

Generally British govt.	50.6
Generally Irish govt.	14.2
It depends (AFTER PROBE)	19.8
(Neither)	9.6
(Don't know/Can't say)	5.2

96. At any time in the next 20 years, do you think it is likely or unlikely that there will be a united Ireland? PROBE: Very (likely/unlikely) or quite (likely/unlikely)?

Very likely	4.6
Quite likely	18.4
Quite unlikely	25.0
Very unlikely	40.4
(Even chance)	3.4
(Don't know)	7.9

CARD Z

97. a) Under direct rule from Britain, as now, how much do you generally trust British Governments of any party to act in the best interests of Northern Ireland? CODE ONE ONLY UNDER COL a) BELOW

b) If there was self-rule, how much do you think you would generally trust a Stormont government to act in the best interests of Northern Ireland? CODE ONE ONLY UNDER COL b) BELOW

c) And if there was a united Ireland, how much do you think you would generally trust an Irish government to act in the best interests of Northern Ireland? CODE ONE ONLY UNDER COL c) BELOW

	(a) British govt.	(b) Stormont govt.	(c) Irish govt.
Just about always	3.9	10.9	2.5
Most of the time	20.9	35.1	16.4
Only some of the time	39.5	26.4	29.1
Rarely	20.3	11.5	19.7
Never	10.6	9.0	22.2
(Don't know/can't say)	4.4	6.5	9.4

36

SECTION EIGHT

NI
ASK ALL
CARD AA

98. Now, a few questions on housing. First, in general how satisfied or dissatisfied are you with your own (house/flat)? Choose a phrase from the card.

Very satisfied	43.6
Quite satisfied	44.4
Neither satisfied nor dissatisfied	3.3
Quite dissatisfied	5.0
Very dissatisfied	3.7

99. a) How about the area you live in? Taking everything into account, would you say this area has got better, worse or remained about the same as a place to live during the last two years? RECORD IN COL a) BELOW

b) And what do you think will happen during the next two years: will this area get better, worse or remain about the same as a place to live? RECORD IN COL b)

	(a) Last 2 years	(b) Next 2 years
Better	18.8	17.4
Worse	17.0	9.5
About the same	63.5	69.3
Don't know	0.6	3.1

100. Does your household own or rent this accommodation? PROBE AS NECESSARY
IF OWN: Outright or on a mortgage?
IF RENTS: From whom?

Owns:	Own (leasehold/freehold) outright	31.9
	Buying (leasehold/freehold) on mortgage	33.9
Rents:	Housing Executive	27.7
	Housing Association	1.1
	Property company	0.7
	Employer	0.4
	Other organisation	0.2
	Relative	-
	Other individual	2.7
Rent free:	Rent free, squatting, etc.	0.7

101. CODE FROM OBSERVATION AND CHECK WITH RESPONDENT
Would I be right in describing this accommodation as a ....

Detached house or bungalow	34.7
Semi-detached house or bungalow	24.3
Terraced house	36.6
Self-contained, purpose-built flat/maisonette (inc. in tenement block)	2.8
Self-contained converted flat/maisonette	1.5
Room(s) - not self-contained	-
Other (WRITE IN:)	-

NI
CARD CC

104. Please look at this card and tell me whether ....
READ OUT a)-c) BELOW AND CODE FOR EACH

	Definitely should	Probably should	Probably should not	Definitely should not	(Don't know)	Skip to
a) .. employers should or should not have the legal right to dismiss people who have AIDS?	19.4	22.3	23.4	22.9	6.3	
b) .. doctors and nurses should or should not have the legal right to refuse to treat people who have AIDS?	11.8	18.2	26.2	38.7	4.6	
c) .. schools should or should not have the legal right to expel children who have AIDS?	9.2	20.4	24.7	38.5	6.7	

105. I am going to read out two statements. For each one, please say whether you agree or disagree.

	(a) Sympathy	(b) Research
a) 'People who have AIDS get much less sympathy from society than they ought to get.' Do you agree or disagree? Strongly or a little? CODE ONE IN COL a)		
Strongly agree	26.9	22.3
Agree a little	33.1	23.7
Disagree a little	17.3	25.3
Strongly disagree	14.8	24.0
(Don't know)	6.6	4.2
b) 'More money should be spent trying to find a cure for AIDS, even if it means that research into other serious diseases is delayed.' Do you agree or disagree? Strongly or a little? CODE ONE IN COL b)		

NI

102. And how long have you lived in your present home?
PROBE AS NECESSARY

		Skip to
Less than 1 year	5.5	
1 year, less than 2 years	5.2	
2 years, less than 5 years	17.0	
5 years, less than 10 years	17.5	
10 years, less than 20 years	25.2	
20 years or more	29.6	

SECTION NINE

103. Now I'd like to ask you about the disease called AIDS. I'm going to read out a list of different kinds of people.

CARD BB
Please choose a phrase from this card to tell you how much at risk you think each of these groups is from AIDS ...
READ OUT AND CODE ITEMS a)-h)

	Greatly at risk	Quite a lot at risk	Not very much at risk	Not at all at risk	(Don't know)
a) ... People who have sex with many different partners of the opposite sex.	70.8	24.5	2.1	-	2.0
b) ... Married couples who have sex only with each other.	0.4	0.5	14.9	81.7	1.8
c) ... Married couples who occasionally have sex with someone other than their regular partner.	13.1	49.3	31.7	1.6	3.7
d) ... People who have a blood transfusion	13.3	25.5	42.5	14.1	4.1
e) ... Doctors and nurses who treat people who have AIDS.	9.3	25.1	41.4	19.3	3.9
f) ... Male homosexuals - that is, gays.	82.0	14.3	0.4	-	2.5
g) ... Female homosexuals - that is, lesbians.	55.9	16.7	11.9	5.6	9.2
h) ... People who inject themselves with drugs using shared needles.	90.4	7.5	-	-	1.6

ASK ALL

902. Apart from people you've just mentioned who live in your household, have you had any (other) children, including stepchildren, who grew up in your household?

NB: INCLUDES CHILDREN NO LONGER LIVING

		Skip to
Yes	34.5	
No	65.6	

902a) Did you ever attend a mixed or integrated school, that is, with fairly large numbers of both Catholic and Protestant children?

IF YES: In Northern Ireland or somewhere else?

Yes - in Northern Ireland	21.1	
Yes, somewhere else	2.7	
No, did not	75.9	
Don't know	0.2	

IF RESPONDENT HAS CHILD(REN) AGED 5 OR OLDER IN HOUSEHOLD (SEE GRID) ASK b). OTHERS GO TO Q.904

b) And have any of your children ever attended a mixed or integrated school, with fairly large numbers of both Catholic and Protestants attending?

IF YES: In Northern Ireland or somewhere else?

Yes - in Northern Ireland	10.2	
Yes, somewhere else	0.5	
No, have not	35.2	
Don't know	-	

ASK ALL

904a) INTERVIEWER: IS THIS A SINGLE PERSON HOUSEHOLD - RESPONDENT ONLY AT Q.39 (p.39)?

		Skip to
YES	9.9	Q.905
NO	90.1	b)

IF NO AT a)

b) Who is the person mainly responsible for general domestic duties in this household?

Respondent mainly	38.8
Someone else mainly (WRITE IN RELATIONSHIP TO RESP.)	39.3
Duties shared equally (WRITE IN BY WHOM)	10.6

c) INTERVIEWER: IS THERE A CHILD UNDER 16 YEARS IN H.H? SEE HOUSEHOLD GRID, Q.901 (p.39)

		Skip to
YES	43.7	d)
NO	46.4	Q.905

IF YES AT c)

d) Who is the person mainly responsible for the general care of the child(ren) here?

Respondent mainly	20.3
Someone else mainly (WRITE IN RELATIONSHIP TO RES.)	17.0
Duties shared equally (WRITE IN BY WHOM)	5.6

SECTION 10

900a) Can I just check your own marital status? ... READ OUT ...

At present are you ...

		Skip to
... married,	63.7	
living as married,	1.0	
separated or divorced,	4.4	
widowed,	9.7	
or - not married?	21.3	

CODE FIRST TO APPLY

b) Finally, a few questions about you and your household. Including yourself, how many people live here regularly as members of this household?

CHECK INTERVIEWER MANUAL FOR DEFINITION OF HOUSEHOLD IF NECESSARY.

MEDIAN: 3

901. Now I'd like to ask for a few details about each person in your household. Starting with yourself, what was your age last birthday?

WORK DOWN COLUMNS OF GRID FOR EACH HOUSEHOLD MEMBER.

	Respondent	2	3	4	5	6	7	8	9	10
a) Sex: Male	47.5									
Female	52.5									
b) Age last birthday:										
c) Relationship to respondent:										
Spouse/partner										
Son/daughter										
Parent/parent-in law										
Other relative										
Not related										
d) HOUSEHOLD MEMBERS WITH LEGAL RESPONSIBILITY FOR ACCOMMODATION (INC. JOINT AND SHARED) Yes	74.7									
No	24.1									

* CHECK THAT NUMBER OF PEOPLE IN GRID EQUALS NUMBER GIVEN AT Q.900b)

195

NI

REFER TO ECONOMIC POSITION OF RESPONDENT (Q.20, page 7)

Top-right boxes: O.U.O. | O.C. | E.S. | S.E.G. | SC/NH.M | SIC | H-C

- If in paid work (CODE 03), ask Q.907 about **present (main)** job.
- If waiting to take up paid work (CODE 04), ask Q.907 about **future** job.
- If on govt. scheme (CODE 02), unemployed (CODES 05-07), permanently sick or disabled (CODE 08), retired (CODE 09), looking after the home (CODE 10), or doing something else (CODE 11) ask Q.907 about **last** job.
- If never had a job, write in at a), then go to Q.908.

907a) Now I want to ask you about your (*present/future/last*) job. **CHANGE TENSES FOR (BRACKETED) WORDS AS APPROPRIATE.**
What (*is*) your job? **PROBE AS NECESSARY**
What (*is*) the name or title of the job?

b) What kind of work (*do*) you do most of the time? **IF RELEVANT:** What materials/machinery (*do*) you use?

c) What training or qualifications (*are*) needed for that job?

d) (*Do*) you directly supervise or (*are*) you directly responsible for the work of any other people? **IF YES:** How many?
Yes: **WRITE IN NO.:**
No: **RING:** 0000

e) Can I just check: (*are*) you ... ... an employee,   79.6
or - self-employed?   11.3

IF EMPLOYEE (CODE 1) AT e)
CARD X2
f) Which of the types of organisation on this card (*do*) you work for?
Private firm or company   43.6
Nationalised industry/public corp.   5.8
District Authority/Education and Library Board   8.7
CODE FIRST TO APPLY
Health Board/NHS hospital   10.7
Central Government/Civil Service   7.6
Charity or Trust   1.1
Other (**SPECIFY**)   2.1

ASK ALL
g) What (*does*) your employer (**IF SELF-EMPLOYED:** you) make or do at the place where you usually (*work*)? **IF FARM, GIVE NO. OF ACRES**

h) Including yourself, how many people (*are*) employed at the place you usually (*work*) from?   (No employees)   7.5
IF SELF-EMPLOYED: (*Do*) you have any employees?
IF YES: How many?
Under 10   18.9
10-24   13.6
25-99   20.5
100-499   20.3
500 or more   9.0
D/K   0.9

NI
ASK ALL

905. How old were you when you completed your continuous full-time education? **PROBE AS NECESSARY**

		Skip to
15 or under	42.7	
16	26.5	
17	10.3	
18	7.9	
19 or over	10.1	
Still at school	0.5	
Still at college, polytechnic, or university	2.0	
Other answer (WRITE IN) ____	–	

906a) **CARD X1**
Have you passed any exams or got any of the qualifications on this card?

		Skip to
Yes	51.4	b)
No	48.6	Q.907

IF YES AT a)
b) Which ones? Any others?
CODE ALL THAT APPLY

		Skip to
CSE Grades 2-5		
CSE - Grades D-G	8.7	32-33
CSE Grade 1		
GCE 'O' level		
GCE - Grade A-C		
School certificate	34.4	34-35
Scottish (SCE) **Ordinary**		
Scottish School-leaving Certificate **lower grade**		
SUPE Ordinary		
Northern Ireland **Junior Certificate**		
GCE 'A' level/'S' level		
Higher school certificate		
Matriculation	15.5	36-37
Scottish SCE/SLC/SUPE at **Higher** grade		
Northern Ireland **Senior Certificate**		
Overseas School Leaving Exam/Certificate	0.2	38-39
Recognised trade apprenticeship completed	6.9	40-41
RSA/other clerical, commercial qualification	9.2	42-43
City & Guilds Certificate - Craft/Intermediate/Ordinary/Part I	4.5	44-45
City & Guilds Certificate - Advanced/Final/Part II or Part III	2.6	46-47
City & Guilds Certificate -- Full technological	0.7	48-49
BEC/TEC General/Ordinary National Certificate (ONC) or Diploma (OND)	1.8	50-51
BEC/TEC Higher/Higher National Certificate (HNC) or Diploma (HND)	1.5	52-53
Teacher training qualification	3.1	54-55
Nursing qualification	3.0	56-57
Other technical or business qualification/certificate	2.7	58-59
University or CNAA degree or diploma	5.6	60-61
Other (WRITE IN) ____	0.2	

43

NI

ASK ALL

908a) Are you now a member of a trade union or staff association?

		Skip to
Yes: trade union	18.4	
Yes: staff association	3.6	
No	77.4	c)

IF NO AT a)

b) Have you ever been a member of a trade union or staff association?

		Skip to
Yes: trade union	27.6	
Yes: staff association	1.6	b)
No	48.2	c)

IF NOW OR EVER A MEMBER (CODES 1 OR 2 AT a) OR b)

c) Have you ever ... **READ OUT AND RING ONE CODE FOR EACH**

	YES	NO	Skip to
... attended a union or staff association meeting?	32.7	18.4	
... voted in a union or staff association election or meeting?	27.9	23.2	
... put forward a proposal or motion at a union or staff association meeting?	12.5	38.6	
... gone on strike?	20.7	30.5	
... stood in a picket line?	9.1	42.0	
... served as a lay representative such as a shop steward or branch committee member?	6.8	44.2	Q.909

IF RESPONDENT IS MARRIED OR LIVING AS MARRIED (AT Q.900a), ASK Qs.909-911. OTHERS GO TO Q.912.

CARD X3

909.a) Which of these descriptions applied to what your (*husband/wife/partner*) was doing last week, that is the seven days ending last Sunday? PROBE: Any others? **CODE ALL THAT APPLY IN COL. I**

IF ONLY ONE CODE AT I, TRANSFER IT TO COL. II
IF MORE THAN ONE AT I, TRANSFER HIGHEST ON LIST TO II

	COL. I	COL. II ECONOMIC POSITION	Skip to
In full-time education (not paid for by employer, including on vacation)	A	0.1	
On government training/employment scheme (e.g. Employment Training, Youth Training Programme etc.)	B	-	
In paid work (or away temporarily) for at least 10 hours in the week	C	35.6	b)
Waiting to take up paid work already accepted	D	0.0	
Unemployed and registered at a benefit office	E	5.2	
Unemployed, not registered, but actively looking for a job	F	0.2	Q.910
Unemployed, wanting a job (of at least 10 hrs per week), but not actively looking for a job	G	0.4	
Permanently sick or disabled	H	1.5	
Wholly retired from work	J	6.6	b)
Looking after the home	K	14.8	
Doing something else (SPECIFY)	L	0.2	

IF CODES 01-02, OR 08-11 AT a)

b) How long ago did your (*husband/wife/partner*) last have a paid job (other than the government scheme you mentioned) of at least 10 hours a week?

		Skip to
Within past 12 months	2.6	Q.910
Over 1-5 years ago	6.3	
Over 5-10 years ago	5.2	
Over 10-20 years ago	3.7	
Over 20 years ago	3.1	
Never had a paid job of 10+ hours a week	2.0	Q.911

NI

REFER TO Q.909 = ACTIVITY OF SPOUSE/PARTNER:

- If spouse is in paid work (CODE 03) - Ask Q.910 about **present main** job.
- If spouse is **waiting to take up paid work** (CODE 04) - ask Q.910 about **future** job.
- If spouse is **unemployed** (CODES 05, 06 OR 07), or **retired** (CODE 09) or **looking after home** (CODE 10), or **doing something else** (CODES 01-02, 08, 11), ask Q.910 about **last** job

Now I want to ask you about your (*husband's/wife's/partner's*) job. CHANGE TENSES FOR (BRACKETED) WORDS AS APPROPRIATE

910a) What (*is*) the name or title of that job?

b) What kind of work (*does*) he/she do most of the time? IF RELEVANT: What materials/machinery (*does*) he/she use?

c) What training or qualifications (*are*) needed for that job?

d) (*Does*) he/she directly supervise or (*is*) he/she directly responsible for the work of any other people? **IF YES**: How many?

Yes: WRITE IN NO.:	
No: RING:	0000

e) (*Is*) he/she ... **READ OUT**

		Skip to
... an employee,	52.9	f)
or - self-employed?	9.0	g)

IF EMPLOYEE (CODE 1 AT e)
CARD X4

f) Which of the types of organisation on this card (*does*) he/she work for?

Private firm or company	26.3
Nationalised industry/public corporation	6.0
District Authority/Education and Library Board	7.8
Health Board/NHS hospital	5.6
Central Government/Civil Service	5.6
Charity or trust	0.7
Other (SPECIFY)	0.8

ASK ALL

g) What (*does*) the employer (**IF SELF-EMPLOYED**: he/she) make or do at the place where he/she usually (*works*)? **IF FARM GIVE NO. OF ACRES**

h) Including him/herself, roughly how many people (*are*) employed at the place where he/she usually (*works*) (*from*)?

(No employees)	6.0
Under 10	13.2
10-24	8.9
25-99	12.9
100-499	13.3
500 or more	6.4

IF SELF-EMPLOYED: he/she have any employees? **IF YES**: How many?

i) (*Is*) the job ... **READ OUT**

... full-time (30 HOURS+),	46.9	
or - part-time (10-29 HOURS)?	9.8	

O.U.O. O.C. E.S. S.E.G. SC/M.NM SIC H-C

NI

911. IF MARRIED OR LIVING AS MARRIED AT Q.900a)

And what about your spouse or partner: is (he/she) the same religion as you?
PROBE AS NECESSARY: That is, Protestant or Catholic?

		Skip to
Yes	60.2	
No	3.7	
Refused	0.6	

ASK ALL

912. Do you, or does anyone else in your household, own or have the regular use of a car or a van?

Yes	74.4
No	25.2

CARD X5

913. Have you or anyone in this household received any of the benefits on this card during the last five years?

IF YES: Which ones? Any others?
CODE ALL THAT APPLY

Child benefit (family allowance)	51.0
Maternity benefit or allowance	11.1
One-parent benefit	3.9
Family credit (family income supplement)	7.1
State retirement or widow's pension	27.0
State supplementary pension	4.4
Invalidity or disabled pension or benefit	11.8
Attendance/Invalid care/Mobility allowance	4.9
State Sickness or injury benefit	9.2
Unemployment benefit	22.6
Income support (supplementary benefit)	18.9
Rate or rent rebate or allowance	14.2
Other state benefit(s) volunteered (WRITE IN)	0.1
NONE	8.3

IF NO: CODE →

914a) Have you ever lived in mainland Britain for more than one year?

Yes	16.0
No	83.8

b) And have you ever lived in the Republic of Ireland for more than one year?

Yes	4.2
No	95.4

46

NI

CARD X6

915a) In the last 5 years, have you visited mainland Britain? IF YES: Please tell me from this card how often?

		Skip to
No, never visited	38.5	
Yes: Once only	17.0	
A few times	34.2	
Many times	9.2	
Lived there	0.8	

CARD X6 AGAIN

b) And in the last 5 years, have you visited the Republic of Ireland? IF YES: Please tell me from this card how often?

No, never visited	37.4
Yes: Once only	10.5
A few times	29.8
Many times	21.7
Lived there	0.3

916a) In the last 5 years, have you thought seriously about emigrating from Northern Ireland ... that is, leaving permanently? IF YES: How seriously have you thought about it ... READ OUT ...

		Skip to
YES: ... very seriously,	8.9	
fairly seriously,	10.4	
or - not very seriously?	7.9	b)
NO: (Never thought about it)	72.0	Q.917
(Don't know/Can't say)	0.4	

IF THOUGHT ABOUT EMIGRATING (CODES 1-3 AT a)

CARD X7

b) Which of these reasons is the main reason why you have thought about emigrating? Please choose the closest reason on the card.
CODE ONE ONLY

Family reasons	3.4
Unemployment	5.3
Fear or violence or crime	8.5
Standard of living	7.3
Health reasons	0.2
Other (AFTER PROBE)	1.9

ASK ALL

917a) Generally speaking, do you think of yourself as a unionist, a nationalist or neither?

		Skip to
Unionist	38.7	
Nationalist	15.4	b)
Neither	45.6	
(Don't know/Can't say)	0.6	Q.918

IF UNIONIST OR NATIONALIST AT a)

b) Would you call yourself a very strong ... (QUOTE ANSWER AT a) ... fairly strong, or not very strong?

Very strong	9.5
Fairly strong	21.1
Not very strong	23.0
Don't know	0.2

— 48 —

NI

922a) In addition to respondent, was anybody else aged 16 or older present during part or all of the interview?

		Skip to
Yes	31.0	
No	41.5	
N/A	27.4	

b) TIME INTERVIEW COMPLETED: WRITE IN: [ ] 24 hr. clock

c) TOTAL DURATION OF INTERVIEW: MINUTES [7 | 5] MEAN:

d) INTERVIEWER SIGNATURE AND NUMBER [0]

e) DATE OF INTERVIEW: DAY [ ] MONTH [0] YEAR [8 | 9]

PLEASE MAKE SURE THAT CASS AND CASS FLAP ARE COMPLETELY FILLED IN. DETACH CASS FLAP AND RETURN IN A5 ENVELOPES.

ATTACH REST OF CASS, MAIN QUESTIONNAIRE AND SELF-COMPLETION (IF POSSIBLE) AND RETURN IN A4 ENVELOPE — AS SOON AS POSSIBLE.

— 47 —

NI

ASK ALL

CARD X8

918a) Which of the letters on this card represents the total income of your household from all sources before tax? Please just tell me the letter.

NB: INCLUDES INCOME FROM BENEFITS, SAVINGS, ETC.

ONE CODE IN COLUMN a)

IF RESPONDENT IS IN PAID WORK (CODE 03 AT Q.20, p.7) ASK b). OTHERS GO TO Q.919

b) Which of the letters on this card represents your own gross or total earnings, before deduction of income tax and national insurance? ONE CODE IN COLUMN b)

N.B. On the questionnaire actually used, and on the show card, income bands were identified by a code letter.

	(a) House-hold Income	(b) Own Earn-ings
Less than £2,000	1.9	2.0
£2,000 – £2,999	7.3	2.4
£3,000 – £3,999	7.0	2.5
£4,000 – £4,999	9.4	4.8
£5,000 – £5,999	6.1	5.2
£6,000 – £6,999	5.0	5.4
£7,000 – £7,999	7.7	4.5
£8,000 – £9,999	6.8	5.2
£10,000 – £11,999	6.9	4.5
£12,000 – £14,999	6.6	4.5
£15,000 – £17,999	7.2	1.6
£18,000 – £19,999	3.5	0.6
£20,000 – £22,999	4.4	1.1
£23,000+	8.3	1.3
Don't know	9.4	0.4

919. Do you (or your husband/wife/partner) own any shares quoted on the Stock Exchange, including unit trusts?

		Skip to
Yes	13.9	
No	85.0	

ASK ALL

920. Is there a telephone in (your part of) this accommodation?

Yes	82.7
No	17.1

INTERVIEWER: THANK RESPONDENT FOR HIS OR HER HELP, AND COMPLETE Q.921–922.

92ia) The self-completion questionnaire: Was it:

... filled in immediately after interview in your presence	50.4
or ... left behind to be filled in later	40.1
or ... refused (WHY?) _____	9.5

b) COMPLETE Q.16 ON CASS ABOUT HOW YOU EXPECT SELF-COMPLETION QUESTIONNAIRE TO BE RETURNED.

Head Office 35 NORTHAMPTON SQUARE, LONDON EC1V 0AX TELEPHONE 01-250 1866 FAX 01-250 1524

Northern Field Office CHARDZEL HOUSE, GAINFORD, DARLINGTON, CO DURHAM DL2 3EG, TELEPHONE 0325-730888

NORTHERN IRELAND SOCIAL ATTITUDES: 1989
SELF-COMPLETION QUESTIONNAIRE

Spring 1989   P.1005

OFFICE USE ONLY:

Interviewer
to enter:

Area No.

Serial No.

Rec.

Interviewer No.

0

To the selected respondent

We hope very much that you will agree to participate in this important study –
the sixth in this annual series. The results are published in a book each
autumn. The study consists of this self-completion questionnaire and an interview. Some of the questions are also being asked in ten other countries, as
part of an international survey.

Completing the questionnaire

The questions inside cover a wide range of subjects, but each one can be
answered simply by placing a tick (✓) or a number in one or more of the boxes.
No special knowledge is required: we are confident that everyone will be able
to offer an opinion on all questions. And we want *everyone* to take part,
not just those with strong views or particular viewpoints. The questionnaire
should not take very long to complete, and we hope you will find it interesting
and enjoyable. It should be filled in by the person selected by the interviewer at your address. The answers you give will be treated as confidential
and anonymous.

Returning the questionnaire

Your interviewer will arrange with you the most convenient way of returning
the questionnaire. If the interviewer has arranged to call back for it, please
complete it and keep it safely until then. If not, please complete it and
post it back in the pre-paid, addressed envelope *as soon as you possibly can.*

Thank you for your help.

*Social and Community Planning Research is an independent social research
institute registered as a charitable trust. Its projects are funded by
government departments, local authorities, universities and foundations to
provide information on social issues in the UK. This survey series has
been funded mainly by the Sainsbury Family Charitable Trusts, with contributions also from government departments, other charitable foundations,
universities and industry. Please contact us if you require further
information.*

N=7780   Qs.201-10

201. Suppose you could change the way you spend your time, spending more time on some things and less time on others.

Which of the things on the following list would you like to spend more time on, which would you like to spend less time on and which would you like to spend the same amount of time on as now?

PLEASE TICK ONE BOX ON EACH LINE

	Much more time	A bit more time	Same time as now	A bit less time	Much less time	Can't choose/ Doesn't apply
a. Time in a paid job?	10.5	9.3	29.5	12.8	3.9	30.8
b. Time doing household work?	2.7	12.3	37.7	18.2	13.3	12.3
c. Time with your family?	22.0	32.2	39.7	1.4	0.1	2.3
d. Time with your friends?	10.3	39.1	44.1	1.1	0.5	1.8
e. Time in leisure activities?	16.0	39.8	33.3	1.0	0.6	6.0
f. Time to relax?	17.6	34.4	39.4	2.8	1.0	2.1

202. Please tick one box for each statement below to show how much you agree or disagree with it, thinking of work in general.

PLEASE TICK ONE BOX ON EACH LINE

	Strongly agree	Agree	Neither Agree nor disagree	Disagree	Strongly Disagree	Can't choose
a. A job is just a way of earning money - no more.	8.8	24.9	13.0	37.4	10.5	2.5
b. I would enjoy having a paid job even if I did not need the money.	11.1	52.3	9.1	17.4	4.1	3.9
c. Work is a person's most important activity.	16.4	34.0	14.3	25.9	5.3	1.8

Please continue ...

---

203. Are you the person responsible for doing the general domestic duties - like cleaning, cooking, washing and so on - in your household?

PLEASE TICK ONE BOX ONLY

Yes, I am **mainly** responsible	46.7
Yes, I am **equally** responsible with someone else	16.3
No, someone else is **mainly** responsible	36.8

204. Think of two people doing **the same kind of work.** What do you personally think should be important in deciding how much to pay them?

Looking at the things below, please write '1' in the box next to the thing you think should be **most important.**

Then write '2' next to the thing you think should be **next most important.** And '3' next to the thing you think should be **third most important.** Leave the other boxes blank.

Write 1,2 and 3 in THREE boxes: leave the other boxes blank

In deciding on pay for two people doing **the same kind of work** how important should be ...

	1	2	3
... how long the employee has been with the firm?	7.7	12.7	19.9
... how well the employee does the job?	49.8	17.9	11.3
... the experience of the employee in doing the work?	12.9	38.1	18.1
... the standard rate - giving both employees the same pay?	11.0	5.8	9.9

OR TICK:

	1	2	3
... the age of the employee?	-	1.2	3.6
... the sex of the employee?	0.4	0.1	1.0
... the employee's family responsibilities?	0.5	0.9	3.5
... the employee's education and formal qualifications?	7.3	9.7	16.4
Can't choose			4.4

3

NI

205. How much do you agree or disagree with these two statements?

PLEASE TICK ONE BOX ON EACH LINE

	Strongly agree	Agree	Neither agree nor disagree	Disagree	Strongly disagree	Can't choose
a. There will always be conflict between management and workers because they are really on opposite sides.	9.0	35.8	19.8	26.0	3.1	5.1
b. Workers need strong trade unions to protect their interests.	14.4	40.6	18.4	18.8	3.3	3.7

206. From the following list, please tick one box for each item to show how important you personally think it is in a job.

PLEASE TICK ONE BOX ON EACH LINE

How important is ...	Very important	Important	Neither important nor unimportant	Not important	Not important at all	Can't choose
a. ... job security?	67.5	29.6	1.3	0.6	0.1	0.4
b. ... high income?	26.2	57.2	11.0	3.1	0.1	0.8
c. ... good opportunities for advancement?	40.5	49.2	4.9	3.3	0.2	0.9
d. ... a job that leaves a lot of leisure time?	7.0	32.3	28.9	25.8	2.4	1.2
e. ... an interesting job?	46.4	46.6	3.3	1.5	0.1	0.8
f. ... a job that allows someone to work independently?	19.6	44.4	21.7	10.7	0.7	1.5
g. ... a job that allows someone to help other people?	25.0	47.6	19.7	5.3	0.6	0.9
h. ... a job that is useful to society?	28.1	48.1	17.3	3.9	0.6	0.9
i. ... a job with flexible working hours?	15.5	31.3	29.8	18.2	2.6	1.7

Please continue ...

NI

207. Suppose you were unemployed and couldn't find a job. Which of the following problems do you think would be the worst?

Please write '1' in the box next to the **worst** thing.
Then write '2' beside the **next worst** thing.
And '3' beside the **third worst** thing.
Leave the other boxes blank.

	Write 1,2 and 3 in THREE boxes: leave the other boxes blank.		
	1	2	3
Lack of contact with people at work	7.6	9.4	13.2
Not enough money	50.6	15.9	7.9
Loss of self-confidence	15.4	21.7	18.0
Loss of respect from friends and acquaintances	1.2	4.9	5.8
Family tensions	5.6	22.5	15.2
Loss of job experience	2.5	5.7	11.4
Not knowing how to fill one's time	3.9	5.5	12.3

OR TICK.

Can't choose	6.5

208. Suppose you were working and could choose between different kinds of jobs. Which of the following would you personally choose?

PLEASE TICK ONE BOX ONLY

I would choose ...

... being an employee	44.2
... being self-employed	46.9
Can't choose	8.0

PLEASE TICK ONE BOX ONLY

I would choose ...

... working in a small firm	53.5
... working in a large firm	29.3
Can't choose	16.2

OFFICE USE ONLY

NI

208. (cont'd)

And which of the following would **you personally** choose?

PLEASE TICK ONE BOX ONLY

I would choose ...

c.

... working in a manufacturing industry — 28.9

... working in an office, in sales or in service — 51.3

Can't choose — 18.2

PLEASE TICK ONE BOX ONLY

I would choose ...

d.

... working in a private business — 49.7

... working for the government or civil service — 33.1

Can't choose — 15.5

209. On the whole, do you think it should be or should not be the government's responsibility to ...

PLEASE TICK ONE BOX ON EACH LINE

	Definitely should be	Probably should be	Probably should not be	Definitely should not be	Can't choose
a. ... provide a job for everyone who wants one?	36.1	39.9	12.4	6.2	4.0
b. ... provide a decent standard of living for the unemployed?	48.4	36.0	7.8	2.6	3.5

210. Do you usually work 10 hours or more a week for pay in your (main) job?

PLEASE TICK ONE BOX ONLY

Yes, I usually work 10 hours or more a week in my (main) job — 48.3 → GO TO Q.13, PAGE 7

No, I usually work less than 10 hours a week in my (main) job — 1.4

No, I don't work for pay at the moment — 50.2

} PLEASE ANSWER Q.11, PAGE 6

Please continue ...

NI

211. Would you like to have a paid job now?

PLEASE TICK ONE BOX ONLY

Yes, I would like a **full-time** job now (30 hours or more per week) — 22.0

Yes, I would like a **part-time** job now (10-29 hours per week) — 15.4

Yes, I would like a job with **less than 10 hours a week** now — 7.4

} PLEASE ANSWER Q.12 BELOW

No, I **would not** like to have a paid job now — 52.9 → GO TO Q.22 PAGE 12

212. If you were looking actively, how easy or difficult do you think it would be for you to find an acceptable job?   N=181

PLEASE TICK ONE BOX ONLY

Very easy — 1.9

Fairly easy — 7.7

Neither easy nor difficult — 6.9

Fairly difficult — 34.1

Very difficult — 47.4

Can't choose — 1.3

} PLEASE GO TO Q.22 PAGE 12

203

7

PLEASE ANSWER Q.13 - Q.21 ABOUT YOUR MAIN JOB.

N=345
Qs.213-21

213. Which of the following statements best describes your feelings about your job?
PLEASE TICK ONE BOX ONLY

In my job ...

... I only work as hard as I have to	7.8
... I work hard, but not so that it interferes with the rest of my life	30.2
... I make a point of doing the best work I can, even if it sometimes does interfere with the rest of my life	58.1
Can't choose	2.0

214. Think of the number of hours you work, and the money you earn in your main job, including any regular overtime.

If you had only one of these three choices which of the following would you prefer?
PLEASE TICK ONE BOX ONLY

Work **longer** hours and earn **more** money	26.7
Work the **same** number of hours and earn the **same** money	61.8
Work **fewer** hours and earn **less** money	5.2
Can't choose	4.7

Please continue ...

8

215. Think of two people doing the same kind of work in your place of work. What do you personally think is important in deciding how much to pay them?

Looking at the things below, please write '1' in the box next to the thing you think is most important at your place of work.

Then write '2' next to the thing you think is next most important. And '3' next to the thing you think is third most important. Leave the other boxes blank.

Write 1, 2 and 3 in THREE boxes. leave the other boxes blank

At your workplace, in deciding on pay for two people doing the same kind of work, how important is ....

	1	2	3
... how long the employee has been with the firm?	10.1	10.2	20.1
... how well the employee does the job?	48.5	23.2	12.6
... the experience of the employee in doing the work?	16.9	38.2	20.9
... the standard rate - giving both employees the same pay?	11.2	5.9	11.7
... the age of the employee?	0.3	2.0	3.4
... the sex of the employee?	-	-	1.3
... the employee's family responsibilities?	0.4	1.0	3.4
... the employer's education and formal qualifications?	4.6	9.8	14.2

OR TICK:

Can't choose	1.5

216. For each of these statements about your (main) job, please tick one box to show how much you agree or disagree that it applies to your job.

PLEASE TICK ONE BOX ON EACH LINE

	Strongly agree	Agree	Neither agree nor disagree	Disagree	Strongly disagree	Can't choose
a. My job is secure	19.7	42.5	12.6	17.7	4.8	1.1
b. My income is high	5.2	12.6	27.7	39.9	12.8	-
c. My opportunities for advancement are high	4.7	16.3	22.0	39.3	14.9	1.0
d. My job leaves a lot of leisure time	2.0	24.0	25.6	35.9	10.2	0.8
e. My job is interesting	21.2	54.1	12.7	7.4	2.9	-
f. I can work independently	21.9	51.4	11.2	11.1	1.5	0.4
g. In my job I can help other people	24.8	50.8	12.1	9.0	1.7	-
h. My job is useful to society	25.8	45.8	16.2	9.0	0.8	0.5
i. My job has flexible working hours	12.6	23.0	12.7	34.2	15.0	0.8

Please continue ...

---

217. Now some more questions about your working conditions.

Please tick one box for **each** item below to show **how often** it applies to your work.

PLEASE TICK ONE BOX ON EACH LINE

How often ...	Always	Often	Sometimes	Hardly ever	Never	Can't choose
a. ... do you come home from work exhausted?	6.7	32.6	44.0	10.8	4.2	0.3
b. ... do you have to do hard physical work?	11.6	17.0	21.0	21.4	27.1	0.3
c. ... do you find your work stressful?	8.7	18.4	47.6	12.1	10.9	0.3
d. ... are you bored at work?	0.9	5.9	26.5	32.1	33.1	0.3
e. ... do you work in dangerous conditions?	4.7	5.5	17.7	17.8	51.7	1.0
f. ... do you work in unhealthy conditions?	4.3	4.3	21.4	20.4	47.7	0.3
g. ... do you work in physically unpleasant conditions?	4.1	7.3	19.0	18.4	49.2	0.5

218. And which of the following statements about your work is **most** true?

PLEASE TICK ONE BOX ONLY

My job allows me to design or plan *most* of my daily work   36.5

My job allows me to design or plan *parts* of my daily work   35.9

My job *does not really* allow me to design or plan my daily work   26.0

219. If you lost your job for any reason, and were looking actively for another one, how easy or difficult do you think it would be for you to find an acceptable job?

PLEASE TICK ONE BOX ONLY

Very easy	2.9
Fairly easy	25.2
Neither easy nor difficult	13.5
Fairly difficult	33.5
Very difficult	22.1
Can't choose	1.4

220. In general, how would you describe relations at your workplace ...

PLEASE TICK ONE BOX ON EACH LINE

	Very good	Quite good	Neither good nor bad	Quite bad	Very bad	Can't choose
a. ... between management and employees?	23.2	42.5	16.5	8.3	3.8	2.3
b. ... between workmates/ colleagues?	39.6	41.6	7.9	0.9	0.5	2.7

221. How satisfied are you in your (main) job?

PLEASE TICK ONE BOX ONLY

Completely satisfied	15.5
Very satisfied	24.8
Fairly satisfied	46.1
Neither satisfied nor dissatisfied	5.3
Fairly dissatisfied	5.2
Very dissatisfied	1.3
Completely dissatisfied	0.4
Can't choose	0.4

Please continue ...

N=780
Qs.222-40

222. Now for some questions on different subjects.
Here are a number of circumstances in which a woman might consider an abortion. Please say whether or not you think the law should allow an abortion in each case.

PLEASE TICK ONE BOX ON EACH LINE

	Should abortion be allowed by law?		
	Yes	No	Don't know
The woman decides on her own she does not wish to have the child	28.7	67.4	0.8
The couple agree they do not wish to have the child	30.0	65.3	0.6
The woman is not married and does not wish to marry the man	27.9	67.7	0.9
The couple cannot afford any more children	24.4	70.3	0.9
There is a strong chance of a defect in the baby	60.5	34.6	1.5
The woman's health is seriously endangered by the pregnancy	76.0	18.7	1.9
The woman became pregnant as a result of rape	70.2	24.1	2.2

223. Suppose a married couple want to have their own child, but cannot have one. Should the law allow or not allow them to use each of the methods below? Please assume in each case that it is the only method open to them on medical advice.

PLEASE TICK ONE BOX ON EACH LINE

	It should be		
	Allowed by law	Not allowed by law	Don't know
They try to have a child by **artificial insemination**, using the **husband** as donor	77.2	17.2	2.9
They try to have a child by **artificial insemination**, using an **anonymous** donor	37.0	55.2	3.2
They try to have a child by having their own '**test-tube**' embryo implanted	71.0	22.4	3.5
They find a '**surrogate**' mother who agrees, **without payment**, to bear a child for them (by artificial insemination, using the husband as donor)	25.5	67.6	2.5
They find a '**surrogate**' mother who is **paid** to bear a child for them (by artificial insemination, using the husband as donor)	13.6	79.5	2.5

13

NI

224. Which of these statements comes **closest** to your views on the availability of pornographic magazines and films?

PLEASE TICK ONE BOX

They should be banned altogether	54.8
They should be available in special adult shops but not displayed to the public	31.8
They should be available in special adult shops with public display permitted	6.7
They should be available in any shop for sale to adults only	4.9
They should be available in any shop for sale to anyone	0.3

225.a) Suppose a person has a painful incurable disease. Do you think that doctors should be allowed by law to end the patient's life if the patient requests it?

PLEASE TICK ONE BOX

Yes	55.4
No	42.6

b) And if a person is not incurably sick but simply tired of living, should doctors be allowed by law to end that person's life if he or she requests it?

PLEASE TICK ONE BOX

Yes	7.5
No	91.1

226. Are you in favour of or against the death penalty for ...

PLEASE TICK ONE BOX ON EACH LINE

	In favour	Against	Don't know
... murder in the course of a terrorist act?	57.4	39.0	1.7
... murder of a police officer?	55.6	39.5	2.1
... other murders?	51.6	43.7	2.2

Please continue ...

NI

227. Please tick one box for **each** statement, to show how much you agree or disagree with it.

PLEASE TICK ONE BOX ON EACH LINE

	Agree strongly	Just agree	Neither agree nor disagree	Just disagree	Disagree strongly
a. Healthy food doesn't usually taste as nice as other food	10.4	25.1	28.4	21.7	13.0
b. Food that is good for you is usually more expensive	21.3	33.7	16.4	19.9	7.5
c. Food that is good for you generally takes too long to prepare	6.3	17.3	27.7	32.7	14.7
d. It is hard to find food that is good for you in supermarkets	4.3	14.6	24.6	38.2	17.2
e. Mothers would eat healthier food if the rest of their families would let them	8.3	21.0	28.6	27.4	13.0
f. As long as you take enough exercise you can eat whatever foods you want	9.1	23.5	13.9	33.7	18.7
g. If heart disease is in your family, there is little you can do to reduce your chances of getting it	4.5	16.4	13.1	34.1	30.5
h. The experts contradict each other over what makes a healthy diet	26.1	39.8	15.8	13.4	3.0
i. People worry too much about their weight	19.1	43.9	18.0	13.6	4.3
j. Good health is just a matter of good luck	4.4	13.4	15.7	30.2	35.0
k. A proper meal should include meat and vegetables	34.2	31.5	14.8	14.3	4.4

228. How worried are you about the sorts of food you eat?

PLEASE TICK ONE BOX

Very worried	3.8
Fairly worried	24.2
Not particularly worried	48.2
Not worried at all	22.0

NI

229. Which one of these statements **best** describes how you feel about the sorts of food you eat nowadays?

PLEASE TICK ONE BOX

I have **never** felt any need to change what I eat	26.9
I have already changed as much as I am going to	33.6
I ought to change more but probably **won't**	32.9
I will probably be changing soon	5.4

230. Please tick one box for each statement to show how much you agree or disagree with it.
PLEASE TICK ONE BOX ON EACH LINE

	Agree strongly	Agree	Neither agree nor disagree	Dis-agree	Disagree strongly
A. Social workers should put the child's interests first even if it means taking a child away from its natural parents.	27.8	44.4	15.4	8.5	2.5
B. Social workers have too much power to interfere with people's lives.	7.6	23.9	34.5	29.0	3.3
C. The welfare state makes people nowadays less willing to look after themselves.	8.1	32.9	25.6	27.1	4.7
D. People receiving social security are made to feel like second class citizens.	15.1	39.6	19.1	20.9	3.8
E. The welfare state encourages people to stop helping each other.	6.6	26.7	26.7	32.9	5.8
F. Doctors should be allowed to give contraceptive advice and supplies to young people under 16 without having to inform parents.	7.6	16.3	13.0	33.7	28.3

Please continue ...

16

NI

231. Please tick one box for **each** statement below to show how much you agree or disagree with it.

PLEASE TICK ONE BOX ON EACH LINE

	Agree strongly	Agree	Neither agree nor disagree	Dis-agree	Disagree strongly
a. Government should redistribute income from the better-off to those who are less well off.	18.5	37.0	18.8	20.7	3.3
b. Big business benefits owners at the expense of workers.	13.8	42.1	20.0	19.6	2.3
c. Ordinary working people do not get their fair share of the nation's wealth.	20.2	48.3	16.2	12.6	1.4
d. There is one law for the rich and one for the poor.	27.1	38.2	16.3	15.2	1.8
e. Management will always try to get the better of employees if it gets the chance.	17.9	37.7	21.5	20.0	1.2
f. Young people today don't have enough respect for traditional British values.	17.1	43.3	26.9	10.5	0.6
g. People who break the law should be given stiffer sentences.	32.8	44.0	17.0	3.2	1.2
h. People should be allowed to organise public meetings to protest against the government.	13.5	41.5	27.7	13.4	2.3
i. For some crimes, the death penalty is the most appropriate sentence.	32.1	26.9	8.5	16.5	14.6
j. People should be allowed to publish leaflets to protest against the government.	13.8	40.8	30.6	11.5	1.9

OFFICE USE ONLY

PLEASE TICK ONE BOX FOR EACH STATEMENT

	Agree strongly	Agree	Neither agree nor disagree	Dis- agree	Disagree strongly
k. Schools should teach children to obey authority.	39.0	49.7	6.4	3.7	–
l. People should be allowed to organise protest marches and demonstrations.	8.5	40.3	27.8	18.2	3.6
m. The law should always be obeyed, even if a particular law is wrong.	9.1	30.2	24.3	29.9	4.6
n. Censorship of films and magazines is necessary to uphold moral standards.	29.2	43.9	14.6	9.3	1.7
o. The government should spend more money on welfare benefits for the poor, even if it leads to higher taxes.	23.1	44.1	19.6	11.3	0.7
p. Around here, most unemployed people could find a job if they really wanted one.	7.3	28.0	18.5	31.5	13.6
q. Many people who get social security don't really deserve any help.	5.1	17.3	21.8	39.5	14.6
r. Most people on the dole are fiddling in one way of another.	8.8	24.8	29.0	26.4	9.7
s. If welfare benefits weren't so generous people would learn to stand on their own two feet.	7.0	25.4	21.0	29.4	16.0

232. Some people think that better relations between Protestants and Catholics in Northern Ireland will only come about through more mixing of the two communities. Others think that better relations will only come about through more separation. Which comes closest to your views ....

PLEASE TICK ONE BOX

Better relations will come about through more mixing	90.0
Better relations will come about through more separation	6.4
Don't know	1.4

233. And are you in favour of more mixing or more separation in ....

PLEASE TICK ONE BOX ON EACH LINE

	Much more mixing	Bit more mixing	Keep things as they are	Bit more separ- ation	Much more separ- ation
a. ... primary schools?	39.6	29.4	28.3	0.9	0.6
b. ... secondary and grammar schools?	40.0	33.1	23.9	1.2	0.6
c. ... where people live?	36.2	37.8	22.3	1.2	0.9
d. ... where people work?	41.3	38.2	17.8	1.2	0.2
e. ... people's leisure or sports activities?	47.1	32.5	18.2	0.5	0.4
f. ... people's marriages?	21.3	24.4	42.1	3.0	6.6

OFFICE USE ONLY

234. People feel closer to some groups than to others. For you personally, how close would you say you feel towards ...

PLEASE TICK ONE BOX ON EACH LINE

	Very close	Fairly close	A little close	Not very close	Not at all close
a. People born in the same area as you	14.7	42.9	21.0	13.8	6.4
b. People who have the same social class background as yours	13.2	52.2	22.8	7.5	2.9
c. People who have the same religious background as yours	16.5	47.7	20.2	9.6	4.6
d. People of the same race as you	15.9	48.3	21.0	8.5	4.2
e. People who live in the same area as you do now	14.2	44.3	26.0	10.6	3.6
f. People who have the same political beliefs as you	11.4	38.7	25.3	14.3	8.0

235. Now a few questions about the disease called AIDS.

Please tick one box to show which is closest to your views about the following statement:

Within five years AIDS will cause more deaths in Britain than any other single disease.

PLEASE TICK ONE BOX

It is highly exaggerated	11.8
It is slightly exaggerated	24.1
It is more or less true	61.3

236. Please tick one box for each statement to show how much you agree or disagree with it.

PLEASE TICK ONE BOX ON EACH LINE

	Agree strongly	Agree	Neither agree nor disagree	Disagree	Disagree strongly
a. Most people with AIDS have only themselves to blame	20.7	35.6	17.6	21.3	3.8
b. The National Health Service should spend more of its resources on giving better care to people dying from AIDS	9.2	48.2	26.8	12.7	2.0
c. Official warnings about AIDS should say that some sexual practices are morally wrong	34.4	38.6	13.7	10.1	2.1
d. Within the next five years doctors will discover a vaccine against AIDS	4.4	27.6	46.9	15.9	3.7
e. AIDS is a way of punishing the world for its decline in moral standards	14.5	25.9	23.6	21.3	13.3

237. As one way of getting to know how AIDS is spreading, it has been suggested that hospitals should be allowed to test any patient's blood (that has been taken for other reasons) to see whether it contains the virus that causes AIDS.

Do you agree or disagree with this suggestion?

PLEASE TICK ONE BOX

Agree strongly	40.5
Agree	40.5
Neither agree nor disagree	9.4
Disagree	6.7
Disagree strongly	1.8

NI

238. Thinking of patients whose blood has been tested for the AIDS virus without their knowledge - should they ...

PLEASE TICK ONE BOX

<u>Not</u> be told the test has been carried out	5.4
Be told about the test, <u>but not</u> be told the result	2.0
Be told about the test, <u>and</u> have the choice of knowing or not knowing the result	34.9
Be told about the test, <u>and</u> be told the result	55.8

239. As far as you know, have you ever met anyone who was confirmed as having the virus that causes AIDS?

PLEASE TICK ONE BOX

Yes	2.7
No	96.9

240.a) To help us plan better in future, please tell us about **how long** it took you to complete this questionnaire?

PLEASE TICK ONE BOX

Less than 15 minutes	10.3
Between 15 and 20 minutes	26.4
Between 20 and 30 minutes	35.0
Between 30 and 45 minutes	16.7
Between 45 and 60 minutes	6.6
Over one hour	4.3

b) And on what date did you fill in the questionnaire?

PLEASE WRITE IN

_____	_____	'89
DATE	MONTH	YEAR

THANK YOU VERY MUCH FOR YOUR HELP!

Please keep the completed questionnaire for the interviewer if he or she has arranged to call for it. Otherwise, please post it as soon as possible in the pre-paid addressed envelope provided.

OFFICE USE ONLY

211

Subject index

214